STONE IN THE KING'S HIGHWAY

STONE IN THE
KING'S HIGHWAY

Selections from the Writings of
Bishop Francis Xavier Ford
(1892-1952)

with
Introductory Memoir
by
Most Rev. Raymond A. Lane, M.M., D.D.
Superior General of Maryknoll

McMULLEN BOOKS, INC.
New York   1953

Library of Congress Catalogue Card Number: 53-8122

Second Printing

*"Grant us, Lord, to be the doorstep by which
the multitudes may come to worship Thee. And
if, in the saving of their souls, we are ground
underfoot and spat upon and worn out, at least
we shall have served Thee in some small way
in helping pagan souls; we shall have become
the King's Highway in pathless China."*

(Bishop Ford's Prayer)

CONTENTS

STONE IN THE KING'S HIGHWAY

Preface

WHEN I WAS A SMALL BOY IN LAWRENCE, MASSACHUSETTS,
one of my chores was to walk a block to Dowling's Notion
Store and buy the *Irish World* for my grandfather. My
mother's father was known as Colonel Doyle. He was tall,
straight as an arrow, neat of dress, slow and deliberate in his
speech, with an impressive head of white hair and a white
moustache. I liked to imagine my grandfather in a military
role; it seemed to fit him so well. As I grew older, I began to
suspect that he might have been a militant Irish patriot.

Years later, when Frank Ford and I were students at
Maryknoll, I met the editor of the *Irish World*, Mr. Austin
Brendan Ford, and I saw a resemblance between these two
old gentlemen. Each had a quiet dignity and a certain self-
assurance that indicated an ability to espouse a cause and see
it through.

At the moment of writing these lines I am at the Maryknoll
parish in the city of Chillan, Chile, a town connected with the
name of another great Irish patriot, Ambrosio O'Higgins, who
was at one time Governor of Chillan. It was here that his
son was born, Bernardo O'Higgins, remembered as a national
hero and leader in winning Chilean independence. What has
all this to do with the present book? Nothing, perhaps, except
that I cannot help linking Bishop Ford with the name of
Austin Ford, his father, and with all great men of thought and
action who earned the title of "Liberator."

The privilege of working on this book has brought me
great pleasure and it has helped to stir up my enthusiasm.

1

Back in student days I little thought that after forty years I would have a hand in publishing the legacy of beautiful spirituality which Francis Xavier Ford was to bequeath to his sons and daughters of the Kaying mission and, through them, to us all.

In the introductory memoir I have tried, as often as possible, to let the bishop tell his own story. For the notes on his boyhood and school days we are indebted to his brother Patrick. The details of his arrest and imprisonment come from Sister Joan Marie, the only Maryknoll witness. My deep thanks go to them and also to all those who collaborated in producing this volume, especially to the priests and Sisters of the Hakka mission who loaned us their letters and conference notes. Sister Mary Just at Maryknoll deserves our special thanks for arranging the material and getting the book into proper shape, and we are indebted likewise to the Sisters in the Administration Office at Maryknoll for their work on the manuscript.

Please God, may this book inspire many young men and women to give their lives as priests, brothers, Sisters, and lay apostles, to serve the cause for which Bishop Ford died.

I dedicate the volume to Mary, the Mother of mankind, whose loving care becomes more and more manifest in the awakened devotion, loyalty and zeal of so many of her children throughout the world. May she bless this work and make it fruitful. Mary, Queen of Apostles, pray for us.

✠ RAYMOND A. LANE

Chillan, Chile
The Conversion of Saint Paul
January 25, 1953

Introductory Memoir

OLD CATHEDRAL COLLEGE STOOD ON MADISON AVENUE, BETWEEN Fifty-first Street and Fifty-second. Fr. James Anthony Walsh spoke to the students of Cathedral College one day early in the year 1912, and told them about a seminary for American foreign missioners which he and Fr. Price of North Carolina hoped to start. The Pope had given the signal to go ahead, and the bishops of the United States were supporting the plan. At the moment, the seminary was still just an idea; they had no building, they had no students, but they were looking for recruits. After the talk, before Fr. Walsh could cross the street and return to the Cathedral rectory, one of the senior students caught up with him. He told him that he was interested; in fact, he would like to sign up. Fr. Walsh had his first recruit. His name was Francis Xavier Ford, and on that day began a career which ended forty years later, on February 21, 1952, in a Communist prison of South China.

These introductory pages will, it is hoped, give a background to the writings of Bishop Ford which have been collected for this volume. There is no question here of a comprehensive and definitive biography. That must await someone with leisure for all the necessary research, someone with a literary skill worthy of reproducing for this generation a complete picture of this missionary pioneer.

Moreover, the story of the Ford family is in itself a thrilling chapter of Catholic American history, far too important and too interesting to be compressed into a hurried synthesis. It will be the task of a trained historian to chronicle the events

3

that began when Eamon Ford and his wife Mary sailed from Galway Bay to Boston in 1846, and brought with them their family of three boys, Thomas, Patrick and Austin, and a baby girl, Ellen. One hundred years of the Ford family history furnish material to fill and overflow an ordinary volume. The student dipping into these memoirs will find himself amid the capital-labor bargainings of nineteenth-century Boston; will smell the furnaces of the New England Type Foundry; he will watch the type setters of *The Liberator*, William Lloyd Garrison's anti-slavery paper, and will read the issues of the Boston *Traveler* of a hundred years ago.

During the Civil War, Eamon Ford, the bishop's grandfather, then over sixty years of age, enlisted with his two sons. Another son, Thomas, was already in the navy and lost his life when the *Cumberland* was sunk by the Confederate ironclad, *Merrimac*. The others were enrolled in the Ninth Massachusetts Regiment.

Austin Ford, the bishop's father, and his uncle, Patrick Ford, founded the *Irish World* in 1870. It was the first paper in the country to reach a circulation of one million. The aims of the paper were set forth thus: "To achieve in this, our day, the independence of Ireland; to bear aloft, as becomes an apostolic people, the standard of the church of God, and to carry the light of Faith into every nook and corner of this land; and, in the political order, to hold the State true to the principles enunciated in the Declaration of Independence."

In those days, when there was no Catholic press such as we have today, the *Irish World* was practically the only messenger of Catholic thought to the exiles of Erin scattered in the far corners of this hemisphere and in other parts of the world, many of them without priests and without the benefits of parish life.

Austin Ford purchased the *Freeman's Journal* in 1892 and assembled a brilliant group of contributors. Fr. Bernard Vaughan and John Bickerstaff Drew contributed articles from London. Gilbert K. Chesterton wrote for it. Msgr. Patrick O'Kelly was its Rome correspondent. Dr. Zahm, companion of Theodore Roosevelt in Africa, wrote on scientific matters.

Non-Catholic readers of the paper would call at the *Freeman* office to discuss its articles. One such visitor was Dr. Benjamin Da Costa, writer and historian, for many years one of the foremost clergymen in the Episcopal Church. These visits led to Dr. Da Costa's conversion. Later, he was ordained to the priesthood at Rome. Father Paul, founder of Graymoor, was also a frequent visitor at the office before his entry into the Catholic Church.

The bishop's mother, Elizabeth Anne Rellihan, had a story almost as interesting. Her father, who had helped to bring the "iron horse" as far as Des Moines, gave up railroading and bought a farm at Keokuk, Iowa. There she was born in 1854, the year the dogma of the Immaculate Conception was proclaimed. When still a little child, she was kidnaped by a band of roving Indians, but was returned the next day.

Later, Elizabeth Rellihan was to read the *Irish World* and to become a contributor. In 1876 she was invited to New York to take a place on the editorial staff. She accepted, and the following year Bishop Loughlin of Brooklyn officiated at the marriage of Austin Ford and Elizabeth Anne Rellihan.

There was never a dull moment at the Ford home. Mrs. Ford was up every day for early Mass, hastened home to get the family's breakfast, and then hurried the youngsters off to school. During spare moments she composed her copy for the *Irish World* and the *Freeman* and wrote a life of St. Jeanne d'Arc. She also wrote for the New York *Times*, conducting a weekly column on Irish affairs. She died on October 2, 1912, just a few days after Francis came to Maryknoll. The bishop's father died in 1934.

1. The Boy

Patrick Ford, the bishop's brother, tells us that Francis was born at 182 Cumberland Street, Brooklyn, on January 11, 1892. His father had just finished reading a life of St. Francis Xavier and was so impressed that he decided this son must have that name. So Francis Xavier Ford was baptized in Sacred Heart Church by the pastor, Fr. Nash. His Uncle Patrick and his Aunt Ellen were sponsors. He was sixth in a family of four boys and four girls. Una, Marie Speranza or "Pansy," Brigid, Thomas Aquinas and Patrick Joseph were older than Francis; Austin Brendan, Jr., and Maura were younger. Of this large family, only Una and Patrick survived Francis and were alive to witness the last chapter of their brother's life. Una died in February, 1953.

In 1894 the family moved to 432 Carleton Avenue, a house that was to be "home" for the next forty years. Patrick Ford, to whom we are indebted for this early history, gives us an idea of life there.

"A typical day at No. 432 began when mother arose to attend 6:30 Mass," he writes. "She used no compulsion or suggestion, but one could see how happy she was if any of the children accompanied her. Then began the series of breakfasts, interspersed with bundling the kids off to school and the departure of others for work. Hours for meals were on a sliding scale, because all did not rise at the same time. Housework followed, and then preparation of lunch for the children.

6

"The evening meal began at six, with all the children and most of the others present. One by one they would straggle in. Father, last to leave the office, if not delayed by some last-minute business, would arrive about seven. By eight the table would be cleared, and the evening's relaxation would begin.

"Some would scatter to the front parlor where the piano stood ready, and duets, quartets or sextets would fill the air. Others used part of the dining room table for a game of Euchre or Forty-five. The children would be outside with the goat or perhaps playing games on the kitchen table. If the boys wanted a more strenuous pastime, there was a set of boxing gloves and a ring roped off in the cellar. When bed time came for the children, Pansy or Una would round them up, say Night Prayers with them and tuck them in bed.

"Father had another corner of the dining room table where he would become immersed in a game of chess. One time he and Dr. O'Kelly were deep in a game when mother left them at midnight to retire. Coming down next morning at six she found them exactly as she had left them. There was no change except in the ash tray, which was heaped higher with cigarette and cigar butts. Only when she called out a 'Good-Morning!' did they realize the time."

The home on Carleton Avenue received interesting visitors. The cause of Irish freedom was there discussed by Michael Davitt, Stewart Parnell, Henry George, John Redmond and Dr. O'Kelly. Mr. Ford supported the Greenback Labor Party. He advocated various labor reforms, the eight-hour day, labor unions, compensation laws, and many benefits that today are taken for granted. He had the confidence of labor leaders like Terence V. Powderly, Samuel Gompers, Edward McGuire, and John Mitchell. So active was the campaign for the Irish land war carried on by Mr. Ford's paper

7

that in Great Britain and Ireland it became a penal offense to possess a copy of the *Irish World*. Correspondent after correspondent was imprisoned by the Birtish. When Mr. Ford took over the *Freeman* he asked Rev. Louis A. Lambert to be editor-in-chief. It was this latter's "Notes on Ingersoll" that blasted Robert Ingersoll, the notorious atheist and demagogue, from the lecture platform. Such was the home atmosphere in which Francis Ford grew up.

He went to St. Joseph's School and St. Francis College in Brooklyn and to Cathedral College in New York. During these years he was blessed with the friendship of outstanding men. In 1910, Fr. Thomas Molloy, now Archbishop Molloy of Brooklyn, was his confessor at St. John's Chapel. When Francis told him of his hopes to be a missioner, Fr. Molloy told him that every priest has the same desire at some time or other. He encouraged Francis to pray for guidance and wisely advised him to defer any decision until graduation time in 1912. Once the decision was made, Fr. Molloy supported him wholeheartedly.

Msgr. Patrick Hayes, later Cardinal Archbishop of New York, was rector of Cathedral College. Frank Ford used to recall the "gentle, firm and calm manner in which he judged all student offenders, the stirring sermons so full of practical advice, the lofty ideal which he constantly preached and constantly lived."

After reading biographies of St. Francis Xavier and Blessed Théophane Vénard, Frank spoke to a priest friend about his own desires for the missionary life. The priest told him that there was plenty to be done in Brooklyn and that he could put in a very fruitful apostolate right there in his home diocese. He encouraged him to think of the priesthood, but the priesthood at home. Fr. William Hughes, vice president of Cathedral College, suggested that he join the New York apostolic mission band, but when he saw that Frank was bent on the foreign missions he gave him full encouragement.

Perhaps the very first idea of a missionary life was implanted in 1904 when as a boy of twelve years he listened to an old European priest speak in his home parish. He mentioned it fifteen years later in a letter from Yeungkong, his first mission assignment: "He was Father Conrardy, a fiery enthusiast, and his subject was his life work among the lepers. He gloried in his love for them and flung the challenge in our face to show our Catholicity by helping him to build a home for them. It seemed harder for him to beg for money than to do the disgusting work of nursing slowly rotting Chinese men and women, but he traveled Europe and America for funds. With a generous impulse I put a nickel in the basket, five times my usual sum, and the rest of the Mass was spent in repeating to myself Father Conrardy's last words: 'My one ambeesch is to die a martyr!' "

2. The Student

A photograph is not always a good medium for recalling one who is no longer with us. A good likeness may awaken memories in one who knew the person, but it has little to tell to later generations. Since his death, there have been various portraits of Bishop Ford in newspapers and magazines. I am thinking particularly of one which shows him in full episcopal regalia, with mitre, crozier and Mass vestments, probably taken after his consecration. It is the ordinary trend of hero-worship to represent our great ones in some commanding pose or impressive attire, but, while it is the accepted thing to portray them so, it helps little, or not at all, toward knowing our heroes.

9

He was twenty-one years old when I first met him in August, 1913. He had a way of walking fast, of talking fast, and it was clear that he also had a way of thinking fast. He did everything rapidly, and his family tells us that he even came into this world in a hurry and arrived so much ahead of time that for weeks he had to be wrapped in flannel cloths soaked in olive oil in the hope that the skin would absorb sufficient nourishment to keep him alive. He was baptized immediately, lest in his rush he should hurry right out of this world and back to God.

He gave the impression of having been hitherto a shy and relatively repressed young man who welcomed the primitive conditions of the first Maryknoll at Hawthorne and the broken-down farmhouse above Ossining. This pioneering atmosphere was a refreshing change from the effete city life of New York and Brooklyn and it appears to have led him to reveal the ebullient nature that up to that time had remained to a great degree under cover. In arguments, humorous sorties, and student pranks he was a match for the best of that early group. At the same time, the beauty of his character, the depth of his feelings, and his thoughtfulness came into view.

By nature he was an introvert, in the sense that he had the habit of reflecting and of finding great satisfaction and value in the inner life of thought and fancy. He was not an introvert if that should mean to retire within himself and close his eyes and ears to the world about him.

While life at Maryknoll was in many ways a big change from home on Carleton Avenue, from the well-ordered school life of Cathedral College, and from the hum and excitement of the *Irish World* and the *Freeman's Journal*, there were at the same time some similarities. His brother Patrick tells us about little Frank's goat. From his earliest days he was very fond of animals and always had a pet of some kind—white mice, pigeons, turtles, dogs, and finally Billy the Goat. Goats were not a rarity in Brooklyn at that time. "The Mounds," as people called the hillside northeast of Prospect Park, were dotted with goats. Billy the Goat was a birthday present from their mother to one of the boys. The goat and Frank took to each other at first glance.

The boys knocked together a two-wheeled cart, hitched the goat to the shafts and led him out to the roadway. Billy refused to budge. The only way to make the goat go was to have Frank walk in front of him. If Frank stopped, the goat stopped. By experience, however, the boys learned that if faced toward home, which meant more oats, the goat would travel fast of his own accord. Frank's only chance of a ride was to lure the goat a good distance down the road, turn him toward home, and then jump into the cart.

One night at supper, with company present as usual, the tablecloth with food and dishes began to move in one direction. It could have been an experiment in spiritism. But no. The goat had left his stable in the yard, slipped into the house unnoticed and was munching contentedly on one corner of the cloth.

When he was a student at Maryknoll, even in his late teens, Frank maintained his interest in pets. Shortly after the beginning of the first summer vacation, Fr. James Anthony Walsh received this letter: "Dear Father Superior, I don't like to annoy you, but would you ask someone to let my turtle free. I left him near the pump and had not time to attend to him. Perhaps Father McCabe might like to train him. A turtle is much more interesting than a canary. F. X. Ford."

Mother Mary Joseph recalls those early days when everyone, priests, Sisters, brothers and students had a busy life. The students had much manual labor to do and they were

11

often called to help the Sisters. Even outside of that, Francis Ford was always on hand. On laundry days especially he would be there to help. In wintry weather when the work was real suffering he would help hang out the clothes. Whenever the question of food came up, so often a favorite grievance with young students—and even those not so young—he always had good arguments to uphold the regime.

His mother died on October 2, 1912, only two weeks after he came to Maryknoll. He idolized her, of course, and missed her greatly, and when Sister Mary Xavier, the first Maryknoller to die, was in her last illness, he asked if he might speak to her and give her a message to bring to his mother in heaven.

He was not a big boy, nor strong, and manual labor must have exhausted him at times, although he never gave any indication of this nor did he show any reluctance. On the contrary, he was always on hand, ready to pitch in.

His confreres at Cathedral College recall his capacity for hard work. He was chosen editor of *The Chimes*, the college monthly. Eight other students were on the staff. Their task was not only to write the copy, but to set the type as well and make up the forms, and do all this by hand. It was hard work for the boys, for none except Frank had had previous experience as printers.

When he mentioned the difficulty at home, his brother Thomas, then working in the *Freeman* plant, told him to bring the copy to the office and he would set it on the linotype after the regular work was done and out of the way. For months things went along smoothly. Frank would bring the copy to the office on his way home from Cathedral. Tom would set it up in the evening. Frank would call for the type about eleven o'clock the same evening and carry it in a suitcase to the subway, then along Fifty-first Street to the College.

12

The watchman would let him in, and there it was, all ready to be made up into forms on the morrow.

One night a broken linotype machine delayed the operation. It was one o'clock in the morning when Frank left the printing plant with his load. He was trudging up Fifty-first Street when a shadow emerged from a doorway. "What have you there, young fellow?" It was a policeman. Frank explained. The officer was skeptical. "Pick up the bag. We'll go to the College. If your story checks, then all will be well. If it doesn't, then to headquarters you go." The story checked, but there was a sequel. The story reached Msgr. Hayes. He objected to Chimers roaming the streets at that hour, and thereafter a printing firm attended to the mechanical side of *The Chimes*.

Frank knew every corner of our fields and woods. He found a spot in the woods which he called his "cathedral" and to it he often stole with his books and his thoughts.

Ordination to the priesthood came on December 5, 1917, at the hands of Bishop Cusack of Albany. Frs. Alphonse Vogel and William O'Shea, the last of the first six seminarians of Maryknoll to reach the priesthood, were of his class. Fr. Walsh was not at home for the ordination. He was in the Far East seeking a field of missionary labor for his young missioners. On Christmas Day he cabled that he had arranged with the Bishop of Canton for Maryknollers to begin their work in a section of his territory.

In those early years of seminary life Frank Ford was already showing the buoyancy which in later years his missioners found characteristic of him. He seemed always able to ride on top, no matter how troubled the waters about him. Whatever contradictions he experienced, whatever opposition and setbacks and failures, he never allowed himself to be submerged by such things. He was never heard to complain

13

about disappointments, reversals, unfairness, which everyone, and especially missioners, are bound to experience.

3. The Pioneer

In June, 1918, it was announced that Fr. Price would lead the first group of Maryknoll missioners to the Far East. Frs. James Edward Walsh, Francis Ford, and Bernard Meyer were to go with him. Three untried young priests were setting out for the East under the leadership of a saintly veteran, who in turn, though skilled through many a skirmish in North Carolina, was himself completely untried in the ways of the Orient.

I recall well that first Departure Ceremony. The big bronze bell, which Fr. Walsh had brought back from Japan, was hanging from a beam on the porch of the old farmhouse, and just at dusk it started its solemn tolling. We crowded into a chapel which was much too small for our own big family and the group of visitors gathered that night. The words of the Canticle of Zachary, used in the Church's prayer for those going on a long journey, were truly appropriate: "For thou shalt go before the face of the Lord to prepare His ways . . . to enlighten those who sit in darkness and in the shadow of death."

Fr. Walsh reminded the young missioners that they were the pioneers on trial before the Catholic world. He said that they had yet to prove that American youth, and the American priesthood have faith, humility, self-denial, and zeal. He pointed out their need of reliance on Divine Providence, their love for the crucified and patient Christ, their devotion to the Holy Spirit as the source of light and strength, to Mary Immaculate, and to their particular patrons.

They sailed from San Francisco, on September 21, on the *Ecuador*. As the boat sailed out through the Golden Gate, the little band of our first missioners gathered on the after deck and sang softly the *Ave Maris Stella*.

Fr. Ford's first letter to Fr. James Anthony Walsh brought some verses written during the voyage and dedicated to "The Pacific":

> *O depths of mystery,*
> *How can you calmly sleep*
> *And sluggish stretch your breadth*
> *Of shining, peaceful deep*
> *Between the East and West,*
> *Between the Day and Night,*
> *Between the Heathen Dark*
> *And God's all-saving Light?*

In Japan, the group divided. Frs. Walsh and Meyer continued to Shanghai, but Fr. Price took Fr. Ford overland by train through Japan, Korea, and Manchuria. When their train passed from Korea, over the bridge of the Yalu River, Fr. Price caught sight of the land of his dreams and he and Fr. Ford together recited the *Magnificat*. When the train stopped in Antung they found themselves in China at last. Fr. Price left the car, knelt down in the railway station and kissed the ground, and he motioned to Fr. Ford to do the same.

As they went along their way through Manchuria, North China, and on to the South, they realized that they were going to be watched. Many Europeans made no secret of their conviction that Americans would never make missioners. One prelate, though kind to them, assured them that he would be at the boat a few months hence to say good-bye to them when they started back for America. That was thirty-four years ago.

15

Our missioners were headed for a place called Yeungkong, a part of Kwangtung Province on the South China seacoast. It is about sixty miles southwest of Sancian Island where St. Francis Xavier died. The section has four good seaports, and the people normally are engaged in fishing, raising geese and ducks, and tilling the soil. Chinese of the neighboring district of Sunning used to leave in crowds for America; many of our New York and San Francisco Chinese are from there, but the people of Yeungkong preferred to stay at home; they were somewhat behind the times, convinced that the whole world revolved about China.

With this provincial mentality they clung to their old ways and were suspicious of novelties. Hence, missionary beginnings were difficult. Protestant missionaries had been there earlier. Their buildings were destroyed twice. Only when pressure was exerted from Canton were they tolerated in the town. The first Catholic priest ran into similar trouble. He arrived in 1898 and for a long time had to hide in a tiny room of an obscure alley. Rumors went through the town that a foreign devil had come to tear out the hearts of children, to steal the eyes of the dying, to poison the people, and so on. His servant was forbidden to draw water from the common wells lest the whole populace be poisoned.

The priest received from a friend in France a hogshead of wine. When the Yeungkongers saw the barrel carried by six men through the alleys, they immediately spread word that the foreigner was laying in a supply of gunpowder. Trouble-makers also reported that French gunboats had been seen at the mouth of the river. Placards appeared in the streets: "Citizens! Do you want to fall into the hands of the foreigner? Arise! Destroy the Catholic chapel and kill the foreign devil!" The missioner warned the mandarin that something should be done before real trouble developed. The mandarin ordered his assistant to investigate, and the investigation came to a happy climax in a soothing drink of old Bordeaux. Quiet times followed thereafter for a few years, but real Catholic family life never flourished in Yeungkong because it was so difficult to approach the mothers and instruct them sufficiently in the faith. It was a hard mission, with much to be done, that awaited our first Maryknollers.

Fr. Ford's experiences during that first year are best described by himself. He was a faithful correspondent, and we have all his letters. "We're home at last and feel it," he wrote after their first Christmas in Yeungkong. "Everything here spells Maryknoll, and I feel that many of us in years to come will walk these floors, and trip on the crooked steps, and soon know the odd twists and dark corners.

"There are positively no people so lovable as the Chinese, at least in the countries I've seen, which isn't much of a record to judge by. Just think of this for a simple character! Our man of all trades, seventy-five years old, shoeless and patched, was hired a few days ago. He asked four dollars a month as wages. When we protested, he said: 'The price of rice is high; when it falls you can lower my wages.'

"Labor is cheap here. There is such a struggle for mere existence that the poor fellows work for almost nothing. They live on rice and vegetables, a pound of rice at five cents and three or four cents' worth of vegetables.

"Our first mission trip! It's as hard to describe as one's first dose of ether, but here goes! We left early Saturday morning, taking dinner close after breakfast for we were dubious about supper. Father Price wrote a long letter, possibly making his will and disposing of his royalties, while Father Gauthier, our French pastor, like a veteran, smoked up to the last minute, and then packed all his luxuries in a neat portable bundle. He insisted we include in our baskets

17

wash basins, blankets, dishes, and Mass vestments, and we looked like Peary and Co., as we set out with our two porters, with A-hon the indispensable Chief Cook and three chairs.

"I have long given up hope of finding the 'why' of Chinese names. Gashiu means 'Elegant Harmony.' It is a village of straggling houses facing a muddy drainage system. Long, long ago the Catholics here numbered twenty-nine, all from the Wan family. 'Wan' means 'to joke'; at any rate, we found 'nary a wan' there, and after ten minutes' rapid questioning, the Rip Van Winkle of the family appeared at the door of the chapel to tell us that one by one they had died in the years since the Mission was started. The chapel is a one-storied, single room, dirt-floored, furnished with two chairs, a table, and a faded picture of the Sacred Heart. It is simply one of the dozen shops on the road.

"How is this for pagan China? In Chungtinnam, after supper, which is late in this busy season, the town crier makes the rounds of the eight or ten streets, but instead of profane remarks on the time and weather, he yells: 'Time for evening prayers—quick, hustle! Time for evening prayers!' Can the Middle Ages show anything better than that? Then the procession. Each man and woman takes a bamboo torch, dips it in the kitchen flame, and lights the dark lanes of the village. That looks more like the catacombs than the Middle Ages, but it's Catholic enough anyway.

"But this crowd of one hundred and fifty does not go to church, because we have no church in this town. Instead, the first twenty people fit into the largest room in town, the next thirty pack into the courtyard and entrance, while the majority throng the alley outside. And this is not on Sunday only, but every single night of the week. Yet these are men and women who have planted rice ankle-deep in mud from daybreak till six in the evening."

Fr. Price died before our missioners had completed one year in China. His appendix had given him trouble for months. In August he realized that he must go to Hong Kong for an operation. He put it off until after the Feast of the Assumption. Then he missed his boat. When he finally reached the hospital in Hong Kong, it was too late. Fr. Ford received a telegram from the Bishop of Canton telling of Fr. Price's death. He set out immediately. He noted: "I had the same little hole of a cabin in the same ship in which Father Price last went away. He died on Friday, September 12th, feast of the Holy Name of Mary. He died happy, saying his last Mass on the feast of Our Lady's Nativity, carefully preparing for Viaticum and Extreme Unction. These he asked for and urged, when the nurses did not see the need. He sank rapidly a few hours later. The Sister remembered how his face beamed when he said, 'I shall celebrate today's feast with our Immaculate Mother. Oh! how happy to die today!'"

No Maryknoller was able to reach him before death. Fr. Tour, the French priest who attended him, said that Fr. Price's last words were: "Tell Fr. Walsh my last thoughts were for them all, and that I died in the love of Jesus, Mary, Joseph, and of Maryknoll."

Because of Fr. Price's devotion to Bernadette of Lourdes, we used to call him Fr. Bernadette. "I feel our saintly Father Bernadette will aid the society now more than ever, by his prayers for us," wrote Father Ford. "In offering Mass for him, I can't help envying his lifetime of preparation for meeting God. His room here will always be an inspiration for us to aim higher, or rather, to trust more in God. God is drawing Heaven and the Maryknolls closer together and we shall all be benefitted by the experience."

4. The Young Missioner

Five years after his departure from the States I saw Fr. Ford again. It was when I landed at Hong Kong. He with others was at the boat to welcome me. Though still boyish in appearance, he had matured beyond his years and had accumulated an enviable wealth of mission experience. The 1920's in Kwangtung were boisterous years: pirates, bandits, Communists, war lords were subjects of daily conversation. All this had its influence on the young missioners. From the hard knocks of an unpromising atmosphere Fr. Ford drew deep thoughts that were to form his views on the winning of China to Christ.

There was turmoil in South China throughout the early Twenties. The town of Yeungkong went through alternate periods of siege, peace and anxious waiting. Soldiers, machine guns, field pieces, trenches, barbed wire—all were part of the daily setting. Despite all this, Fr. Ford opened St. Thomas' School at Yeungkong for boarders and for day pupils. It was called after St. Thomas Aquinas, the patron of schools, and St. Thomas the Apostle who labored in the Far East and even perhaps as far as China. The name also kept Fr. Ford and his companions reminded of Fr. Thomas Frederick Price, their beloved leader who had his heart set on having a first-class school in order that vocations for the native priesthood might be encouraged, that catechists might be trained, and also that the dormant intelligence of Chinese boys might be developed.

He started a "Grandmothers' Home" for old women folk. A girls' school was opened later, an orphanage, too, a home for the blind, and other works of charity were multiplied as the years went on.

The Maryknoll Sisters arrived at Yeungkong in 1923. Fr. Ford's school boys, all in uniform, were at the boat to welcome them and escort them to their new home amid the din of bursting firecrackers. The convent which Fr. Ford had ready for them was a three-story building, something new in those parts, and during the day of open house, when the people were permitted to roam through the three floors, there were various amusing incidents since many of the villagers had never before been so high in the world.

Mother Mary Joseph visited Yeungkong after the Sisters were established there. Fr. Ford made her visit a gala event for the mission and for the town. He may have wished to show some appreciation in return for the attention which Mother Mary Joseph bestowed on himself and the rest of us during student days. "I doubt if any other Mother Superior has had such experiences and such a welcome," he wrote. "When we left Maryknoll for the missions, Mother had only a small group of Sisters to distract her, and she found time to mother every one of us boys. In fact, we still remember her Sunday desserts and feast-day specials; we remember the lean days, too, when an unexpected influx of visitors taxed her ingenuity with hasty puddings; we recall the huge piece of pie that somehow crossed our path in reward for extra labor done—the thorough understanding of the growing boy."

In 1925 a new field was assigned to Maryknoll, to the north of the territories already occupied. Fr. Ford and Fr. James Drought were designated as the first to enter it. This was the beginning of the work in Kaying, the Hakka mission, a particularly interesting region in China.

In a relatively high and mountainous country blessed with cool evenings, back eighty miles from the coast, these energetic and keen-witted people live their lives. French missioners had gone among them in the middle of the last century. There

21

were several thousands of third-generation and even fourth-generation Catholics awaiting the Maryknoll missioners when they arrived.

I was in Hong Kong to see Fr. Ford and Fr. Drought start for their new field. Rarely have I seen anyone so filled with joyful, vivacious interest. They were literally following the Gospel advice to "take neither scrip nor staff." They had the lightest equipment imaginable, hardly more than you would take for a day's picnic. But for Fr. Ford it was the real beginning. He had been experimenting, thinking over methods, sizing up the situation. The conversion of pagan China was a vast enterprise. It appeared so big, so impossible, and his own little efforts in Yeungkong seemed like nothing. But he had seen the problem, he had measured the difficulties, and he had his plans.

Fundamentally, his plans followed the methods used by the Church throughout the world, and throughout China, but he emphasized certain angles of approach. He took a course which ultimately became a distinctive method and attracted attention throughout China. Years later, Archbishop Riberi, the Internuncio in China, was to speak of him as the most advanced missioner in China.

Frs. Ford and Drought worked out their policy for the new work among the Hakkas. It consisted of four principal points: they would take care of the Christians and train them to be self-supporting by mission work on their own part; they would prepare a native Chinese clergy and Chinese sisterhood; they would insist on direct evangelism on the part of the missioners, despite the labor entailed in ministering to those already in the fold; they would introduce Maryknoll Sisters, not merely for schools and institutions of mercy, but for direct evangelism among the women. He and his fellow missioners had a big field before them: almost three million souls in nine cities, 178 towns and several thousand villages.

5. The Bishop

When the Hakka mission was erected into a separate ecclesiastical territory, Fr. Ford became its first superior; later, he became its first bishop. Bishop James Anthony Walsh, presiding at the consecration ceremony on September 21, 1935, must have felt great joy in raising his first student to the episcopacy. He may have foreseen that it would be one of his last public functions, for his health had been failing steadily; he died the following Easter. The ceremony was in the chapel of the Sisters' Motherhouse, the temporary chapel of the seminary being much too small. Co-consecrators chosen by Bishop Ford were Bishop Thomas Molloy, his director during high-school days in Brooklyn, and Bishop Stephen Donahue, a classmate at Cathedral College.

Bishop Ford turned to St. Paul for his episcopal motto. He chose the word "*condolere*," meaning "to have compassion," "to sorrow with," taken from Hebrews 5:1: "For every high priest taken from among men is ordained for men in things that appertain to God, that he may offer up gifts and sacrifices for sin: who can have compassion on them that are ignorant and that err, because he himself also is compassed with infirmity."

Better than anything else, perhaps, this motto tells us Bishop Ford's estimate of his vocation and his relation to his people. As a missioner he identified himself with his people. He had begun to feel ill at ease outside of China. I realize now that he was completely in earnest in his opinions about the Chinese, which at the time I thought were exaggerated and spoken mainly to entertain us. He could feel for and feel with the Chinese, and his ability to do so seemed natural, although it must have been the result of an effort, the logical working out of the implications of his vocation as he saw it.

23

Most interesting was the quiet and unobtrusive way in which he built up his little realm. There are many ways in which men may govern. Some centralize authority and initiative in themselves and by their strength, resourcefulness and, inspiration set a pace which their co-operators would by themselves never reach. Others distribute the responsibility among those about them, and thus awaken initiative in others. They seem thereby to touch unsuspected depths, and so arrive at great accomplishments.

Bishop Ford leaned toward the latter method. His hand, always firm when necessity required it to be so, was hidden; men's minds were happy and at peace when they worked with him, yet at the same time they were alert and fired to activity. His priests found pleasure in coming to him, and no one discovered him unready to sit and chat unendingly about mission problems, books, home, Chinese horses, cooks, catechists, or anything under the sun.

"We missioners are here for a double purpose," he said, "first of all to found the Catholic Church and, secondly, to make converts. I thought for a long time that our main purpose was simply to make converts, but Rome in her repeated advice to missioners insists that our main purpose is to build the foundations of the Church. The impetuous Celt or German would throw himself into activities. The Roman says: Organize, get your nucleus of Christians functioning smoothly and regularly. In the event of persecution, it is the organized Church that can withstand attacks."

From his first years in Kaying he had worked hard to build up the Chinese priesthood. He had his preparatory seminary. He sent his students to the major seminary at Hong Kong and some he sent to Rome. No doubt, while he was the first foreign Bishop of Kaying, he sincerely hoped that he would be the last and that his successor would be one of the

Hakkas. "Kaying has one building," noted Bishop James Edward Walsh on a visit to the mission. "It is not the residence of the missioners, with the seminary in the cellar or in a mat shed. The building is the seminary, with the missioners falling into the odd corners."

He did not hesitate to use new methods but was always careful, of course, to safeguard the fundamentals. When he was drawing up the constitutions for his Chinese Sisterhood, he had to state their general and particular purpose. The Maryknoll Sisters said: "Why not make them just like ourselves? Limit them to direct missionary work." It was done just as simply as that. Again at the Sisters' suggestion, he prescribed a new departure in the way of novitiates: instead of shutting the Chinese novices up for two years of intensified spirituality and cloistered life only, he decided that they should spend some of the time in actual work among non-Christians as apprentices under the older Sisters.

In ages to come, scholars looking back on the missionary work of the last hundred years may possibly charge us with three big defects. They may say, first of all, that we did not always seem to know where we were going, or at least, if we did know, that we did not always take the shortest road. Christ gave as one of the proofs of His mission that the poor had the Gospel preached to them. Have our methods really brought the Gospel to the great masses? Secondly, future historians may charge us with lack of enthusiasm when they compare us with the Christians of the early Church and with the missioners of the sixteenth century. Finally, it may possibly be alleged that we failed, at least to some extent, to identify ourselves with our people, to become all things to all men.

Obviously, there have been missioners in our own day, and especially in China, against whom these charges cannot

25

be laid. I am thinking in particular of Fr. Vincent Lebbe, and his confreres, and others like him. I am thinking of some of our own men, now passed to their reward, and I am thinking of Bishop Francis Xavier Ford. He was truly worthy of the great name he bore. "He wanted us to bring the Faith to the people," one of Bishop Ford's helpers wrote. "The Faith was to be a living reality, lived near the people, and something that they in turn could copy. He encouraged us to think up ways of making the Faith real to the common country people, that their humdrum lives might be lived on a higher plane. He wanted them brought into the inner life of the Church. He urged us to mix with the people, to walk through pagan villages, for he said that when a baptized person goes through one of these villages something good happens to it. This was his way of making us conscious that we were not only messengers, but also Christ-bearers."

In 1937 alone, Kaying reaped a harvest in the baptism of 3,300 well-chosen, well-instructed men and women. Word went around that Kaying had evolved an effective method of presenting the Faith. When a neighboring missioner asked for the secret, the reply was: "Bishop Ford." When he asked for details, the Kaying priest told him: "We sum it up in three points: 1) every member get a member, 2) come to dinner tonight at seven, and 3) don't just let George do it.

"Bishop Ford has trained us all to put the task of winning China up to our people. A part of every Sunday sermon goes to urging the congregation to convert their relatives and friends. In the back of the Kaying City parish church, a bulletin board carried a list of every man in the parish, and beside each name was a space for the non-Christian to whom he was pledged to bring the Faith. Bishop Ford's name was at the top of the list; he did his bit when he brought his barber into the Church.

"When we ask someone to call on us, we make it definite. Instead of 'come over to dinner some time,' we say, 'Come to dinner tonight at seven.' Finally, if we just let George do it, it won't be done right. Catechist teachers are zealous and good, but not good enough unless guided. Bishop Ford insisted that his priests and Sisters have a part in every study course for new Christians."

He insisted that the missioner's primary purpose should not be overlooked. "We are in China to present a Gospel," he explained. "We are not school teachers, or medical doctors or philanthropists. We have no right to present a distorted notion of the Gospel especially for first impressions. My stand on charity may sound a bit hard-hearted and therefore unchristian in its appearance to the hopeless, but the point is missed completely if such a conclusion is drawn. I have no quarrel with charitable works. Here, as everywhere else, it should be our aim to dot China with hospitals and clinics and asylums, or rather it should be our aim to energize our people into dotting China with such institutions. My sole contention is that we are merely directors of charity, trustees or counselors of our Chinese Christians in their service of the poor."

The bishop impressed upon his missioners the importance of the language for preaching effectively and for reaching the people intellectually; at the same time he emphasized the need of reaching their hearts through kindliness. He urged his helpers to study the customs of the people, their philosophy of life, their history, their religious beliefs. They were to change nothing in the life and customs of the people so long as there was no conflict with good morals and right belief. The missioners were simply to lay the foundation for the people's transformation into Christ.

Bishop Ford commissioned the Maryknoll Sisters in Kaying to participate actively in the work of converting souls.

He felt that they should not be limited to directing schools and staffing charitable institutions. They should go among the people. He wanted them to go not only into every village but into every home where the Name of God was not yet known. They were to build up a friendship between the people and themselves and eventually lead them into the Church.

This idea was not new. The Catholic community in the little fishing village of Aberdeen, for example, on the island of Hong Kong, owes its beginning to the presence of two Italian missionary Sisters who had their tiny convent there and went daily among the people. They had Mass once a week, on Wednesdays, when a priest from Hong Kong would reach them on his rounds. Bishop Ford's idea was to make this the Sisters' principal work, and in a few years he had thirty Maryknoll Sisters and Chinese native Sisters working out from thirteen different missions.

This form of apostolate called for a great deal of adaptation on the part of the Sisters. In this the Mother General of the Maryknoll Sisters co-operated fully. The Sisters went out through the villages, two by two. They would be gone for days, and this meant that they had to miss daily Mass and Communion. At such times, the Divine Office, spiritual Mass and Communion, the Rosary and other pious exercises helped to maintain their recollection and religious fervor. Periodic returns to the convent kept them fresh in the stream of religious and community ideals. The "cloister" in their convents was always safeguarded, but at the same time there was also a section in each convent which was the rallying place of women and children.

Religious schedules were adapted to the needs of the people. Everything possible was done to let the women and children feel that the Sisters were always at their service. The Sisters taught catechism at night, if the people were busy at work during the day. On their visits to the villages, the Sisters lived in the homes of the people.

The religious garb was simplified to fit the needs of mission travel over mountain paths, in river boats, adapted for wading rivers, for pedaling a bicycle, or riding on the back of China's newly introduced taxi-bicycle. The work-free periods of the people, such as after the planting or after the harvesting, or during the Chinese New Year holidays, were the times used by the Sisters to instruct new converts. They did some visiting all the time—to make friends, to follow up inquiries, to call on the poor, the rich, the sick, the dying, the good, the sinner, the educated, the uneducated, everyone who needed the word of God and His faith and hope and love.

The plan was approved by Archbishop Anthony Riberi, the Papal Internuncio in China. He asked that the same plan be adopted by bishops all over China, convinced that the Church in China would grow much more rapidly if more Sisters were made to participate in this direct apostolate of convert-making.

Such was Bishop Ford's method as shepherd of Kaying. He preferred to distribute the responsibility among those around him, arouse their interest, direct their efforts, and awaken new initiative in his eager helpers. There remained in him always a certain shyness. He would have found it easier to curl up in a corner and read and write, and would have preferred it to appearing in public and filling the role of captain and leader. His enthusiasm for his people and for his work among them, however, never allowed him to retire into anything like a hermit's life. He was a superior who could be eagerly obeyed and loved with lasting devotion.

6. The War and After

When the Japanese armies marched through China during the long war from 1937 to 1945, Hakkaland was affected only indirectly. The land forces did not approach Kaying. It was blessed in its strong natural bulwark: the home of the Hakkas is a pocket in the mountains, and the great routes across China do not pass this way. War planes flew overhead, however, and there were bombings.

"War has its purifying element," the bishop wrote in 1941, "not only that resulting from pain and misery shared with others, but also that from lighter moments shared in common. In every dreadful incident there is usually some comical mishap that relieves the strain and irons out the anxious lines on every face. This is especially good for us Westerners in China who have a tendency to solemnity and aloofness and who lack the natural simplicity of the average Chinese crowd.

"We like to feel that our restraint betokens coolness under fire and calmness in emergencies. Where others shout, we stolidly smoke our pipes; where others wave their arms and point out the approaching airplane, we content ourselves with a squinting glance and a grim appraisal of its direction and speed; while others frankly run in all directions, we uphold our pride by sauntering, content with our estimation of ourselves.

"In a hole dug for four, ten already are crowded, but they generously squeeze as only Chinese can, and fit you in. Of course the roof was built for smaller occupants, and to stand upright would be to lose your head, so you add the final touch by attempting to squat as do the Chinese. The sudden blast of the bomb and the curious silence after it that stills all natural life drive introspection off. You become conscious, in a detached way, of the centipedes and other insects shaken from the roof; you peek out the doorway and notice how green the grass is, and how clear the sun; the hush of the frogs and birds and crickets is startling for the moment.

"Then you glance at your fellow cave men and suddenly grin, thinking of the sight you must present to them, disheveled and dirty. As though this gave permission, they unleash an outburst of laughter. Your answering smile becomes a chuckle, then a full-blown laugh; and soon the dugout echoes and melts the sounds until you are one with the crowd. Laughter levels as surely as a bomb. As all scramble for the light and then slowly meander home, you feel closer to the people and understand them better."

His missioners point out the bishop's constant buoyancy and say that it indicated that his spirituality was securely anchored by the virtue of hope, the virtue which he himself referred to as the essential missionary virtue. "Hope at all times, and not merely in a crisis; this is the essential missionary virtue," he would tell them. "The danger that hounds us continually is reliance on self. We are God's coadjutors, not that He will do all the work, but that He will make up for what is lacking in our strength. With hope, we work as though all depended on ourselves, yet knowing without any doubt that all depends on God. With hope, we throw ourselves into our work with confidence."

During the war, his missioners worked among the refugees. Food was the great need. Many of the refugees were sick, underfed, excited. Mothers were looking for their children. Children were crying for their parents. They were all tired, frightened. "It's a grand opportunity to plant a little hope in these hopeless hearts," his missioners wrote, "to ease in some way the heavy weight of their sorrows, to bring a smile to their sad faces, to have some part in giving shelter to those

31

driven from their homes. What a privilege is ours! We sleep soundly at night; we know that in this work we are fulfilling part of the same noble mission for souls."

During those long anxious years of the war we were in the habit of looking forward to the postwar period as an era of great missionary activity. On August 15, 1945, Feast of the Assumption of Our Lady, when we were told that the war was finally ended, we said to ourselves: this is the beginning; from here on the Church will strike roots deep in Chinese soil. The outlook was good; we felt justified in our optimism. Bishop Ford, as usual, was looking ahead. His missions had grown steadily during the war. There was valid reason for believing that with normal times restored the Church in Hakkaland would flourish. It was indeed a magnificent vista.

"As new China will turn to the United States for examples," he wrote, "with more emphasis than heretofore on engineering projects, co-operatives, social Westernization, Western music and entertainments, and the whole gamut of modern American city life, it might pay us to emphasize somewhat that phase of education among our seminarians. Much good can be accomplished by priests equipped for handling social service, industrial problems, and youth service."

The cathedral of Kaying, which Bishop Ford had been planning over the years, began to take shape after the war. For twenty years the cathedral parish had been what he called "nomadic," using rented temporary quarters wherever possible. It started originally in a small house, where six Catholics could sit comfortably; it was a room under the pastor's bedroom. Next, the chapel was moved to a dwelling that would seat fifty persons. A former bus station, large enough to hold 100 worshipers, then became the parish church. Finally, the congregation moved into a house with a covered courtyard into which 400 persons squeezed to hear Mass.

When the new cathedral basement was more or less ready, the bishop and the pastor conducted a solemn ceremony, a sort of liturgical "moving day." At the end of Mass, the pastor invited his people to take up their pews and walk. "Of course, the business was conducted with liturgical flourishes," Bishop Ford wrote. "Vested in cope and towering like Saint Boniface before the druids' oak, the pastor sprinkled holy water on each group as the different sodalists came, two by two, burdened with a pew between them. He even improvised a 'Procedamus in Pace,' the signal for the procession.

"The old men and women were given the lighted candles from the altar, the missal and altar cards, the Stations of the Cross, and holy water stoups, to carry. The carpets were lifted in their dusty clouds of glory, and the sanctuary rail was taken in sections. The younger men and women raised their pews and, led by the cross-bearer and acolytes, in somewhat unliturgical procession moved through the fields and streets. At a decent interval, the pastor followed with the Blessed Sacrament, and then a new life began for the parish." Meanwhile, the official name of the diocese had been changed from Kaying to Meihsien.

During this postwar period Bishop Ford had the Sisters intensify their efforts of seeking out the people in their homes and bringing to them the joys of our Faith. His conferences to the Sisters brought out his own practical view of life. He made them realize the practical problems of life. He acquainted them with the moral tone of the pagan women of the district and the task of helping to Christianize them. He taught the Sisters to face reality without being shocked. During these instructions one became aware of the bishop's reverence for all God's creatures. For him, every creature was a sacramental. He used to say that everything we look upon or touch is holy, even inanimate creatures. He discouraged gossip. Gossipers and tale-bearers are the devil's agents, he said. It was easy for him to distinguish between the sin and the sinner in his reverent handling of souls; the souls were to be saved, not despised. He made his helpers conscious of souls and the price paid for their redemption.

"The joy of a missionary Sister must be mixed with gall and wormwood and must bear heavy on her strength," he told them. "It is the peace of victory, even with the smarting marks of combat. It is the joy of the rainbow seen through the storm. It is the calm cheer that tranquilizes us in times of stress or apparent failure, the peaceful assurance of God's Will that compensates abundantly for otherwise overwhelming discouragement. No matter how dark the world around us, how huge the task ahead of us, the thought that 'God is good' can send us smiling through life. We have the uproarious secret to thwart the devil and all his vanities. We know the answer to the world's riddles and we can afford to smile at so-called calamities. Like children playing hide-and-seek with God, we know we shall be tagged by God and caught in His embraces, and life becomes literally a game and a test and even a hard endurance test, but with the consciousness that God is judge and watching from the side-lines, that God is Himself the prize.

"We greet Mary daily in the *Ave* and wish her 'Ten Thousand Joys' and we should say it with a cheerful smile. We have companions with us everywhere, if we but will it, to keep us company on our mountain roads, a laughing, joyous troupe of friends of God. Again, if we but see it, the whole world about us is singing God's praises. The whole of nature is at our feet a sermon for our lips."

Bishop Ford built a pagoda at his central mission. "We

34

claim that it is the only useful pagoda in China," he explained. "Our pagoda is hollow. The first floor is a garage and has the pump installation for our water supply, connecting with a deep well underneath. The second floor contains the generators for the mission's electrical plant. The third floor is our repair shop. The fourth floor is for storage space. The fifth floor is a workroom. The sixth is completely occupied with our water storage tanks. The top floor is ready for the still unbought bell.

"The whole structure is crowned by a huge cement cross. Last Christmas we illuminated the cross with electric lights and it could be seen four miles away by villagers coming in for Midnight Mass. The cross is the highest point in the whole city.

"Pagodas, like the round towers of Ireland, are usually picturesque but useless, except as landmarks for footsore travelers, telling them they are near their destination. Chinese architectural principles did not permit us to put a steeple on the church. The pagoda solved the need for a landmark, especially as it is situated on a bend of the river and can be seen for miles.

"Besides, the Church here in Meihsien needed to get out of the catacomb stage. The graceful pagoda has become the prize subject of hundreds of Chinese kodak fans. As time goes on, hundreds of thousands will talk about the Catholic mission and its pagoda in their daily conversation, whereas formerly the Church was hidden away in low buildings."

7. The Red Tide Rolls In

Russian Communist influence reached China shortly after the Bolshevik Revolution. In 1919 large numbers of Chinese

35

students accepted an invitation to Moscow and Irkutsk to investigate the Soviet system. The Baku Congress of Nations of the Orient, held in September, 1920, at which twelve Eastern countries were represented, including China and Turkey, was conducted by George Zinoviev, President of the Executive Council of the Third International. Its purpose was to prepare Asia for participation in the world revolution. Among the guest members from other parts of the world signing the resolutions at this conference were Communists from the United States. From 1920 to 1925, the work of the Communist Party in China was entirely sub-surface; its campaign was among students and laborers.

At this time, the newly formed Kuomintang Government in China was struggling for existence. Dr. Sun Yat-sen was having a difficult time. He needed help from outside. In 1923, he sent one of his assistants, Morris A. Cohen, to the United States and Canada to recruit World War veterans to modernize his army. He also sent his English secretary, Eugene Chen, to Hong Kong and London to seek British aid. Both missions failed. He sought assistance from the Germans, again without success. It was then that Sun Yat-sen turned to the Russians.

Karakhan was Soviet Ambassador at Peking. He had Michael Borodin appointed as special advisor to Dr. Sun Yat-sen to negotiate eventual Russian help. Borodin saw that it was mostly a question of organization. He promised to get Russian arms and munitions on easy terms. With characteristic Soviet largesse, he also promised to provide a corps of military and civilian experts to help reorganize the government along Soviet lines. Thus the Reds got their hold on the country. By 1925 Borodin had acquired dictatorial powers; he had Russian and Chinese Communists in every pivotal position. Later, when Chiang Kai-shek became champion of the anti-Russian feeling among the people and became strong enough to act, he broke with the Communists. Borodin was forced to leave the country. But Chinese Communism lived on, even though outlawed, and during the next twenty years the Reds plagued their countrymen with outrage, terror, and cruel civil war.

Japan's invasion of China brought new opportunities to the Communists, who fought the Japanese mainly as part of their own campaign to conquer China for themselves. They used the war as an excuse to build up their military strength, although their military operations were of very minor importance; they gave far greater attention to political and economic propaganda. By the end of the war they were very strong.

I was in Manchuria during the entire war. I saw the Russian army come in. The Soviets took over the country and held it until the Chinese Reds had marshaled a large army there in the north, and to this army the Russians turned over great stores of confiscated Japanese arms and munitions. The Russians balked the Chinese Government forces when they tried to take possession of this part of China. According to a treaty signed by the Soviets, November 14, 1945, was the date set for the Russian forces to retire and the Chinese Government forces to enter Manchuria. The Russians kept putting off the date until, finally, the Nationalist forces found that they had to fight their way into Manchuria against a large Chinese Red army armed and equipped by the Russians.

The rest of the story is known. The Marshall mission helped to establish the Communists even more firmly. General Marshall's instructions from the Secretary of State referred to the "so-called Chinese Communists." Washington's Far Eastern experts, such as they were, urged support of this party of "agrarian reformers." This title and subterfuge was rejected even by Mao Tse-tung, China's chief Communist, when he finally achieved what he was after and thereupon announced

37

to America and to the world that Chinese Communists were *real* Communists.

President Truman had already made a public statement insisting on fair and effective representation for the Chinese Communists in a coalition government. Chiang Kai-shek knew that a coalition government with Communists was hopeless and impossible, but he agreed to make the experiment. To a Communist, "coalition" means to infiltrate and invade and eventually to take over completely.

The Reds, of course, played their part extremely well. When they came into Manchuria, they were deferential, friendly, they were of the people and for the people. To General Marshall's field teams, with which it was aimed to negotiate peace all around and friendly co-operation, the Chinese Reds appointed military and civilian representatives who were very likeable men, intellectual, sociable, great mixers, and they impressed the Americans. The Communist cause in China, as presented by these men to their American confreres on the Committee of Three, was going to be a great boon for China. China was going to be saved at last from corrupt officialdom, and there would soon be a nation of happy, prosperous small farms.

The Reds' friendly approach in Manchuria was merely an opening wedge. This quickly changed when they passed on to the next step of increased restrictions, and this in turn gave way to the reign of terror and complete domination. This was the pattern all over China, and it was the pattern in Hakkaland.

They came into the Kaying section first as guerillas. They posted proclamations saying that they were bringing complete freedom of religious worship. When their armies arrived, they put up notices signed by the commissar saying that Church property was to be protected and nothing to be removed without his authorization. The front of friendly co-operation was soon cast aside. Christians found themselves the object of discrimination. The missioner's altar boys were told to keep away from the church; it would go against them later in school if they went to the mission for evening prayers, and they would be barred from winning any prizes even if their marks should be the highest.

Bishop Ford was soon prevented from traveling around his diocese. He could still send out his monthly letters, exhorting his priests to be ready to suffer, just as Christ their Leader had suffered. At Pentecost 1949, shortly before Kaying was taken over by the Reds, he wrote: "Pain and suffering may be God's plan to purify our motives. Pain accepted in advance may be God's way to unite us more clearly to Himself. 'If they have hated Me, they will also hate you.' You must not expect Heaven on earth. As Christians we should share the Cross. Perhaps suffering is the only way we can expiate the sins of the world, our own and others. This should not worry or terrify us. 'I can do all things in Him who strengtheneth me.'"

He had watched the Reds' tactics in other territories and now he saw them at work in his own diocese. Freedom of religion was advertised at first, but then came anti-religious propaganda, followed by absolute suppression of any adverse criticism, and a rigid control of all news and information. Surplus food supplies were confiscated, the people were left helpless and hungry, and the control of the whole area was in the hands of a small group of officials who maintained their authority by armed force and terror.

On the first Christmas after the Reds took over, there was a record high attendance of Christians at Mass. Their fervor had increased steadily with the Reds' stepped-up persecution. The people now fully realized the Communists' hatred of religion; they realized that they were in danger of losing their Church, and it suddenly became more precious. Masses were crowded. More and more non-Christians came for instructions. Night classes of catechism were started. The people knew that their very presence at the Catholic mission would mark them as suspected foreign agents, and still they came.

Bishop Ford summed up the situation at that time: "Perhaps the most glorious page in Chinese history is now being written by the devotion of both Chinese priests and Chinese Catholics. There has been little panic and there is a surprising demonstration of fidelity to their Faith. Almost overnight the Catholic Body has been recognized even by puzzled pagans as the one anti-Communist force in evidence throughout China, not necessarily an endorsement of the Nationalists' regime, but clearly taking a stand on moral and doctrinal grounds. The Church, hitherto perhaps too aloof and esoteric, could soon become a practical way of life that pagans can understand."

In December, 1950, the Reds issued orders freezing all American property in China, movable and immovable, and in January, 1951, they issued another order confiscating all American institutions. On December 3, 1950, some of Bishop Ford's priests and Sisters were seized and put in prison. His Chinese priests, too, were imprisoned.

Two days before Christmas 1950, Bishop Ford and his secretary, Sister Joan Marie, were seized by the Reds, who invaded the church and rectory of Kaying to search the archives and to "discover" evidence that the bishop was engaged in anti-Communist, counter-revolutionary, and spy activities. Meanwhile, the other priests and Sisters of the Center Mission at Kaying were placed under house arrest.

The bishop was kept in solitary confinement, during which he was subjected to constant questioning. Several men went through his files day and night. He became pale, gaunt, and haggard. The Reds were building up a great propaganda campaign against him. They had "found" evidence to show that he was spying for the United States, that he was harboring Kuomintang agents, organizing a "black army" to rise up against the Communist Government, and preparing a plan to sabotage the Communist reforms of the newly established National Church. This was printed in newspapers throughout the whole country and, of course, in Moscow.

On the morning of April 14, 1951, Bishop Ford and Sister Joan Marie, both bound like criminals, were taken to court under an escort of thirty soldiers, and there judgment was pronounced on them. Then they were paraded through the main streets to the bus station. Students, soldiers, and some of the townsfolk had been planted along the way to create a demonstration and shout, "Down with the imperialists! Down with Ford! Death to the spy!"

Sister Joan Marie said afterwards that one incident of that journey from Kaying to Canton left an unforgettable picture in her memory. They were surrounded by the escort of thirty soldiers. The people along the way had their hands clenched and were yelling at them. The bishop was walking a few paces ahead of her. His hands were bound tightly behind his back; they were attached to a rope around his neck, and the two bonds were tied together in such way as to pull the head backward. In this awkward position he had to carry his bedding, a heavy bundle wrapped with a bamboo thong, and this cut through the skin of his fingers.

Sister knew well that if the bishop's hands were free they would certainly be raised in blessing over those people; even so, he did bless them before he left Kaying. He had never at any time shown any resentment for the injuries heaped on him. He had previously said that we should not be too hard on the Communists. He had said that they are not allowed to think, they are simply obeying orders, and they should always have our forgiveness. Even in those darkest moments, the bishop's patience and forgiveness must have predominated over any contrary feeling. "I was struck by the contrast," Sister Joan Marie said later, "the love of Christianity and the hatred of Communism. Love was bound, and hatred was free." Still bound, they were put aboard a bus and driven away.

8. On the King's Highway

Their first stop was at Hingning, where they were met by another military escort. The two prisoners had to carry their own baggage and walk from the bus stop outside the town to the jail at police headquarters. Preparations had been made for a demonstration. Middle-school students lined the road, armed with sticks, stones, and refuse. The bishop walked through the lines, slowly and deliberately, followed by Sister Joan Marie. Both were struck repeatedly and severely beaten. One of the students thrust a stick in the bishop's path to trip him; when he fell, he was subjected to a vicious clubbing.

The crowd got out of hand. Even the soldiers of the escort were beaten in the confusion and they ran away, leaving the bishop and Sister Joan Marie in the hands of the frenzied students. The bishop rose and continued calmly on his way, refusing to hurry. At least three times on that terrible journey through the streets of Hingning, Bishop Ford fell to the ground. Each time he would get up with great effort, and without turning to look to one side or the other would proceed on his way. Not once did he try to defend himself.

That night, in the prison at Hingning, the two prisoners were placed in different sections of the building. Sister, still very much disheveled from the beatings along the way and the refuse thrown at her, was made to sit upon a sort of improvised throne. The people were brought in to insult her and as they passed, one by one, they called out: "Where is your God now? What is He doing to help you? Our god is the devil. Our god has power over your God!"

The next day they were on their way again. Other stops were made, and the routine of abuse repeated. At Waichow the ropes were changed for heavier ones, but they were first soaked in water so that when they dried they might bind more tightly. The Reds tied the bishop's ropes in such a way that the end of one would hang down in back from his padded gown to look like the tail of a monkey. At Chung Muk Tau they went through it all again, with added humiliations. The journey finally ended in the big prison of Canton. During the confusion at the prison entrance, the bishop had a chance to speak to Sister Joan Marie. He said: "We're going to prison in honor of Christ, and it is no disgrace."

In the cells of the provincial prison at Canton the prisoners slept on the stone floor. There were no beds. Like all Chinese prisons, it was a place of punishment, and the prisoners' comfort was not a matter of official consideration.

The physical trials of this prison life were many, but they were a welcome distraction from a fear that haunted the prisoners daily, the fear of what they might say, what they might do, as a result of the physical and nervous weakness produced by long hours of forced Communistic indoctrination. Ordinarily, this lasted for about twelve hours every day, beginning at six in the morning and continuing, with short breaks for rice and rest, until ten-thirty at night. Fortunately, this regime did not continue through the entire period of imprisonment.

Some days no account would be taken of the hour, and the sessions would go on indefinitely, even until two in the morning. If there happened to be what the Communists called a "search faults" meeting, it might go on and on without end. Or there might be a trial, and that would last for days; one lasted for thirteen. At this time the leaders would help the prisoners to become good Communists, or, to translate their expressions literally, they would "carve out their defects" and "wash their brains." These were always horrible affairs filled with hysteria and physical violence, punctuated with screamings and denunciations. The constant questioning, the tension that came from the unrelenting effort to think up answers, plus the already weakened condition of the body owing to lack of food, placed a severe strain on the whole human system.

To make it all the harder, there seemed to be no common bond among the prisoners of the Communists. There was no friendship, no moral or spiritual link to hold them together, with the result that they yielded to the inducement to snoop and spy on one another with the idea of getting something to report. New prisoners coming in, apparently of good breeding and upright character, would little by little be influenced by the indoctrination, robbed of their personality, and transformed into repulsive creatures of suspicion and hate and deceit.

Sister Joan Marie caught a glimpse of the bishop a few weeks after they were put in prison. She did not see him again until January, 1952, nine months later. It was a quick furtive look through a crack in the high gateway; she saw him in the next yard, very close to the gate at which she was standing. "I was standing right in back of him. His neck was very thin and his hair was white, but I couldn't see too much of it because he was wearing a little woolen cap. His padded gown hung loosely on him as though he were very thin.

"He had a stick in his hand. There was another prisoner with him, one of the trusties. I recognized him. The bishop stood up and wavered on his feet as though he were trying to get his balance. He put both arms out. The prisoner laughed and told him to hurry. He walked a few steps. The sentries were in the center of that yard which opened on four cell blocks. The other prisoner started toward the sentries, then stopped and told the bishop to come. The bishop replied that he could not. The prisoner turned and pulled the bishop, who then stumbled and fell to his knees.

"When I looked through the gate again, I saw the other prisoner squatting down to let the bishop throw his arms around his neck. Then the prisoner stood up and carried the bishop on his back to the cell block. I supposed he was bringing him to his own cell.

"I didn't see his face. His legs hung limp like a rag doll. He was painfully thin and very limp. He seemed to have hardly the strength to straddle the man's back and hold on. He must have been very light, because it was apparently no effort at all to carry him, and on the way the other prisoner turned to the sentries and laughed. The sentries laughed, too. That was about January 19 or 20, 1952.

"Two days later I saw him again, the same way. I had to maneuver a little ruse to stand near the gate, because it was against the rules for us to peek through to the other yards. The gate had been boarded up and paper was pasted over the latch hole, but fortunately there were some cracks in the wood and spots where the paper was torn.

"This time I saw him plainly. His right arm was linked in the arm of another prisoner, and he had a cane in his left hand. He was walking with great difficulty, taking very small steps. I got a good view of his face. He was emaciated and weak, and looked like an old man of a hundred years. He had a beard that looked like white cotton. His hair was long and white. He seemed to be saying something to the prisoner. I had the fleeting impression that his face was peaceful.

"He walked with the prisoner toward the sentries, and

then back into the cell block where he had gone before. He was wearing his black padded Chinese gown which he wore to prison. He also had a clerical overcoat, and he was wearing a pair of warm bedroom slippers, brown, the kind with sheep's wool lining and zipper front. I recognized these things as sent to him from Kaying.

"I saw him once again. He was being carried up the stairs from the lower end of the cell block. He was over another prisoner's shoulder. I cannot say clearly just how he looked. I know it was Bishop Ford, but I cannot describe definitely his appearance. I was ill myself at that time, and confused. He was not being carried on the prisoner's back as on the former occasion; this time he was slung over his shoulder."

That was the last time Bishop Ford was seen by friends, so far as is known at present. On August 16, Sister Joan Marie was called to the warden's office for interrogation. There she was told that Bishop Ford was dead. She was shown six photographs taken of the bishop, supposedly in the hospital. One showed him in bed, with a doctor and nurse at his side. The bishop's head was swathed with bandages. The little woolen skull cap, which he was fond of wearing, was on top of the bandages. His face was clean-shaven, but emaciated. His cheek bones were very evident. His eyes were sunken. Two other photos were closeups and showed a dying man or one already dead.

She asked for copies of the photos. At first the officials said they would get her some, but later she was told that the negatives had been damaged. She asked for some of his personal effects; these also were promised, but none were given to her. They told her that the bishop had died on February 21, and they gave her a testimonial to sign saying that he died of illness and old age despite the medical care they had given him.

46

After this, Sister Joan Marie herself fell quite ill and for two weeks was in a Canton hospital. On September 1 she was brought to an old public cemetery in an isolated spot outside the city and shown the bishop's grave. There was a rough granite slab like those commonly used for grave markers. Painted in red letters were the characters of the bishop's Chinese name, plus the one word, "grave." It also had the date: February 21, 1952. That was all. The paint was still fresh. Soon afterward, Sister was ordered out of the country and escorted to the border.

A memorial Mass for Bishop Ford was celebrated in the cathedral at Hong Kong on September 14. It was the Feast of the Exaltation of the Holy Cross, and the cathedral was decorated with a great display of red color. There was a striking symbolism in the liturgy of that day, appropriately significant as a memorial service for the dead missioner.

Archbishop Anthony Riberi delivered the eulogy. He said: "Today, there is a temptation to gloom and despair among those of us who are weak in faith as we see the sturdy oaks of the Christian Church, such as Bishop Ford, being cut down, and the Cross, that was planted with such great labor and pain, uprooted by a grim and relentless foe of God and religion.

"Let us have courage and confidence in the One who said: 'Fear not, I am with you all days, even to the consummation of the world.' Bishop Ford's death is not in vain. In God's plan it is the planting of a seed that will yield a great harvest. Thanks to his inspiring example the soil of China will sprout with crosses that will make it the fairest field of Christendom. Have we not this assurance from Christ Himself? He said: 'Unless the grain of wheat fall into the ground and die, it remains alone. But if it die, it brings forth much fruit.' "

THOUGHTS ON THE MISSION VOCATION

" 'Go ye into the whole world' was spoken to the present-day youth just as much as to the disciples of our Lord in Galilee; and the response to this call will bring forth in American young men the very qualities that are needed most today— zeal for souls, and a manly spirit of sacrifice."

The Normal Life of the Church

"FRANK FORD WAS A THIN, WIRY, BLACK-HAIRED TYPE. HIS EYES *were penetrating but kindly; they told of reserve, of power, and of piety that was innate. He was a gifted lad, whose studies came easily to him, and who soon became very popular with his fellows,"* reminisces one who was a classmate of the future bishop in 1909-12.

At the graduation dinner, one after another of the young men spoke of the careers they had chosen. There was general surprise and even embarrassment when Frank Ford announced his intention of joining the newly founded Maryknoll Society. His decision to become a missioner was vaguely felt to be odd and even rather freakish. Many of Frank's relatives and friends shared his classmates' opinion.

In the later years, recalling his own earlier experience, Bishop Ford repeatedly emphasized the fact that the mission career is in nowise an extraordinary one. "It is the normal life of the Catholic Church," he wrote. "The Church has been a missionary organization from the very first setting out of the seventy-two disciples. There was never a time when the Church did not have missioners. . . . Granting that the missioner is a necessary part of the Church, it follows that the mission vocation is not intended by God as something rare or extraordinarily difficult, and therefore only for the few."

51

Qualities of the Successful Missioner

THE ABILITY TO PHILOSOPHIZE OVER HEAT AND COLD, TRYING conditions of travel, and lack of ordinary comforts is more valuable to the missioner than mere good health. A man who knows the need of ordinary precautions is going to do longer work than a recklessly healthy individual. Thus the physical qualities of the successful missioner may be limited to fair health, without either fastidiousness or heedless ignorance of nature's laws.

The spirit of study is a greater asset than actual knowledge, though it is true that no knowledge is wasted in China. The best missioner is one who realizes his ignorance, and is determined to better his condition. The worst mistake a man can make intellectually is to feel either that he has a sufficient working knowledge of theology for mission activities, or that a smattering of the Chinese language is his goal. A missioner should have more than the average priest's taste for worthwhile reading; without a well-thumbed library of standard theological books, he will quickly retrograde. Missions today have the complexity of modern life elsewhere, without the opportunity of letting others think for you.

Unless the intellectual attitude of the missioner is humble and inquiring, much of the native philosophy will escape him. He should have reasoned it out with himself clearly that his initial work is to know, love, and serve the Chinese people; then only will he be equipped to teach Christianity to pagans and to save their souls. He must be a student, as well as a teacher. He must keep in mind that he is primarily a missioner to souls, not a social reformer.

Spiritually, the missioner should be sufficiently humble to distrust his own powers; he should be grounded in the spirit of persevering sacrifice; and he should have acquired a habit of prayer that is independent of mood or outward circumstance. In other words, over and above the qualities of any good priest or religious, the missioner must have those that will carry him on when he is alone. He may be the only "other Christ" his Christians have as their model.

From a social viewpoint, the best missioner is a gentleman. He is considerate of others, guards his tongue and temper, and has breadth of outlook. The ultra-sensitive, the slovenly selfish, the secretive, the cocksure, or the surly man is unfit for mission life. Most mission work today is carried on among highly civilized races; and the man is mistaken who thinks that the missions need a backwoodsman type. The spirit of a St. Francis de Sales or of a St. Charles Borromeo is required for modern missions. (*1928*)

A New Approach Is Needed

THERE IS A SCIENCE OF SANCTITY, AND ITS LAWS MUST BE observed by those who seek to become saints. In this connection, we can with profit recall three laws of physics: (1) a moving body has a tendency to continue in the same direction; (2) a moving body tries to seek its own level; (3) all bodies seek to be at rest. Persons, as well as other "bodies," have a tendency to go along in a straight rut, not to strive for higher levels, and to become content with static routine. We missioners, too, need a new approach to our work, a renewed vision of the apostolic vocation, both for our own spiritual advancement and for the success of our labors for Christ.

Christianity is the most revolutionary doctrine in the world; the man who follows its laws is spiritually born anew. All through the Christian centuries the Catholic Church has given birth to new religious orders, to remedy some malady of the time. Each of these orders was at the period of its foundation a startling innovation, introduced not because it was new, but because it was needed. Such a Church is not well served by static missioners.

Now I do not mean that we should all become innovators; but each one of us should seek a fresh approach to our own relations with God and to our mission work. Am I really praying to God, or rattling off formulas? Do I try to vision God as I shall see Him on Judgment Day? Do I realize that each time I teach the mystery of salvation to pagans it is for them startlingly new tidings? Do I keep a childlike thrill of novelty in my own spiritual life and in my apostolate, or have I become cast, like cement, in adhering to certain preferred formulas?

We have to fight against human inertia and adherence to a drab, stale routine. Nothing is more insipid than the left-overs from a former meal; a picnic grounds after the crowd has gone is a sad place. We have to clean up our own soul and our own work as often as possible, in order to keep spiritually young and energized. We have been entrusted with the most glorious work possible, and in its performance, there is no room for tedium or monotony.

Each of us has to shoulder the salvation of the world, in so far as its people come into contact with us. We cannot seek refuge in routine and custom. The responsibility rests on each one of us as an individual. We must act as God's representative in interpreting His mind here and now, in this particular case. The obligation cannot be viewed as a burden, but rather as a thrilling challenge. God wants us to put life into our work—His Life. He wants us to become His Life. (1948)

God Needs Us

THE HARDEST CROSS TO BEAR IN LIFE IS THE THOUGHT THAT WE are wasting our time, that we are useless, that the world is rushing along and we, apparently, have not yet found our feet. For the missioner, the monotony of merely marking time, of facing petty tasks, or even of manufacturing small jobs to kill time, can be especially disheartening. Yet the nature of our work here in South China among farmers without leisure at planting or harvest time, the isolated situation of our chapel sites, the fewness of our Catholics, and the preoccupations of pagans elsewhere, compel us to pass many hours and sometimes days in humdrum monotony.

This monotony readily suggests to a nervous conscience that we could be doing better work elsewhere, that we are not really appreciated at our full worth, and that we are not given a chance to show what we could accomplish in busier circumstances. All of us have our daydreams of ideal conditions in which we modestly achieve wonderful success through our own plans, and in these dreams it is difficult at times to distinguish between inspiration and vanity. We all have our moments of dreadful tedium, when even our favorite books are distasteful and when we favor a chance visitor with unusual cordiality.

At such times we could recall with profit the words of the blind Milton: "Thousands at His bidding speed, and post o'er land and ocean without rest; they also serve who only stand and wait." God needs us where we are; we are active even in being merely on call; and the Omnipresent God is beside us even when we feel alone. God has willed to save the souls of men through their fellow men; and in the spiritual

55

warfare for the conquest of souls, sentrywork is essential though seemingly inglorious.

There is a tendency in modern moods to emphasize the emotional side of religion; and we are all somewhat tainted with this error. We are only too prone to look for sensible consolations in our mission work, and in their absence we are tempted to take a grim view of life. The remedy for this self-centered condition is contemplation and service of God. Contemplation takes us out of ourselves and focuses our attention on God; service of God instinctively issues from our contemplation. We see that God needs us in His redeeming of the human race; and we forget ourselves in satisfying God's needs.

Thousands would never hear about the true God were we not standing on call even in our most tedious hours, waiting for stray pagan visitors. The thought that God needs us is a heartening appeal to our healthiest emotions. No one is so useless that he cannot help God in His salvation of the world. The sooner we are conscious of the call to help God in His children, the more quickly we shall be able to react against moody emotions.

God needs our prayers, if simply to fulfill the prophecy that from the rising of the sun to its setting a clean oblation will be offered. God needs our adoration and thanksgiving and contrition and petition, to voice the duty of all creation and to obtain His favors contingent on prayer. God needs us as His arms and feet and eyes and voice, to demonstrate the love He bears all men. He needs us as companions in His life on earth, a life of sitting on the hillside and watching the heedless crowds pass by, as well as of active sharing in His apostolic work. Christ needs us to stand by His Cross when He allowed Himself to feel forsaken.

God needs each one of us here and now in a hundred small

ways, though the slightness of each need is no measure of its essential greatness. Our habitual reaction to this need, if the conviction of its urgency has been rooted in our souls, will stimulate our days to sharing in the life of God on earth, as useful and necessary members of His Mystical Body. (*1949*)

The Personlity of the Missioner

"No MATTER HOW WORTHY YOUR CAUSE MAY BE, YOU HAVE TO attract people to it; you have to make people like you." That is a bit of homely advice from Joe Smallwood, the statesman who united Newfoundland to Canada early in 1949. He spoke from experience, because the people of Newfoundland were very reluctant to give up their independence. They are more clannish and homogeneous than continental Canadians, and the rougher climate of Newfoundland and hardship of fishing on the banks have bred a reserve with strangers and distrust of polished, city-reared mainlanders. It took years of patience before the islanders could be won over to vote for union with Canada.

Looking at our own life in China, missioners are pretty much in the same situation as were the Canadian statesmen. We are trying to introduce an alien way of life to a people settled in personal habits and local customs, who are rightly cautious of strange notions. No matter how worthy our cause may be, it cannot be weighed on its own merits until attention is brought to it; and attention is attracted by personal contact with the missioner. It all comes down to this: people will be attracted to consideration of our religion only if they are attracted to us. A businessman's integrity invites dealing with him, and we missioners are essentially promoters or salesmen.

The missioner cannot afford to let personal traits interfere with his salesmanship. I recall a missioner who was meticulous in his priestly duties, but so cold and reticent with strangers that few pagans ever came to see him. He was concerned at their aloofness, and said a special Mass every week imploring God that he might win their attention. Yet when visitors did approach, he received them with stiff formality, with no unbending to their rustic ways. He was soon left undisturbed in his rectory.

I once asked Bishop Fulton Sheen the "secret" of his many conversions. It may be unfair to quote him without permission; but he gave, among several other reasons, two that struck me especially: people expect a priest to talk religion, so he should not hesitate to introduce the subject into his conversation; and secondly, people are interested only in those interested in them as individuals, so we must show our personal interest in potential converts.

How, then, can we attract our Chinese pagans? The desirable approach is not one of stiff decorum, or a bustling, efficient manner, or, in fact, any mannerism that calls attention to ourselves except as being interested in our visitors. The attitude we must strive after is the one that will make the stranger feel at ease with us, and unaware that we are mentally sizing him up. If nature has endowed us with a tight, straight-lipped face, or if cares have carved seams in it, we'll simply have to practice smiling. Silence can be golden in a monastery, but on the missions it will rarely draw out a bashful stranger. On the other hand, a hearty laugh, or at least a smile that starts from the eyes down, may win over a nervous visitor.

I've noticed, in traveling by bus here, the difference that a smile makes. When the struggle for a seat unconsciously registers on my face as a frown, and I pass off the inconvenience with a smile or a joke, soon the whole bus is chatting with me.

We are really blest in our people. They break into a smile so easily that it takes effort to beat them to a pleasant expression.

There are other ways of attracting strangers, of course. Few men have had greater success as a politician than Jim Farley, and one of his foremost assets is the ability to remember peoples' names and faces, and where they live. Cardinal Spellman once remarked that the conversation a stranger appreciates best concerns his own name and his home town. The casual acquaintance whose name we remember is immediately drawn to us. This may seem a small matter, but too many missioners go through life without attempting to become personally interested in individuals; we simply cannot treat strange pagans as a mob or a group, and then expect them to be attracted to our religion through a liking for us.

St. Paul described the labors of the Christlike apostle as "spending and being spent" for others. No one can resist the person who reveals a deep interest in him as an individual, a sincere, spontaneous interest that does not count the cost. (*1949*)

The Apostolic Vision

A GENERATION IN THE UNITED STATES HAS GROWN UP TO WHOM the concept of the Church as a missionary organization is familiar. In our Catholic schools, among the clergy, and in religious institutes, studies of mission problems, symposiums, and mission rallies are the order of the day. All these activities have driven home to the conscience of American Catholics their duty to continue the Acts of the Apostles. The present generation, then, takes an increasingly important part in the spread of God's Kingdom.

We are apt to forget that this is a new development in the life of the Catholic Church in the United States. It has been accomplished within two generations. Fifty years ago, when young Fr. James Anthony Walsh began his missionary career as Boston Director of the Society for the Propagation of the Faith, the vision of a message to pagan nations had not yet been given due attention by Catholics in the United States. The Church in our country had been absorbed in the struggle to make provision for floods of needy immigrants; and she did not emerge from her own missionary status until the year 1908, when she ceased to be under the jurisdiction of the Sacred Congregation of Propaganda.

The Society for the Propagation of the Faith was nominally established in many dioceses, but in only two or three was it functioning with any success. The reason for this was, as St. Thomas puts it, that "the preaching of the Word must proceed from the fullness of contemplation"; and as yet the notion of a world-wide mission was too vaguely grasped by the American Catholic. When Fr. James Anthony Walsh entered on his duties as Boston Director of the Society for the Propagation of the Faith, he quickly sized up the situation and attacked the problem with fundamental remedies.

He realized that the unknown cannot attract, that interest and sympathy must first be developed, and that knowledge would lead to co-operation in mission endeavors. He understood, too, the superficiality of a merely emotional appeal, so he emphasized the need of convinced sacrifice for the mission cause. He began his life-long campaign for volunteer missioners. Few American Catholics had ever seen a foreign missioner, and when they had, his English was broken, his beard was usually luxuriant, and he hailed from some unpronounceable corner of dim Asia or Africa. Fr. Walsh saw that American Catholics needed to be given a corrected vision of missions and missioners, and that this would require calm, steady instruction, without sensational approach.

Fr. Walsh launched a mission magazine, intriguingly entitled *The Field Afar,* as an organ of information. With his quick eye for news toned to the American sense of humor, he presented the mission cause without oratory, using terse, pointed understatement, and a conversational style that presented the whole argument without preaching. He was possibly the first to present the missions in language akin to the American taste. His magazine was readable and widely read, while the Catholic press began to appreciate his mission items as news, apart from their religious origin.

Fr. Walsh was objective in all his varied interests, and he carried that unemotional, impersonal touch into his mission arguments. He had an ax to grind, but it was the Church's cause, not his own aggrandizement. His statistics were verifiable and his conclusions were cautious. Insensibly, he convinced the Catholics of America that the Church is essentially apostolic, and that the furtherance of the mission cause is normal to our spiritual life and necessary for its growth.

As part of his task of making Catholics of the United States mission-minded, Fr. Walsh journeyed through Europe, studying mission problems as solved by older nations. He presented to American Catholics their first broad view of Europe's great missionary organizations. His descriptions of the valiant efforts of little Holland to staff the mission fields were literally an eye-opener to complacent Americans. He entered into wide correspondence with outstanding missioners throughout Asia and Africa; and in depicting these seasoned apostles in *The Field Afar* he gently corrected many misconceptions of mission life.

Fr. Walsh began publishing books—lives of missioners that portrayed their subjects as human, and thus comprehensible to modern American readers. His writings were devoid of pious platitudes and spurious foreign atmosphere. Today the general literary trend is to write the biographies of saints in this fashion, but Fr. Walsh's treatment of saintly missioners was in those years a refreshing novelty.

Perhaps most characteristic of Fr. Walsh's traits as a missioner was his patience. He did not expect to revolutionize America overnight. He appreciated fully and used successfully the means of modern publicity for promoting his cause; but he was careful to give it only due proportion, along with the rest of the many-sided life of the Church. Thus he aroused little or no antagonism by his presentation of mission needs.

For many years, Fr. Walsh considered himself merely as a promoter of the mission cause. One of his chief motives in journeying through Europe was to enlist the aid of any European missionary society that was willing to establish a branch in the United States. He doubted his ability to launch such a society himself; and it was only after frequent urging from prudent counsel that, in despair of outside aid, he seriously entertained the notion of a native American society. Even then, he acted only at the insistence and with the co-operation of a veteran North Carolina missioner, Fr. Thomas Frederick Price.

Once Fr. Walsh's decision was made, he showed his vision in the prudent choice of professors to form the spirit of the new institute along missionary lines. He obtained mentors from the Paris Foreign Mission Society, the English Mill Hill Society, and the French Dominicans. Fr. Walsh studied the methods of all the larger missionary societies abroad, consulted leading prelates and priests in the United States, and leaned gratefully on the experience of seminary directors and heads of religious orders. Thus he gracefully knit the combined missionary aims with the spirit of Catholic America.

Fr. Walsh continued to be content to cope with problems as they arose, never forcing the issue. Whether as a Director

of the Society for the Propagation of the Faith, or later as
Founder and Superior during the formative period of the new
Maryknoll Society, he always demonstrated a practical vision
of the time when the Catholic Church in the United States
would attain full apostolic stature, by assuming her due share
in the expansion of God's Kingdom on earth. (*1950*)

The Lure of the Missions

THERE IS A CURIOUS APPEAL IN THE LIFE OF A MISSIONER, PURELY
accidental and very often absent in fact, yet so associated the
world over with mission life that it were hard to think of one
without the other. It is best summed up in the phrase: "The
Lure of the Orient"; it has two phases: the exotic mystery of
the East, and the hardy life of the missioner. Such a view of
mission life, partly true and largely false, is in itself harmless.
The world has absorbed the thrilling letters of the *Jesuit Relations* and their continuation in the *Annals* and in more modern
mission biography, all of which strive to be objectively true
even when colored by unconscious bias. But it is not the whole
story, and in these irreverent days of general debunking the
question presents itself: Is the missioner's life one of exciting
adventure?

To form clear ideas on a missioner's life, we must see his
work according to the Church's pattern, which has been drawn
soberly in Encyclicals from time to time. The experience of
centuries of mission effort is also a sure guide to the general
policy of the Church, for she does not allow abuses to harden
into habits but continually remolds and freshens and rejuve-
nates her personnel. There is probably no secular organization
so alive to the changing moods of nations and fashions, so
willing to experiment along new lines, so insistent on adjust-
ing her methods to national customs and fusing her own with

native new blood; her pioneering and tutelage are as short as possible, and usually several generations ahead of political policies adopted by governments with colonies. But the secret of her assurance in launching new endeavors, humanly speaking, lies in her blueprints that have conserved essentials, and noted well-tested experiments, and allowed leeway for accidentals. Radical innovations, to a forgetful world, are merely pages from her logbook of 2,000 voyages.

Her apprentice, nevertheless, must meet her measurements; the articles of indenture are very definite, though sometimes couched in language whose import is beyond his experience, but he may confidently sign on for life and identify himself with a cross. This does not mean, however, that the Church seeks adventurers or impulsive innovators. The success of her enterprise in new fields depends on the assurance that her personnel will carry on in normal obedience. This is their real test of courage and enthusiasm. If the missionary sailor is to venture into strange circumstances, he must be content with the restraints of teamwork and steady monotony; the sea to be charted is new, but the routine is without glamor. Too frequently the unseen horizon is forgotten in the tedium of the nearest wave, and the hand becomes calloused and the eye weary keeping the wheel pointed with the compass.

To be successful, then, must a missioner be a mere automaton; must the distant lands be debunked of their lure and the spirit of adventure in normal veins become anemic? Must the sailor forget his characteristic gait, his ready humor, and his boyish grin; must his dreams be disillusioned at the outset; will it help him to learn that, though of all men the world over the sailor is most welcome, yet in every port he is considered fair game for native guile? Must the salt and holystone and scurvy grub be his daily portion, without sight or smell of jungle palms or exotic oddities; must the spice and zest of tropic isles be sweated out of him by scraping barnacles, before he be granted shore leave?

No, a thousand times! The supernatural builds on nature and there is inevitable enticement in strange lands, the air is heavy with scents and the eye with sights; the blood is quickened with peril and the toughest skin dyed a deeper tan, especially in the seasoning first contacts with the Orient; and he who sails as a missioner is denied none of the colored impulses that touch newcomers to the tropics. It is God's will that the East allure, and that the mist and haze beglamor land and people at the outset. Too soon and thoroughly the day becomes a brazen heat, and shade or night is dark; the wilted godlessness of man and scene is a burden to the soul, the very stars are strangers, and the natural cry arises for some familiar sight. The contrast is startling at times between the opal and sapphire tinge of sky reflected in the light jade of the sea, that greets the missioner on his land fall, and the same sky and sea that have somehow become a drab unfriendly, lifeless scene to eyes later jaundiced by malaria.

In a sense, neither view of the Orient is true; each sins by excess, and it is only from the Church's level that they can be reconciled and shaded with God's palette. The Orient is mystic to a heart aflame with the zest to woo it, and dismally silent and cold when the echo of God's voice is spent. From the captain's deck and seen at a certain distance, as a whole, the lands of the East are a challenge to be met for Christ; too near and heedless of a pagan sun, the perspective is lost in the dust and glare, and the stamina to fight is weak, as the task looms gigantic in the tropic heat.

Should disillusionment, then, be in the training of a missioner, or should he wait until the noonday sun has chased the cooling shadows from his work? It matters little, provided he be trained to work objectively with the Church's aim before him. The types of men that make the missioner are so varied that there is room for both approaches to the problem: the prosaic, stolid character may prefer to face facts without coloring; the sanguine, on the contrary, is enamored with the setting —either is hopelessly immutable, and would feel cheated if treated as the other wishes. Whether the soul of the phlegmatic is steeled to the blows that inevitably come to every man, or the imagination of the enthusiast is kindled with high romance, it is an even chance for successful work, provided both seek Christ in the East.

The one test of service in the Orient is willingness to take whatever comes in fair and foul weather. The local conditions beyond the missioner's control do not alter the contract; and his success is gauged under such difficulties by his perseverance, not by measures to avoid them. This test in theory seems easy and reasonable; but as it covers the varied demands of life in the Orient, it resolves into monotonous fidelity, along lines familiar to all priests from childhood. The sacraments must be administered and, though the setting be changed, the essentials remain the same. The poverty and uncouthness of pagan surroundings, indeed, distract and dampen enthusiasm rather than quicken it. In the abstract, it would seem thrilling to bring Viaticum over steep mountain paths to a distant village; in fact, however, the inconvenience of heat and weariness, the incongruous squalor of a village hut, and the pagan neglect of sick neighbors, robs the sense of poetry. The poetry is there, of course, if seen by faith; but the beauty is all within and in spite of external nuisances, and it strikes the missioner according to his viewpoint.

If he be the type that leans heavily on emotions, he will often feel the weakness of his staff; if he prosaically live in the will, he misses much of the overtones that modify monotony. Blessed is he who can seek the beauty of a supernatural spirit informing the meanest clay; and if his missionary life is motived by this search, as it drives him up and down the mountain trails seeking and seeing Christ in his work, he is successful, whether or not the world ever hears of him.

The natural allure of strange lands and peoples is the least enduring of mere physical sensations, and based on emotional reactions it may come and go in an instant—yet it is this that the unthinking call the "lure" of the Orient! It may bring the missioner to the nearest Oriental port, but rarely beyond the gangplank. There is a far stronger attraction that animates some ardent souls; they vision easily the enormous pagan throng and confidently, by some gap in reasoning, see themselves as Xaviers in spiritual conquests, tired with the physical strain of the very rite of baptism. Such dreams touch the outer confines of the neurotic, and are no more sustaining than the physical lure. They may be more harmful, as masquerading under a spiritual halo that would eventually make actual conditions drab and slow by contrast.

A motive that not only strengthens the will but also sustains it through the humdrum dog days of the tropics is that of sharing in the obedience of Christ; this obedience need not rob the missioner of the poetry of his life. Indeed, it is the only factor that brings out the essential beauty of his vocation. It is the Mystical Body of Christ that is comely and that makes the work desirous; this vision lost, the missions of the globe are colorless at the very least, if not totally disheartening, and paganism shows itself an ugly mass or a monster with unhealthy ulcers. There can be no beauty in a Christless world, as even nature borrows of His raiment in reflecting God; a truly pagan atmosphere is sulphurous and gloomy in despair. There is no purely natural beauty left on earth anywhere, because corruption is inevitable where the Cross has not been planted.

The attraction, then, of mission life lies essentially in its opportunity to share in the work of redemption, which, after all, is common to the Church's mission everywhere. The added zest of work in pagan lands is real, of course, and due perhaps to the concentration possible on the purely spiritual without the attractions of normal home life, but in its essence it differs not at all from apostolic work in any land. Paganism has its own distractions, not attractions, which perforce emphasize by contrast the missioner's ideals, and thereby purify his motives by repulsion.

He is thrown for mere companionship more into his own communion with God, and breathes his native air in his chapel and finds there even natural links with home. Out in pagan alleys, or on the mountain trail, he must bring his God with him in his thoughts to keep above the natural. It is the dilemma of every Christian, of course, and not peculiar to the missioner; but it is brought home to him perhaps more vividly, as a necessary safeguard to his sanity of mind and body. He steps into a void without sustaining helps, once he deviates from this close union; and he lacks the correctives of a Christian atmosphere to steady him. His very peril, so to speak, is an added incentive to straight reasoning and clarifies his principles, so that it can be said his way is simple and less complicated, his duty clearer and hence more squarely met; he sees more visibly the need, and senses tangibly the strong hand of God.

If directness of aim and a life untangled by mixed motives, helped, too, by the physical aid of tropical humidity and heat, are more than accidental concomitants of mission work, a missioner may indeed be said to lead a well-balanced life, when all is raised above the natural in obedience to Christ. A successful missioner, then, is measured by standards other than this world's, but perhaps more easily evaluated in a balance marked by divine degrees. (*1942*)

The Mission Vocation

THE SUMMER VACATION PERIOD IS A TIME OF DEEP THOUGHT AND resolution on the part of Catholic young men and girls just graduated from our schools in the United States. The all-important question of vocation demands an answer. And, of the million Catholic graduates, some few will hear the words of our Lord, "Go ye into the whole world, and preach the Gospel to every living creature," and will interpret these words as a personal call from God to offer themselves for His missions.

Some, hearing this call, will pass it by as too hard for their feeble nature; some will deem it presumptuous on their part to aspire so high, feeling that the vocation to the missions is a rare one, given only to specially chosen souls; while others will fear the criticism of being odd, and out of the ordinary, and somewhat freakish, and will be unwilling to invite the smiles and surprise of relatives and friends.

It behooves all of us, then, to come to a right understanding of what a mission vocation demands. Whether we stay at home or offer ourselves to the cause, we all need to have a correct idea of mission work, so that we may not hinder, but may even help ourselves or others to answer the needs of the Church in distant lands. It is doubly important at the deciding point of life to have a just picture of the mission vocation, in order that our judgment may be accurate and always satisfying. We owe it to God and to ourselves to find out what He asks, in the invitation to preach the Gospel throughout the world.

First of all, and what is perhaps the most surprising of all to many, the mission career is not an extraordinary one, fit only for specially generous souls. It is the normal life of the Catholic Church. The Church has been a missionary organization from the very first setting out of the seventy-two disciples, even before the Last Will and Testament of our Saviour was announced on the Mount of the Ascension. The Church has had its missioners from Sts. Peter and Paul down to the present day. There was never a time when the Church did not have missioners; there was never a country that was not converted by missioners—in plain words, then, the missioner is part and parcel of the Church's organization, and is no more extraordinary, no more a luxury, than any other workman for God.

And the reason for this is easily seen. The Church is One, Holy, Catholic, and Apostolic. It is One because its doctrines are always the same, no matter where practiced, and this requires the transmission of the truths from converted to pagan minds by missioners. The Church is Catholic because missioners have spread its truths throughout the world, and have not reserved salvation to a privileged few. In other words, the Church of today is One with the Church of all time, because its priests have been missioners.

Hence, the attitude of unthinking minds, expressed in the idea that mission work is a new-fangled fad, is totally at variance with the essential note of the Catholic Church. The missioner has been part of the organization of the Catholic Church from the beginning; is today as necessary to the very life of the Catholic Church as he always was; and will remain so till the Gospel shall have been preached to every living creature.

Granting, then, that the missioner is a necessary part of the Church (and by necessary we mean that without him the Church would no longer be the Catholic Church), it follows that the mission vocation is not intended by God as something rare or extraordinarily difficult, and therefore only for the few. If America were to realize that mission work is the ordinary, *normal* life of the Church, our seminaries could not contain the applicants offering themselves.

I stress this point, as it answers at one blow most of the objections against the mission vocation. If mission work is the normal life of the Church, then it cannot make demands that are impossible to human nature; if it is the very life of the Church, then it is not enough that a scattered few offer themselves. Our Lord chose seventy-two out of the few hundred who followed Him, and sent them forth. Where work requires the co-operation of many (and mission work demands thousands, and literally hundreds of thousands of new recruits), it is evident that it can be accommodated to the abilities of the many.

And, finally, for those who fear being termed odd and freakish were they to embrace a mission career—it is important to repeat again and again that the Catholic Church is a missionary Church, and that aspirants to the missions are really the logical type, and those who seek to prevent them are acting against reason.

This brings us to another important point, the fact that the qualities needed for a mission vocation are practically those required for any priest. The missioner has a double life: that of the ordinary parish priest, with its steady, unvarying demands on the patience and perseverance of the priest in the daily administration of the sacraments; and, secondly, his more missionary occupations. Even the first phase of his ministry is, or can be made, romantic. The absolving of sinners, and the most sublime act on earth, the celebration of the holy Sacrifice of the Altar, should never be considered as dull, prosaic duties. Whether performed in New York City, or in the heart of

Africa, the administration of the sacraments raises the priestly life far above all natural occupations, and the sacrifices demanded by such duties ennoble the priestly soul.

A missioner shares with his clerical brother at home all the romance and sacrifices incidental to the care of souls; if both this joy and hardship are increased on the missions, they but give the missioner so much the greater right to the sympathy of priests at home. But, in parochial matters, the missioner is more than a parish priest. He concentrates in himself not only the pastor, but also the school principal of a dozen schools; he is besides janitor, and teacher, and sometimes his own catechist, and cook. He usually runs a medical dispensary, an orphanage, and an old folks' home of one sort or other. In short, even in the usual parochial matters, he has more than his share of experience, and the qualities that make for a successful parish priest at home are necessary in a missioner.

But, over and above all this, he has duties that are peculiar to his own vocation. He must learn a foreign language, adopt the ways of his new field, put up gracefully with all its seeming shortcomings; he must become acclimated to strange weather conditions; and learn to adapt himself to the different manners and customs of his flock. He must school himself in the hard discipline of loneliness, and learn the value of renunciation. He must become all things to all men, that he may gain all.

I have put the demands of a mission vocation clearly on the table, to make you realize that there are practical difficulties to be faced by every missioner, and to establish the point that mission work requires previous training along special lines. The virtues sought for and instilled in foreign mission seminaries are especially these: humility; the sturdiness of character which will enable the missioner to "go it alone," without much supervision; cheerfulness in adverse circumstances; and adaptibility, or the power of accommodation. Add to these qualities prudence in administering finances, and a practical judgment of relative values, and the result will be the ideal missioner.

This subjecting the mission vocation to severe scrutiny, and dissecting it in a heartless way, may appear to give too lifeless and dry a presentation of the work, and that is very true. There is another side to mission life—the side that makes it so attractive to the missioner, the side that brings out all his loyalty for the cause, and brings on a feeling of homesickness and dismay when he is absent from his mission. There is both a natural and a supernatural attraction peculiar to mission life.

Ask the fur-clad priest in his igloo in the frozen north, or the white-robed missioner of the tropics, ask the patient, plodding apostle among the almost hopeless Mohammedans, or the apparently forgotten worker among our Negroes in the South. There is no need to ask them—one can see in every eye a peculiar joy in their work—and it is the joy of sacrifice for God. Any sacrifice begets peace and contentment, and this is true even of self-inflicted sacrifices; but there is a special reward for unplanned and undeliberated sacrifices, imposed by others and suffered for God, and mission sacrifices are of this order. They come unexpectedly, and under the guise of pagan lack of sympathy. They are met with even in the thoughtful love of Oriental Christians, whose etiquette makes heavy demands on the missioner. It is the constant, inseparable sacrifice mission work demands that gives it such an attraction, even naturally, for human nature likes to be challenged to a test.

This call on the missioner's better qualities makes of his life a real romance. Of all priests his activities are, on the average, the most varied. Up at all hours before dawn, how often must he say his Mass on an improvised altar, in a barnlike structure that is bare of inspiration and lacking even in essentials. How often must his day's work include a harrowing ride for twenty or thirty miles on mountain paths, or pathless plains, down steep valleys, or fording swift streams. How often do his travels oblige him to long fasts, and scanty meals of unpalatable foods, and, tired in every muscle and bone of his body, he must find his rest as best he may on the roughest of beds.

This is the glorious side of mission life, the petty, constant sacrifices that make the missioner's day profitable for souls almost unavoidably. His work is a continuous call to hearken back to the sturdy qualities of the Apostles; it demands a manly spirit, and repeats that demand throughout his life, until the missioner rightfully has taken on the aspect in our eyes of a creature above the natural.

He has inherited the crusaders' cross from St. Bernard, the spirit of adventure from St. Brendan, the laughing eye and tongue of St. Sebastian, along with his gridiron. The missioner espouses Lady Poverty with St. Francis of Assisi, renunciation and isolation with the Trappists, and fasting with the hermits. In all reverence and justice, we may say the mission life is the quintessence of them all; the one field wherein all the activities of the Church are united, and flourish side by side. It is a startling truth, and shows the excellence of the mission vocation, that the missioner combines in himself all the varied phases of the Church's work. He fasts with St. Jerome, and preaches with St. Paul; he is more alone than many a recluse, yet exercises all the social graces of a St. Francis de Sales. It is no mere rhetorical statement to say that the multiform activities of the missioner are a sign that he is necessary to the Church, that he is essential to the Church, or rather, even, that the Church herself is essentially a mission organization, and finds her true growth and flourishing in mission endeavor.

The mission vocation is a hard one, though not beyond human strength. It makes demands of a very practical nature on the body and soul of the missioner, but it is also a most logical vocation, a necessary vocation, and incidentally, a heroically romantic vocation.

"Go ye into the whole world" was spoken to present-day youth just as much as to the disciples of our Lord in Galilee; and the response to this call will bring forth in American young men the very qualities that are needed most today—zeal for souls, and a manly spirit of sacrifice. "Pray ye therefore the Lord of the harvest that He send forth laborers into His harvest, for the harvest indeed is great, but the laborers are few." (1935)

IN TOWNS AND LITTLE VILLAGES

"The lanes and roads and streets of China are worn by passing thousands, the air is loud with the busy cries of vendors, countless careworn hearts are weary as they pass along; but few among them have ever heard of the one True God. Ours is the most thrilling vocation in the world, the privilege of making straight the way of the Lord in these towns and little villages."

Seen from Hakka Hilltops

As Bishop Ford journeyed over narrow trails of the Hakka hills, he delighted in looking down on some teeming Chinese city or little village surrounded by its rice fields. In the towns, worshipers sought their pagan temples, jostling crowds pushed by small shops overflowing with merchandise of every sort, and the sampans on the cluttered water fronts swarmed with boat-dwellers. The green of the village rice fields was dotted with dark clothes and big hats of toiling farmers. Everywhere there were people, people; and sometimes not one of them knew about the True God.

Often, Bishop Ford was struck with compassion for these pagan towns and villages, but his yearning had not the sadness of Christ's longing for obdurate Jerusalem. These Chinese souls had not rejected God's prophets; it was simply that no messenger had yet reached them with glad tidings of the Kingdom of Heaven. At such times, new plans for establishing contact with the loved pagans made Bishop Ford's heart glow with fresh apostolic confidence. When the Communists took over in that section of South China, he and his missioners had brought Christ to over 20,000 souls in Hakka towns and hamlets.

Representatives of Two Faiths

The Buddhist monk slowly unbent and stood up straight and held out his wet, yellow robe. The river was low and he had to lean far over to wash the garment for services on the morrow. He was really too old, the neighbors said, for washing properly, and reverence was forgotten while watching his awkward attempts. But the old man heeded no remarks; besides, he was almost deaf. His sixty years of cloistered life had dulled his ears to the noises of the busy Chinese about him; though his eyes were keen and under bushy, whitened brows, they took in much of what was lost to hearing or to touch.

He was no sluggard, and usually worked steadily, but today his eye had caught a strange sight passing. Perhaps it was the startled snort of a water buffalo that attracted his attention and made him look up, for the peaceful animal is usually majestic in its self-control. He saw a boat approaching one of the many sampans that squirm like beetles on the river, and at its prow a stranger stood—a Western foreigner. A long, black robe differed somehow from the Chinese scholar's gown, and a black sash with a dash of red at the fringe caught the eye as it fluttered in the breeze.

The old monk paused and the yellow robe lay unnoticed against the slimy rocks. A foreigner in these parts! How the world was changing! He had heard a monk who had journeyed to Yeungkong tell of the advent of the "foreign devils," but here was one at his very elbow. Were the stories true, he wondered, that were told of these white men, their fast ships and flying vehicles and instruments that told the hours of the day; and the stranger tales of occult powers, of medicines made of children's eyes, of a bitter drug that cured the chills and fevers of this marshy land, of salty water, signed and prayed over, that put devils to rout. At any rate he would find out whatever could be learned, for little passed unnoticed by this old, rheumatic man.

The stranger landed a few feet away and picked his cautious steps up the slippery rocks. The monk was near the landing, but seemingly intent again on pounding the virtue of cleanliness into his faded tunic.

"Pardon me, Elder Brother," said the stranger to the monk, "can you tell me where the Catholic church is in Chiklung?"

The monk, though deaf and busy, caught the words and answered in a deep, clear voice: "The dwelling next my own has such a sign above the door, but I have never seen a Christian enter yet." And encouraged by a smile, he added: "Are you a Catholic priest?"

"Yes," answered the missioner, "and I am glad to see you, for I shall be your neighbor for awhile. Which is the house of which you spoke?"

The monk, with the inbred courtesy of a Chinese, wrung his wet robe, still far from spotless, and, shoving his feet into his sandals, began the ascent to the row of houses above them. He paused at the back of a little shop and pushed open its broken door. A water rat rushed out and roaches fled into corners. A spider's web with dusty rays was stretched from doorsteps to lintel, while, within, the moss-green paving had sprouted scrawny weeds.

"This is your home, and that is mine next door," said the monk, "and you will excuse me for a moment."

"Be it ever so humble," the missioner tried to say as he registered a tired smile. A wave of his hat cleared the cobweb, and the mission of Chiklung had a resident priest.

It was a new venture in the rapidly expanding Maryknoll mission—a peaceful penetration into fields where white man never yet had lived. It was a résumé of the history of the Catholic Church the world over, a hearkening back to apostolic times when first the Gospel had been preached in pagan parts. "Thus far and no farther," cried Canute to the unheeding waves; and with like success can anything stop the progress of God's message of salvation to all men.

81

But the moment was one of no exaltation for the missioner. A night on a draughty boat had robbed the sun's halo of its poetry, and with a grim smile the priest began to set up his simple altar. His "boy" had followed from the boat with hand-bag and the day's provisions, and soon the tapers brightened another altar to the Unknown God. The tinkling of the *Sanctus* reached the neighbors' ears, and the shadow of the Buddhist monk peeped in as the consecrated hands raised the saving Host. The monk stood reverently till the end and then quietly slipped out, and when the priest had unvested, he returned with tea and cakes.

They were an odd sight as they sat down to tea, the aged monk and the younger priest; symbolic, too, of the two reli-gions. The monk with shaven head and dull gray gown, ascetic and austere, looked like a figure from the past, a past that had grown old and withered; while the priest, although he, too, was simply dressed and accustomed to austerity and prayer, had about him the grace of a living Faith, a religion ever young and never more vigorous. It was like a valedictory repast for the old man; he had ministered to the simple-minded natives, as generations in the monastery before him had done, and now the newer religion was, in God's good time, to sup-plant the old.

They talked little during the meal, except in smiles, for the priest was engrossed in plans for the future and the monk was too long habituated to silence to be a ready talker. A silent meal is soon ended; besides, it was so scanty it did but whet the appetite of youth, and already the boy was preparing some eggs and coffee on a more generous scale. The old monk withdrew and soon through the open door could be heard the dull tom-tom and the droning chant in which he spent half his day.

The priest had a busy morning ahead of him. An hour's war on uninvited guests rid the house of its age-long animal and insect tenants, of three pans of dust, and of a motley collection of broken jugs and crockery. It was a simple house to clean, with no panes of glass or draperies, no pictures on the walls or dusty furniture, no rugs or varnished floor; simply and solely four walls with a loft and three openings that served as doorways and windows. Before the day closed there was matting near the altar, four chairs and a table and bed had been installed, the walls were whitewashed, and locks had been put on the doors.

The Christians of this mission were not so few as the monk had imagined, though even the altar boy was a pagan. Within the town of 7,000 souls there was one Catholic; and scattered in villages were fifty others, baptized, some of them, more than twenty years before by a passing missioner.

That sums up the start of the Chiklung mission. Before a month had passed there were twenty catechumens, and a school of thirty boys; Christianity had begun to take hold in Chiklung. (*1921*)

Tabernacled in China

IN THE MANY TOWNS OF THE CROWDED SHORES OF CHINA, GOD IS tabernacled among men. He is as truly present there as in the more glorious churches of our own cities. The lanes and roads and streets are worn by passing thousands, the air is loud with the busy cries of vendors, countless careworn hearts are weary as they pass along; but of the throng of Chinese souls so close to God's own dwelling, few among them have ever heard of the one True God. Their eyes are held that they should not know Him.

The divine patience of our God, who desires that all men should be saved, yet decrees that they be saved through man! How little do we know Him! Are not our own eyes held that we do not know Him? Else, how is it we do not hunger more to bring souls to Him? Is not His daily, silent sojourn in the pagan towns of China a strong enough call to us to do our utmost to show the passing throngs that He alone is the Way and Truth and Life?

Their eyes are held, but not willingly. They know Him not, but they would gladly hear of Him. Their eyes are held —let us say rather, we withhold their eyes from knowing Him, for unto us is given the keeping of their souls. The pity of their state—they sit in darkness and in the shadow of death, and within reach dwells the Light of the World.

Who shall open the door to them? Who shall roll back the stone that they may approach their Redeemer? Grant us, Lord, to be the doorstep by which the multitudes may come to worship Thee; if, in the saving of their souls, we are ground underfoot and spat upon and worn out, at least we shall have served Thee in some small way in helping pagan souls and we shall have become the King's Highway in pathless China. (1923)

A Kaying Ramble

WHEN I SUCCEEDED AS PASTOR OF THIS DISTRICT, I ASKED THE retiring priest what parishioners would not be able to come in to Kaying for the next feast day. He mentioned offhand the Catholics of three or four places, among others of Tsung Yan on the Fukien border. So I wrote the little group of Christians there that I would spend Christmas Day with them, as the other priests at the seminary could take care of the main reunion at the center.

It was a dip into a section I had never visited before. It has often been said up here that much of the local scenery equals or surpasses some of the best in the United States, so I am not trusting only my own judgment in claiming one of the most beautiful sections as our happy hunting ground. The path mercifully follows the lower levels, but even from the valley the view is framed in ever-changing mountain peaks, some Montana-like, with craggy spires; others domed in the dark green of autumn spruce and pine, with sword-like flashes of clear waterfalls, relieved below by bright green fields of winter wheat. The paths throughout this section deserve the name of roads, though often cutting nervously along a fault in the cliffs and peeping boldly above sheer chasms.

This mission is isolated, as missions go, but to most city bred that adds to its attractiveness, and makes us wonder why the Lord set us in such undeserved surroundings. As we look on the virgin scene we are reminded of Jogues and Rasle. Still, it is not a desert, for you can sense the reassuring presence of woodsmen as they burn their charcoal in almost hidden gullies. It is a land that Doré could have painted in fine black strokes, had he but used the warmer-toned and kindlier Chinese brush. Enjoyment of the scene is enhanced by the realization that no bungalow will obtrude itself, no tooting horn blaspheme, no picket fence, no matter how forlornly picturesque, will jar the symmetry.

I sometimes ache for you at home who must put up with noisier life, and yet, lest you envy me too readily the beauty of these hills, I must confess they are Carthusian, not Franciscan lands. We must learn to love silences that are sometimes hard to bear, silences that last until the ear has magnified the rustle of leaves, the switching of bushes, and the almost forgotten sounds of former conversations, until the wee small voice of conscience seems almost to roar aloud in the utter silence. Happily, there is not the gloom of heavy forest to oppress, or fear of physical danger to accentuate the loneliness, but the absolute absence of sound that sometimes settles like a void on nature brings home sharply the fact of our isolation. Not that I want sympathy, for the mountain fastnesses here cannot compare to the cold nights of Alaskan lands, or to the clammy darkness of tropical forests. In fact, this country resembles rather the still, sublime regions that Boniface and Columban crossed, or the trails Marquette first glimpsed; it is eminently a livable spot, if you can learn to live with your own thoughts as company.

Along the route, the sellers of tea in the Chinese counterpart of American roadhouses seem more sociable up here, where visitors are less frequent. And speaking of the great national dissipation of China, it has often struck me as a strong proof of the innate refinement of the Chinese. Now, "tea house" should not connote for you a languorous, Oriental dive, the exotic, effeminate product of a degenerate nation. On the contrary, the Chinese have raised a cup of tea to the manly plane of a German stein of beer—we have nothing like it in America. Tea is present at all business transactions and friendly visits; it is on tap in every home and shop from dawn to midnight, it is poured at every moment of the day, except at meals. Chinese tea is drunk without sugar or milk. I think it would be very easy to prove that the Chinese are the most temperate people of the world—"mortified," perhaps, would be more exact than mere "temperate." They are content with unmattressed wooden beds, hard pillows, dark, cold rooms, stone floors, cushionless chairs, and cumbersome modes of traveling. Not that they could not have softer surroundings; it is a deliberate choice.

I realized this strongly as we trudged the mountain paths

and rested at the inns. The benches were often occupied by well-to-do Chinese sipping tea; they were of every age, uniformed officials and high-school boys and a sprinkling of the older type of classical scholars; many had been in Singapore or Borneo and had seen Oriental and Western luxuries, yet one and all sat on hard benches sipping sugarless tea. And you notice with surprise how delicately they go about it. A pot of leaves is placed before each customer and boiling water poured on it. The cup is warmed and symbolically cleansed with a dash of the steaming brew, and the libation is then thrown on the ground. We all, of course, like our tea hot; the Chinese drink it scalding.

Perhaps this is truer of the Hakkas then elsewhere, for the folks up here, like Rev. Mr. Stiggins, have a "peculiar vanity" —an abnormal love of hot water, both in the teapot and for ablutions. The poorest of them will have a kettle of boiling water on the fire at any moment, though firewood is relatively dear, and it is a treat these cold days on mission trips to find a basin of hot water for the morning shave. We are up in the unfrequented mountains that mark the natural boundaries of the province, so a stranger is treated much more cordially than in the sophisticated valley of Kaying.

Because the road passes through the inn, every one must enter it. The inn is a four-walled structure with openings on two sides, and usually situated on the top of a hill, to catch the breeze and give refreshing shade after the climb. There is good psychology in the site, as naturally the panting, sweating walker pauses to rest awhile before descending. The room is lined with stone slabs, or wooden benches, while to one side a smoky fire heats the kettle behind a rough counter. The innkeeper is often a toothless, unkempt, dried-up old codger, too old for more active work, who spends his time fanning the flame with a worn-out spray of palm while he eyes the weary visitors. Whether you buy or not seems to make no difference in your right to sit in front of him until you are rested.

For possibly twenty miles we passed through the lumber region of this section. It is often said that China is deforested, and the shore line seen by travelers confirms this view, for naturally the ease of transportation has denuded lands adjacent to the cities. But the statement must be qualified in Hakka territory. As we edged our silent way above the gorges, we could see below us pigmy men like beavers astride a log, directing with their poles a regiment of bare trees that quivered and bobbed in the racing current. There was something uncanny in the swerves and leaps the logs made to avoid the rocks, and when a jam demanded nimble daring as the men dislodged the obstructing timber, the scene became an epic, and the rough beams that are so commonplace in Chinese roofs will seem in future to reflect the glory of their birth.

China is an Eden in more ways than one, especially Southern China. The Middle Kingdom is like to a treasure hid in a field, by which we may value human knowledge; not a mere relic of a past civilization, but a living history of man's reign on earth. I, for one, shall not hasten the gory wheels of progress in this section. The Chinese hereabouts are addicted to papering their walls with last year's copies of American dailies. They are a distraction to you in every house, with their recitals of murders, divorce and rot. Thank God, the Chinese cannot read them, and I sometimes pray: "Lord, that they may not see."

My thoughts ramble as much as does the roadway, but on a walk like this there's plenty of time in which to think. The steady monotony of silent plodding, with no mileposts to check the distance, and the natural silence of your Chinese companion, who out of respect insists on walking a few paces behind, conduce to uninterrupted thought. My companion on this trip is my house boy, Fook Lim. I may be prejudiced, but Chinese names to me sound sonorous and their meaning is usually poetic. My house boy's name means "a cloud," and his given name is "a happy forest."

We passed his native village on the way, and I asked him how many relatives he had there. He answered truthfully, "about a thousand." (The village we stopped at for the feast had 8,000 by the name of King.) The boy, in defense of the smallness of his clan, explained that a neighboring village of his relatives was much more numerous. I wonder what a Mayflower descendant would pay to be able to trace his lineage through 5,000 living relatives? It is a strong argument for the solidarity of the Chinese family that several thousand of the same name live in comparative peace within a village. (*1929*)

Kaying City from a Mountaintop

I slowly climbed to the summit of Pat Li Ridge, to the east of Kaying City, and paused to breathe a while. The view from our mountains is slightly intoxicating. Whether it be the colder air, or the clouds that vault the outlook, or the depths of the valley below, or the haze of the distant hills and, farther still, the almost hidden mountains; whether it be relief at the sight of home a short hour's walk below after a day of winding paths, or the natural faintness from a pounding climb, I do not know; but it is true that, this ridge attained, I feel urged to smiles and song, and easily see vistas in the sun-drenched clouds. A shaft of light reaches down from heaven, seems to strike the city, and is reflected in the square white pools of water in the rice fields.

Kaying City, then, is fair to see; its walls that rise up

naturally from the clay have taken on a coat of moss, and are as permanent as the hills behind it; within the walls the solid field of tiled roofs, all smoking with the evening fires, spread a pall of gray between the dying sunlight and the streets. Distance robs the memory of the city's dingy spots, and at each descent I discover Kaying anew.

We yield our love to places in China for the very reason we withhold it elsewhere. The soul must seek its God, and in Kaying the only thing that God can claim is the view; it has not been marred by man. Yet the thought marks zero hour in my day's walk. Jerusalem, Jerusalem, how often would I have gathered thy children as a bird doth her brood under her wings, but thou wouldst not. In all the city of Kaying there is not a spot that belongs to God; He must be content with a rented room.

And this is the center whence Christ's work in this mission is to radiate, the center to which the missioners should come for strength of heart and body after tiring work in the mountains.

A mission center in China is an interesting entity. It is more than a cathedral—that can wait; it is more than a chancery building, for the volume of such work is slight. It is, or rather should be, the one building in the entire mission that the missioners can call home; the one place where overnight accommodations can be offered to emigrating Catholics, where room can be found for visiting priests, and where a few of the comforts that build up the soul may be got.

It may be news to some to learn that the average missioner's house is not a home, that it lacks all but the barest necessities —a bed, a table, and some chairs of the rudest sort. Not that the priests complain or even feel conscious of extraordinary sacrifices. They do not, but on reflection it should be evident to anyone that the loneliness of such a life in the mountains of China is a real hardship that calls for remedy.

And the remedy is a center house large enough not only for the superior and local needs, but also for the priests and brothers of the mission, that they may come and, in the quickening companionship of prayer and rest, regain their courage for another siege. The greatest battles for Christ's Kingdom in Kaying will be won at the center.

We can do with temporary make-shifts elsewhere; we can skimp on catechists and chapels if need be, or on schools; but the center is an urgent, inevitable need that cannot wait longer. We have provided a seminary for our Chinese students for the priesthood; we have built a convent for our Chinese novices. We are then justified in concentrating on this permanent mission center.

As the sun lies flat on the valley and the clouds rise higher above the city, Kaying seems invested in a new light with the promise of a Resurrection Day, when for the first time in 700 years its streets will lead to a House of God at our center. (1929)

To Readers of Dickens

I AM SURE THAT TO ANY OF US WHO HAVE EVER SAT TENSE AND wide-eyed while deep in the fascinating tales of Dickens the thought has come, some time or other, that the queer scenes in which the plots are laid have never had existence outside of the author's and his readers' minds. Certainly in America today there are few links with England of the early nineteenth century as pictured by Dickens.

It is true that he dwells by preference on the slums and the seamy side of London, and is most at home among the poor, the orphans, and the denizens of prisons and parish work-houses. Yet, even in his happier scenes of normal life, the pen-pictures are of a country remote from America. There is an ancient, smoky flavor not to be found in our spick-and-span New England towns, and hence much less in the younger sections of the West.

But over in China, at this very hour, there is much that recalls the English life of Dickens' tales, and passages borrowed bodily from his books might fittingly describe the commonest sights in China. I do not mean in the port cities of the East, which have been Westernized within the past few decades, but the village and town life of inland China is still strikingly like England before the discovery of steam and electric power.

Take this passage from *Our Mutual Friend:*

"It was market day. The ground was covered, nearly ankle deep, with filth and mire; all the pens in the center of the large area, and as many temporary ones as could be crowded into the vacant space, were filled with sheep; tied up to posts by the gutter side were long lines of oxen, three or four deep. Countrymen, butchers, drovers, hawkers, boys, thieves, idlers, and vagabonds of every low grade were mingled together in a dense mass; the whistling of drovers, the barking of dogs, the bellowing and lunging of oxen, the grunting and squealing of pigs, the cries of hawkers, the crowding, pushing, driving, beating, whooping and yelling, and the unwashed, squalid, and dirty figures constantly running to and fro, and bursting in and out of the throng, rendered it a stunning and bewildering scene which quite confounded the senses."

The foregoing is hardly descriptive of American life, not even of such rare events as that of the circus coming to town, for America has plenty of space and elbowroom for all. It is, though, a fairly accurate picture of many of our market towns in China, except for the presence of the sheep, and of the thieves and vagabonds. There is noise and bustle enough in our markets over here, but all is in good humor, and restrained.

It is a pleasant sight to glimpse at dawn the gathering of the farmers, each wending his way behind a cow or before a flock of geese, with perhaps a pig or two swung in baskets from his shoulders. They come as far as ten miles to the market from all points of the compass, and soon the temporary sheds are filled with mooing cows, and the river that always skirts the town is gray with geese, seemingly unconscious of restraint, yet always within sight of the gooseherd's flagstaff.

There seems to be very little unnecessary cruelty to animals, either because the ducks and geese and pigs and cows have lived so close in daily company with man that they have lost all fear, or else because the Chinese is by nature calm and gentle. Then, too, generations of kind treatment have bred a strain of animals that can walk unconcerned in a jostling crowd, and not tax the patience of the driver.

The permanent shops in the market towns are not unlike those patronized by the *Uncommercial Traveller:* "Shops where an orange or a half dozen nuts, one cake of fancy soap, and a cigarbox are offered for sale," or further down the alley another, "sheltering in one corner an irregular row of ginger-beer bottles." I doubt if America, with its pure food laws, can prepare one for any adequate conception of these Chinese shops.

If there is anything a Chinese youngster likes, besides eating unsterilized dainties, it is undoubtedly to fondle the same. Near one of our mission chapels each afternoon an old man passes by, or rather lingers, for the gatekeeper and he are cronies. The neighborhood awaits his coming anxiously; he no sooner settles himself in the warm sun than a flock of scantily clothed urchins surround his stand, and try to hypnotize the sugared cakes for sale. They get bolder as their mouths water, and, one by one, they pick over the little pile of cakes, and suck the sweetness that adheres to their paws. What a red-letter day it was when one of the group could proudly wave a cash or two, and buy a cake.

Each was disposed to eat it by himself, but generously offered a bit to the Maryknoll pastor. And when the missioner, accepting it, broke the cake in two, and divided his half into as many portions as there were mouths, what a lesson in charity they learned! It is to the credit of these Chinese street-urchins that they profited by it on other occasions, and, without prompting, shared the precious morsels among themselves.

The view down one of our mission alleys in South China is like a page from *Barnaby Rudge*. America is too brand-new to figure in such a story. Old China has the gnarled trees, and crooked lanes, and ruins at every turn, where foundation bricks have been eaten away by saltpeter and doorless arches are choked with tropical weeds. The very newest dwelling looks age-old when built, for paint is a stranger in inland China, and the heavy rains soon coat the bricks with moss.

But it is at night that China is most like England of Dickens' time. As Barnaby Rudge would gallop through the London streets, "long stands of hackney-chairs, and groups of chairmen obstructed the way." America has not seen that since the days of Martha Washington; while, in many sections of China, it is still the sole mode of travel, unless one has a pony.

Then, too, in Barnaby's time, "shops still adhered to the old practice of hanging out a sign." Indeed, Dickens would be at a loss for a word to introduce his chapters if there were to be no comments on the swinging signboards. The main street of any town in China looks like a lumber yard on strike. The streets are none too wide at best, yet are narrowed by two rows of jostling sign-boards that threaten to hurl themselves from rusty hinges, the better to catch your eye.

Dickens says: "The streets were very dark. Many of the

courts and lanes were left in total darkness. Quiet folks had great dread of traversing the streets after the shops were closed."

In inland China, after nightfall, a rash stranger who ventured out of doors would imagine a plague had struck the town—deserted streets, except for squealing rats, the shops all boarded up, and not a light in sight; pitch-dark on moonless nights, and silent, unless the watchman happens to be striking his gong and beating the hour on a drum, just as in Dickens' London.

We who have blinked our eyes as babies at the arc lights have no idea how black real darkness can be on the first nights of a Chinese month, when the new moon hides herself in fear. Even little Nell and Lizzie Hexam had an oil and cotton lamp, or a tallow candle, to light them along their way.

In China we find enough queer characters to rival any of the Pickwick Club. Mr. Micawber cannot begin to compete with the Chinese in their passion for pawning clothes. A boy who slept at one of our missions for a few nights could not rest easy until he had exchanged the pastor's blanket and his extra suit for a pawn check.

Then take such characters as Silas Wegg, who nightly reads to Noddy Boffin the stirring deeds of Belisarius, or "Bully Sawyers," as he anglicizes the general's name. Where, out of China, would you find such conceit as is concentrated in the village schoolmaster; and where else are the people in such admiration at his ability to read the Chinese scrawl? And, if he knows English over and above his native tongue, he is hopeless.

One of our mission schoolteachers, proud of his stock of English, enhanced his reputation by teaching the children to recite "*do, re, mi, fa, sol,*" blindly persuaded that he was speaking English.

Perhaps some of us today do not relish the quaintness of

95

Dickens' tales to the fullest. Might I suggest an aid to this? Living in up-to-date surroundings, in an atmosphere of sophisticated modern life, with its latest improvements in dwellings and comfort, we are apt to miss some of the flavor of ye olden times. You must come to China for local color, in order to read Dickens as he should be read. (*1933*)

About a Block Away

IN CHINA, EVERY CITY DWELLER KEEPS CLOSE TO COUNTRY LIFE. A block or two away, the country begins—not as a dump for discarded scrap iron, but in genuine fields where each householder grows his daily vegetables. Every tinsmith and cobbler keeps a chicken or two in his shop to eat the scraps left over from his meals; the average family can feed a pig frugally on the odds and ends that otherwise would be thrown away; the richer the man, the less anxious he seems to waste this profit, so that it can be confidently asserted that there is at least one pig hidden in every house. In fact, the Chinese word for "family" is composed of two characters signifying " a pig under a roof." There is no sadder sight than an empty house, no more hollow sound than the shutting of its door, no more cheerless mockery of homecoming than the turn of a latchkey in a deserted flat, yet this is the daily experience of the cliff-dwellers in the modern West. How different the Chinese home, where a closed door is the sign that all are housed for the night, where throughout the day the children and chickens are seen in the shelter of the inner courtyard, where practically all the home life except sleep is lived out in the open.

In the spacing of its houses, China has many pointers for the West. The Chinese population is still eighty percent farmers, and a nation that can keep its farmers has solved a problem that has stumped the West. Perhaps one of the main causes of China's success is the spacing of her houses. Farm life among Westerners, at least before the days of airplanes and radios, was thought of as lonely and isolated: the growing generation had to go far afield for companionship; the older folk had to resign themselves to lonely vigils; help in the emergencies of sudden sickness or death was out of reach; stout hearts were needed in the womenfolk; men grew taciturn for lack of friendly neighbors. Yet such an unattractive picture has always been alien to the Chinese, and almost inconceivable. They have established themselves as farmers for forty centuries without the drawbacks that have desolated some American farms, simply by spacing houses.

Chinese farmers build, it is true, in the valleys near their crops, but they group houses into a village surrounded on all sides by common fields for grazing grounds and hills to supply firewood. Such a village has an artificial pond well stocked with fish, and usually it has a temple and a school. Fifty or a hundred boys call to one another from their doorways and need seek no pleasure in a distant town; two-score women do their washing at the brook, and their chatter is as lively as the stream; a score of thin-blooded, old cronies sun themselves in company and forget the aches of age while minding greatgrandchildren; the village is alive, and a unit, and a hive of mutual service. Such can be said of few countries elsewhere.

Give any man a hundred friends with whom he works as an equal, let him be owner of his time and fields, and he will not go afar off to strangers for his pleasure. The Chinese have actually reversed the Western concept; the village to them means home and friends, and the city is a hostile exile. So much is this true that the towns have that ghostly, forlorn look of abandoned mining centers that have petered out; the smaller cities are alive only on market days, and then only until sundown. (1942)

97

Down on the Farm

SOME YEARS AGO I PASSED THROUGH THE UNITED STATES IN company with a group of Chinese undergraduates, sent by their government to specialize on economic subjects. They were keen young men, anxious to appreciate America, and somewhat regretting that there was an impression here impugning their own country's supposed lack of culture.

I was faced with a dilemma. I did not want to dampen their enthusiasm for their American venture by reminding them of the many advantages China had, and took for granted; nor could I compromise with truth; so I took the safe course of emphasizing the material comforts of our living conditions which they would share. As many of them were engineers, their main interest was in structure and bridges, and I dilated on the few outstanding edifices they had heard of during their schooling. I was more than ready to see the good in everything in my homeland, the young students were ready to admire anything, but the bleak shanties that blotched the treeless plains were indefensible—aesthetically, morally, or even economically. A square, box-like structure of unpainted wood and tarred-paper roofing, stuck on top of the ground, surrounded by lean-to sheds of motley shapes, and repeated at random every few miles, scarred the horizon interminably. These were not squatters' huts thrown up in emergencies, or the cabins of the poor whites of the south, but homes on prosperous farms.

The blank dismay on the faces of the Chinese students was striking, until I realized the contrast such a scene made with their own homes in China. These boys were not wealthy; they ate only one meal a day on the train, because of the prices. Every Chinese is a farmer of one sort or another and keeps close to the soil even in the city. And he is accustomed to look on home as a substantial building with courtyards and many rooms clustered around large guest rooms, with patios and cool corners.

The essential purpose of a home is to provide a place where children may be born and reared, and old folks find their peace encircled by their children and their children's children. First of all, the Chinese homes have enclosed gardens, where the children can romp to their hearts' content in the sunlight without fear of autos; they have roofed walks and open rooms, where the babies still can play in the open air when it rains. The infants' laughter and noise locate them, when necessary, though they are at a distant part of the house; the "parlor" can be forbidden ground against sticky fingers and mischievous curiosity, without condemning frisky natures to inactivity; the children are not always under foot, nor is there fear of their falling downstairs, yet they need never be out of sight or far from their mother's voice. As they grow older, there is plenty of room for the pets every child should have—chickens, and ducks, and dogs, while the nearby trees invite all sorts of birds, and the unripe fruit from his own garden gives every Chinese boy his quota of stomachaches.

The Chinese know the meaning of the word "home," even though they rarely use the word. They settle down with the intention of seeing generations living in the same house, and they plan the house accordingly. If possible, they buy adjoining fields and learn to know every stone therein, expecting that their grandchildren will also plow the same. They locate their graves beside the field and are united even in death with future generations of their kin. And such adhesion to the soil begets a loyalty and sense of responsibility, and a common interest in the locality, foreign to Americans.

But, it may be wondered, how can the poor Chinese, whose profits are so small, build such large houses, when the industrious American farmer finds a square, wooden box the limit of his possibilities? The answer lies partly in the unwritten archives of the Chinese family, which bears hardship for one generation that the next may enjoy comforts, and partly in the material used in building. The Chinese build of earth, whether in the form of mud bricks, or adobe, or in adobe made with lime. When the summer crop is harvested, the family turns to making bricks. The average family usually takes years to build the house, and years more to plaster it; but the labor is unpaid, the material gathered locally from the fields, and even the lumber for rafters may come from a pine grove planted for that purpose close by. There is a sacramental symbolism in a home built by a man's own hands from his own soil, in which the very trowel marks and irregularities are the expression of his ideas. I can think of no more fitting bequest to leave for sons and grandsons.

But is there not danger of amateurish bungling and monstrosities at the hands of unskilled farmers? Incredible as it may sound, the Chinese farmer is not unskilled or without a sense of form. The average Chinese house rarely offends against the canons of good architecture, simply because the Chinese are well grounded in fundamental principles of balance. A Chinese village is as though planned by one mind, including the bamboo grove and cool ponds that surround it, with a resulting harmony attained only by costly landscaping in America.

Such construction, if adopted more generally in America, would solve many problems. It would beget a pride in our homes, to counter the restless urge to move; it would focus and thereby intensify the natural instinct in all of us to own something permanent; it would localize and color childhood memories, now dissipated over a dozen dwellings; it would be the expression of a family's united aim and harmonious labor.

Morally, it would be a bond between the present and future generations, a tradition which every nation needs to flourish healthily; it would be the lodestone for restless youth and a safeguard of its communion with parents. Economically, it would prove the solution of financial difficulties for pioneering couples and, in the long run, obviate unsatisfactory and costly repairs and constant painting of gimcrack, shoddy woodwork; it would abolish the numerous middlemen who now control house shortage. It is an investment that enhances the land and the stability of its dwellers. (*1942*)

STURDY CHINESE CATHOLICS

"In China the stricter morality of an anciently civilized race that has conserved much of the stoic in its conventions demands less vigorous reform outwardly in customs than in the case of a degenerate race. Christianity happily adds the finishing touch of charity to an otherwise too rigid outlook, and perfects the 'truth in charity' that gives a balanced life. The Church is naturally human, and the Chinese is naturally Christian; the assimilation of the two will produce a reassuring new Catholic China."

The Glorious Resistance

BISHOP FORD ALWAYS HAD FIRM CONFIDENCE IN THE STERLING *quality of China's Catholics. His faith was amply justified by events after the establishment of the Communist regime in the Kaying diocese. As long as the Catholic churches were left open, they were so crowded that extra Masses had to be added. In spite of severe penalties imposed in the public schools, altar boys refused to stop serving Mass. Christians continued to visit the American missioners, though they knew that the Reds might accuse them of being foreign agents. The Hakka priests resisted every effort of the Communists to enlist their co-operation in the founding of a National Catholic Church.*

Now, all the American priests and Sisters have been expelled from the Kaying region. More than half of the young Hakka priests trained by Bishop Ford are in jail, condemned to forced labor. The ones still in their homes are not allowed to say Mass publicly. But the Chinese Catholics continue to be faithful to their family prayers. The Blessed Sacrament is carried from village to village by courageous members of the Hakka Sisterhood, or by Catholic itinerant peddlers.

"The devotion to their faith of both Chinese priests and Chinese Catholics parallels the most glorious annals of Christian martyrdom," wrote Bishop Ford before his imprisonment by the Reds.

The Chinese at Prayer

At home I have listened to Polish Catholics reciting their prayers in unison, the men commencing and the women on their side of the church answering, and the sound was a prayer, though I could not join in it with them. I have heard the Rosary given out in the soft Galway tongue that seems to be made for communing with God. And in the same polyglot city of New York I have knelt and heard the thunder of the heavy German gutterals that fit the deep faith of the Teuton. Even in Japan and Korea, the chant of many praying natives was solemn and seemingly without cadence, like the cloud of incense that rises to a height above the ministering thurifer and rests suspended before the All Holy.

But the din of Chinese prayer is nerve-racking to the Westerner, accustomed to the puritanic severity of American services and laying undue stress on external decorum. To the Chinese, prayer is a personal talk with God, and though united in body with his fellows at Mass he seems to forget the union as he prays. This morning I tried to make my thanksgiving after Mass while the Christians prayed at the Mass that followed, and soon I found myself nursing a grudge against certain individuals in the congregation. With my eyes shut tight in concentration, I could still see the men behind the shouts that pierced my eardrums.

One old man in a corner prays as though Heaven were as deaf as himself; a good old woman in the back insists on chanting through her nose in a key that whines above them all. An urchin near the altar rail shouts out, exulting in his memory of the prayers. Meanwhile, our old gatekeeper chimes in strong on the "Our Father" whenever it occurs, and subsides for the rest of the time. Thus they pray on, one man answering the litany before the invocation is ended, and his neighbor drawling out the "Amen" when the others have finished.

This morning, picking up the prayerbook, I followed their words. And it made a difference. Here were young innocents and old sinners, men who had lately been baptized and others whose fathers before them had known the blessings of faith. And all were saying: "Thanks be to God for creating me and taking care of me! Thanks be to Him for the blessings of the Incarnation and Redemption! I thank Him for the forgiving of my sins and the giving of His grace, in that He led me into His Church and to the road to Heaven! I thank Him, finally, for His unnumbered blessings from the day of my birth up to the present!"

And the expression of each thankful soul colored the prayer. The old man in the corner could look back upon the score of years through which God led him by the road of Job and loss of fortune to resignation and to daily Communion. The good old soul at the back had seen her sons and their sons kneeling to the one True God and peace had smoothed the wrinkles of old age. Perhaps the noisy urchin did not realize how much he should be thankful for, but it was fitting that his thanks be loudest who had been spared a life of pagan worship. And our old gatekeeper in his simple wants had found a home with friends, and work that kept him close to the altar and its God.

And then the words of St. Paul to the Romans came to me: "The Gentiles are to glorify God for His mercy, as it is written: 'Therefore will I confess to Thee, O Lord, among the Gentiles and will sing to Thy name.' . . . And again: 'Praise the Lord, all ye Gentiles, and magnify Him, all ye people.'"

And the solemn hush at the Consecration showed that these Christians could pray as well by silence as by noise, and rebuked my carping criticism. It is true that St. Paul elsewhere warns his new Christians: "Let all things be done decently and according to order"; but until such time as these zealous Chinese are disciplined to order and moderation, I am sure the good God understands and accepts their thanks. Thanks in any form makes a sweet prayer. (*1920*)

Holy Week in the Orient

DURING THIS WEEK THE HEART OF THE WESTERN WORLD TURNS toward the Holy Land. We have in our thoughts the familiar names of Gethsemane, Golgotha, Jerusalem, the Pasch, and the Cenacle. We have for the moment transferred ourselves in spirit to the scenes immortalized by the physical presence of our Saviour, and there is none among us who would not like to know better the places and times and conditions sanctified by the Passion and Death of our Lord.

Our Western life is so different from that of Palestine, our commerce and industry, our dress and habits, our manner of speech so alien to the Oriental life, that it is hard at best to visualize the people to whom our Lord preached and by whom He was rejected. We find it difficult to realize the meaning of such common Biblical terms as "the portico of the Temple," the "washing of the feet of the disciples," the "gate of the city," the "thirty silver shekels," and the "court of the house of Annas."

Now, it is one of the consolations of the missioner who spends his life in the Orient that much is still left to remind him of our Lord's times. It is especially true of China, and perhaps more true of China than of anywhere else, that the traditions of the East have been handed down unchanged. And it is surprising how many of the customs of Biblical Palestine are common to the whole of Asia, and still retained by the Chinese, while, on the other hand, the Westernization of

108

Palestine and the inroads of commerce and manufacturers have destroyed in great part the local color of the Holy Land.

Once we have penetrated into the interior of China, we are struck by its Oriental atmosphere—not Oriental in the modern sense of exotic, luxuriant, languorous sensuality, but like the Orient in our Lord's time. A land devoted to simple agriculture, with a barefoot people who walk, not ride, who bear the heat of the day and the burdens, who gather the crops by hand and winnow the chaff in the wind, who yoke the ox to tread the corn, who draw water from the pool, who make bricks with straw and burn the grass of the field; a land whose temples have porticos, and whose cities are girt with walls, whose blind and lame sit begging at the city gate, and whose lepers are a common sight.

Even the parables of our Lord are more easily understood in China, where the fishermen let down their nets, where fishing boats are tossed by typhoon winds, where the sower goes out to sow his seed, where, in a word, the simple patriarchal life, uncontaminated by modern inventions, is still preserved.

All this is a helpful background for a missioner's understanding of Biblical allusions, and the Sunday Gospels take on a local color and life from the Chinese surroundings. Especially is this true when we stop to consider the Passion and Death of our Lord. The first Holy Week found the Gentile converts all turning to Jerusalem, as to the holy city of God. The narrow streets of this small city were crowded by two million strangers. China today preserves its streets made narrow by the fortified walls of its cities, and China's population gives us frequent pictures of huge crowds that block the alleys.

On Monday and Tuesday of Holy Week our Lord preached in the portico, or the exterior corridor, of the Temple, and this style of architecture is still in use in China. As the disciples began the Paschal Feast, our Lord took water and towels to wash their feet; in China it is the invariable custom to wash the feet when the footsore traveler arrives. After the Last Supper, our Lord passed through the southern gate into the narrow gorge of Kedron, and walked between the city wall and the brook. In China this narrow path between the city wall and the surrounding moat is a favorite walk, a refuge from noisy, crowded thoroughfares.

Our Lord was priced at thirty pieces of silver, the market price of a slave. In China we deal in silver coin, and slaves are still bought and sold. The crowd led by Judas came to the garden with swords and clubs and lanterns and torches. Even now in China lanterns and torches are seen at night in the dark, unlit alleys of the interior. The house of Annas, the high priest, is essentially on the same plan as Chinese houses—several flagged courts, surrounded by brick buildings. Like them, it was entered from the road by the archway closed by a massive gate. While the trial was proceeding, Peter warmed himself in the court at a brazier of charcoal, such as we use in China. The house was lit by lamps of olive oil, while in China we use oil ground from nuts; both give the same steady but faint light.

These are small details, and each in itself is of no moment, but it is the accumulation of many such details met with every day in our life in China, that makes the Holy Scriptures so much more living and pertinent.

Holy Week as observed in the Orient differs very little from the ceremonies in use in the United States. In China of the interior, where the rude chapels and lack of priests do not permit elaborate ceremonies, the liturgy of the Church is still faithfully observed as far as possible. The Christians come more than a "Sabbath day's journey" afoot; for many of them it means a four or five days' journey. Holy Week is the best observed of the Church's feasts in China. The Christians are especially fervent on Holy Thursday. In all the churches where the Blessed Sacrament is reserved there is nocturnal adoration, and as sometimes the Christians are very few it means three and four hours of adoration for each. They pass the entire night in vocal prayer, chanting the litanies and special prayers to our Lord, or reciting the Rosary aloud, or singing hymns in Chinese.

All during Lent in China there is a strict fast, but on Good Friday nothing is taken until noon. At the adoration of the Cross all the men and boys approach barefoot to the altar, making the three prostrations up the aisle. During the Mass, the Passion is recited in Chinese by the catechist. In the afternoon all assemble again for the Stations of the Cross.

Holy Saturday sees the entire congregation at the altar rail, and the long services are faithfully attended. The Easter fire is lit with flint and steel, and baptisms usually take place on this day, following the ancient custom of the Church. During the morning the houses of the Christians are blest, and also the foodstuffs for the feast-day meal.

Easter is truly a joyous feast in China. Many who because of distance cannot come on other Sundays are present; and all, including the newly baptized, receive Holy Communion. In many churches the Consecration is honored by the setting off of firecrackers, both within and outside the church. The crackers in China, however, are not merely explosive; they sound like the rapid beat of muffled drums, and are not an unseemly salute in the Chinese fashion to the Risen King. The churches are decorated in a cheap but not unpleasing style, and every one dons his best robes. As the Chinese silks are beautiful in their subdued colors, the long, flowing robes of the men and boys add a dignity to their natural seriousness.

Holy Week in the Orient takes on a new meaning when

we are brought face to face with catechumens and pagans for whom the Church prays on Good Friday. Holy Saturday's long prayers presuppose the presence of new converts, and they are in fact the final step in the instructions before baptism. Above all, the lamentations of *Tenebrae,* the yearning of God's love for man in psalms and canticles, have a wider meaning when the missioner finds himself in a pagan city. The heedless throng of pagans marketing on Good Friday, ignorant of the special application of the day for them, brings home to us their spiritual need. Christ loved them and gave Himself for them; the Last Supper and Calvary were in vain for them, if they be not evangelized.

Holy Week is essentially a mission week—"Behold I come to do Thy will"; it is the manifestation of divine Love to the utmost. "God so loved the world as to give His only begotten Son." And the missioner's task is to preach God's love to the pagans; to prove God's love; to extend the radius of its reaching until it include every man of every clime. (*1933*)

All Things to All Men

CHRISTIANIZING A COUNTRY IS A COMPLEX WORK. IT LEADS TO all sorts of branching side lines that are conclusions from simple premises. It means essentially preaching the word of God, and that appears plain and artless, but its application to various circumstances develops endless possibilities. Catholic culture is a living, applied science that runs counter to a pagan civilization; and the proved habits of Catholic culture must be the norm of the new lives of converted pagans, until they have reformed their customs and purified their underlying, original pagan motives.

A new convert in Western lands was unconsciously influenced by many Catholic ethical beliefs even before his conversion. But the converted pagan in Asia has lacked that leaven to grace his actions. When once he applies the new touchstone to his daily life, he finds alloy in everything, so true is it that outside of the supernatural life in God all is vitiated. In proportion to his effort to live his new life in accord with truth does the converted pagan meet the challenge of a literal putting off of the old man.

Paganism in any country gives absolute control based purely on possession. In the patriarchal family system of China implicit obedience to elders from childhood has often prevented in souls that first impulse towards conversion that would end in baptism. Again, centuries of custom have consecrated numerous pagan festivals and superstitions which the Catholic catechumen must discard. Even the realm of thought is invaded by Christian morality. Covetousness, envy, pride, and all interior acts of the will are now subject to a control hitherto unexperienced in pagan life. Justice is revealed as something more comprehensive than mere commercial probity, a principle motived less by fear of penal sanction than by the dictates of conscience.

Perhaps it is in simple examples of ordinary living that the difference between Christianity and paganism is startling. The Christian home in China outwardly differs little from any other, but the life within its walls is poles apart from that of pagan neighbors. The respect for women, the refining influence of Catholic modesty, the spirit of sacrifice, the recognition of evil habits as more than a mere infraction of conventions—all these Christian attitudes of mind gradually change family relations in a household of new Catholics. It sometimes takes generations of Catholicism to transform completely the atmosphere of a home, although from the very beginning keen eyes can discern a warmer relationship among the members of a family of converts.

Fortunately, in China, the stricter morality of an anciently civilized race that has conserved much of the stoic in its conventions demands less vigorous reform outwardly in customs than in the case of a degenerated race. Christianity happily adds the finishing touch of charity to an otherwise too rigid outlook, and perfects the "truth in charity" that gives a balanced life. The Church is naturally human, and the Chinese is naturally Christian; the assimilation of the two will produce a reassuring new Catholic China. (*1944*)

APPRECIATION OF THE CHINESE PEOPLE

"The stamina of the Chinese has that good-humored element in it of the Poverello: smiling hunger, nonchalance in pain, endurance unconscious of heroism."

A Great Missionary Heart

SOON AFTER BISHOP FORD ARRIVED IN THE ORIENT AS A YOUNG *priest, he fell in love with the Chinese people. On the rare occasions when he returned to the United States, he was restless and homesick for China. His own writings about his adopted country were alive with a warm optimism, and he often protested the gloomy news of China commonly displayed in the Western secular press.*

His Chinese seminarians and students were surprised to discover that this American prelate manifested a better appreciation of Chinese culture and customs than most of them possessed. He did not like to hear them joke about the national dread of "losing face," or ridicule other ancient Chinese traditions and fine points of etiquette.

Bishop Ford discerned good even in Chinese bandits. When a thief stole money from his pocket, he did not wish the offender to be caught, but said: "The money is not lost; he can use it, too." For years he endured the unsavory concoctions of an inept Chinese cook, because he knew the wretched man would be unable to find any other employer.

The real explanation of Bishop Ford's deep devotion to his adopted people is found in the following tribute of a young Chinese Catholic: "Those of us who knew him intimately can attest that his love for China was so affectionately genuine and singular that it could only come from a man who had a great missionary heart."

117

More Picturesque Speech

A MISSIONER IS MORE OR LESS A MAN OF ONE BOOK—HIS dictionary in whatever dialect he uses in his ministry. All dictionaries the world over are, of course, intensely interesting; this is especially true of Chinese ones. Every missioner spends hours over his dictionary; even the least bookish does, and he perhaps more than the Sinologue, for the latter has learned to curb his curiosity and maintain discipline of the eyes. The common or garden variety of missioner opens his book to look up a word, and immediately becomes sidetracked by the first word that meets his eye. Where every word is useful and necessary, it is hard to pass by the ninety-nine in search of the urgently lacking one that caused him to thumb the index.

In Webster's unabridged, the chief distraction is the derivation of the word; in Chinese dictionaries, the danger lies in the multitudinous meanings of a word and the arresting poetry in every one of them. This might be thought an imperfection in a language, but the purpose of words is to convey a vivid image, and poetry is the language of the seer. English, by comparison, is a pure memory feat, as the word in itself so often conveys no meaning except to the lexicographer. One example must suffice. None but a Latinist could reconstruct the picture of a "bachelor" as "a young soldier too poor to have retainers," so the word in English is no aid to the reader; in Chinese, however, the two characters used signify "a solitary leaf on the family tree," which defines the poor creature nicely in a country of ancestor worship.

The primary aim of words is to clarify an image, yet what boy of school age in America can make anything out of the military terms so abundant in the press these days, such as colonel, corporal, battalion, brigadier general, and a host of others taken from Italian and French? In Chinese the words mean something to the mere civilian: a corporal is the "tent chief"; a captain is "head of one hundred men"; and a general is the "master" or "model chief." There is quite a psychological value in this latter term; any one who can go through life bearing the title of "the model" has a lot to live up to. Of course, "general" in English has poetic kinship to "genuine" and "family," but only a linguist would revert to it.

The poetry in Chinese words is present almost always. An American boy learns that Washington is the capital of his country and that capital punishment is meted to malefactors; a Chinese boy speaks of his capital as "the eminence linked to the people," as sailors are wont to draw a ship through the gorges, or, to change the metaphor, he may call it "the heights that are crowded." Chesterton mentions the affinity between "police" and "politeness," yet to the average man both words convey no notion of their origin; the Chinese term their police "the people's soldiers," and they call a soldier "the brave." While it is true with English-speaking people that such origin of words is rarely, if ever, averted to, the opposite is the case with the Chinese; the latter delight in playing on the derivation of words. My name, for instance, in Chinese, is "Happiness and Virtue," and every possible occasion of festivity, whether holiday or holy day, begets some expression of greeting that joins happiness and virtue to the celebration.

It is a pity that in English our saints' names have lost their primary meaning. Were we conscious always of the meaning of our names, they would present a goal to aim at in many cases and lead us to cultivate at least the natural virtues; John (the gift of God) or Austin (reverence) would have an added message for us. In China all names are chosen with that end in view, and though the end attained by pagans is merely picturesque in some cases, it is surprising how frequently the

119

virtues are drawn upon. It sounds at first a bit highfaluting to call your house boy "Clear Justice," but it is no more outlandish than "Milton" or "Hercules," and of course the words in Chinese are sonorous.

This use of a living terminology, of vivid current speech couched in poetic form, is seen to advantage in our Chinese catechism. Catechisms have to be theologically sound, even at the sacrifice of style or simplicity, and at first blush it would seem that poetic Chinese would present insuperable difficulties. As a matter of fact, the pioneer missioners solved the problem much better than did our Western theologians; the former avoided Latinisms and they translated ideas into current language. They were helped in this, no doubt, by the fact that the literary language in Chinese is already fixed, while the English language is more fluid; at all events it was a happy choice that enables even a pagan Chinese to grasp the meaning of our religious terms with less need of explanation than might easily have happened. "The holy action" signifies more to a pagan Chinese than does the word "sacrament" to an American of no literary pretensions; "firm encouragement" means more to a boy than "confirmation"; and "the last applying of oil" is clearer than "extreme unction." "To harbor the harborless" is translated "To welcome the stranger" and is immediately self-evident in Chinese.

A mere reading of the Chinese catechism is refreshing even to the missioner who realizes with something of a jolt that "Chief of Religion" is an accurate term for the Pope, and that the "Founding Companions" of our Lord describes more clearly the Apostles than does the Greek word. It would do every one good occasionally to restate religious terms in non-technical language, that the vigor of the ideas might be brought home to us anew. The need of studying the Chinese text does that for the missioner, and he sees that "grace" means a benefit and "virtue" is related to conduct; by using such synonyms he avoids the rut of routine thoughtlessness.

The missioner is especially refreshed by the poetry inherent in the Chinese language, for this makes for picturesque speech. If the virility of a tongue is gauged by the clarity of its common, current terms that still retain the cultured elements of their original meaning and express ideas in striking metaphors, then Chinese is indeed a living language, capable of absorbing bemuddled terms from Western languages and transmuting them to nervous idioms for Oriental ears. (*1941*)

How Old the New

To the last generation of study clubs in America, Dr. James J. Walsh used to exclaim: "How old the new!" His purpose was mainly to show the young twentieth century that fundamental inventions are things of the past and that we live in the age of adaption, that much of our modern technique is simply the logical outcome of ancient inventions, and that very complicated mechanical processes may be reduced to a few basic functions; in fine, that we are not the inventive geniuses we like to imagine ourselves to be.

Many an Occidental has so muddled a mental picture that China means to him either a baffling Confucius or a still more mysterious Fu Manchu. The Chinese are not galley slaves chained to a pulley; they are inventive, even though their inventions are not streamlined. To them, inventions are not contraptions to be sold, but practical household requisites. They make worn-out materials perform tasks hitherto unthought of.

What Westerner, as he pulls out of a skid, would ever consider consigning his threadless tire to a cobbler to be remade into innumerable rubber soles and heels—the inevitable fate of tires in China? What Westerner would take despised tin cans and deftly fashion them into serviceable lamps or kitchenware? What foreigner would make a taxi of a bicycle and pedal passengers a dozen leagues a day? Or use charcoal to run his automobile at one-fifth the price of gas?

Inventions? Of course they are—the inventions of local craftsmen who use their own hands and brains for their own needs! A thing doesn't have to be copyrighted and patented with its individuality stamped out of it to be called an invention. An invention is a new use for an old thing, and the simplest farmer in China is inventing half his lifetime. (*1942*)

Chinese Stamina

IT IS STAMINA, MENTAL RATHER THAN PHYSICAL, THAT ENABLED China during the Sino-Japanese war to thrive on an invasion exhausting to her enemy. The mere will to survive, or the consciousness of a righteous cause, could not have sustained China against overwhelming odds under such a long strain. The bare physical strength of her manpower could not have withstood the mechanized superiority of her enemy. But as both mental and physical stamina were combined with a Spartan philosophy of living, the endurance was without weakness and the tension was never a strain to the point of incapacitating injury.

China retained her poise as only an agricultural nation can. After her countless homes were destroyed, she calmly rebuilt on the ruins. The slaughter of defenceless women and children welded Chinese resistance to a united stand. There was never a moment's weakening of resolve. This stamina is inbred in the Chinese through generations of hard living. From birth to death, even moderately well-to-do Chinese, if not influenced by Western life, conform to a severe regime.

The furnishings of a middle-class home can be summed up as: wooden beds without mattresses, wooden, straightbacked chairs, a few tables, several large, boxlike containers, and a multitude of baskets. Tableware and kitchen equipment will include an abundance of rice bowls and plates, two or three pots and several buckets, a cleaver and a wooden meatblock, weighing scales, and a large pan to cook, fry, steam, and roast the meat and vegetables. Pictures on the walls are rarely more than a few photographs and a calendar. There are some pots of flowers in the courtyard, and possibly a vase or two, to represent the arts. There may be a dozen books, all told, in the house. A dog and cat, five or more hens and ducks, and the inevitable pig enliven the place.

Such is the Spartan simplicity of the average middle-class home in China. On entering it, one does not receive an impression of poverty—much less, of unhappiness. It looks planned and balanced, with deliberate avoidance of frill or frippery. The Chinese enjoyment of life is in human beings, not in incidentals.

Even in social visits, the Chinese do not relax. Neither men nor women settle down to an afternoon's chat with folded hands, at their ease. Men will stand for an hour or so discussing news. The one pipe will be passed around, each one contenting himself with a single filling and handing the pipe to his neighbor. The women do not relax even to that extent, but chatter away while preparing the next meal, and their visitor joins naturally in the chores.

A grueling test of Chinese hardihood is the daily bath. In many homes the bathroom is out of doors, and is simply a cubicle of poor construction. In cold weather, it conserves the north winds and intensifies their dampness. Though hot water is dipped from a bucket, the chilly atmosphere more than neutralizes the warmth. Yet this purifying ritual is rigorously gone through without fail.

After General Grant's two terms as President of the United States, he toured the Far East. He remarked on the ability of the Chinese to make long trips afoot with the simplest food sustaining them. What strikes a foreigner resident in the interior of China is the people's ability to eat the same, unvarying diet for weeks and months and years, with practically no change even in the method of preparing it. Several bowls of rice and an ounce or two of vegetables, with a side dish of soup consisting of the water they were boiled in—that is China's staple diet. The Chinese do not fill up on bread or potatoes or dessert. Sugar seems to be lacking completely in their diet, as are also milk and butter and fruit.

The national custom of tea-drinking can be best likened to the American habit of swallowing a glass of water off and on during the day. The tea is taken hot or cold, without milk or sugar, and though usually it is sipped slowly, the rite takes but a moment or two, as the teacups are minute.

Yet on such abstemious fare the student and laborer and farmer work steadily, and the coolie carries heavy loads all day. What the foreigner finds most trying about the daily meals is the long wait for "breakfast," until nine or ten o'clock, although school and work have begun at daybreak. Three hours' walk and work on an empty stomach would exhaust most Americans. Such a Spartan regime in eating is not due to poverty, but to custom, as even those who otherwise are liberal spenders content themselves with simple meals.

Such a prosaic enumeration of sparse living, however, fails to bring home the contented spirit with which the slim dieting is endured. It is a Chinese reaction as spontaneous as laughter to a Negro; and this economy permeates every act, without puritanical moroseness. It expresses itself even in such unconscious states as sleeping and walking. No Chinese lounges, or sprawls, or slouches along, or sleeps beyond sunrise.

The oldest hag is sprightly on a narrow plank thrown across a stream. A toothless crony of uncertain age will hop into a rowboat that ferries the river, and land upright and smiling on the square foot of space still vacant as the boat pushes off. Occasionally among Westerners there is found that attitude of not yielding to old age in creature comforts, but too often from the motive of not wishing to appear feeble or senile. Among the Chinese, where age is revered, the spryness of old folks does not ape nimbleness, but comes from supple pliancy of co-ordinated nerves and muscles and a lifetime of effort.

Inconveniences that in Western lands would call for indignation and litigation are not so much suffered, as ignored, in China. The annual flooding of the river that brings its turgid water waist-deep into hundreds of homes is philosophically accepted, with less comment than would be given a leaky faucet in America.

The stamina of the Chinese has that good-humored element in it of the Poverello: smiling hunger, nonchalance in pain, endurance unconscious of heroism. It is an impersonalized outlook on life. It is unselfish in the sense that it is more akin to romantic chivalry than to realistic materialism. It retains zest for adventure even in prosaic daily happenings, and keeps the nation supple. (*1943*)

Kindergarten of Hard Knocks

MISSIONERS IN CHINA HAVE AMPLE OPPORTUNITY TO OBSERVE child life. So long as a youngster does not actually appropriate things, he is allowed by custom to range at liberty through his neighbors' houses; the bishop's residence is not exempted from these daily visitations. In fact, it would be impossible to shut the tots out; our houses here are built in the Chinese style, and the doors are open throughout the day. All the neighborhood comes to draw water at our well, so every child on his mother's back grows familiar with the layout from birth. As soon as he can toddle on his own uncertain legs or even crawl around exploringly, he finds his way to the mysteries of our desk. These days my dog is getting old and resents too boisterous an uproar, so there is a semblance of discipline in their explorations.

In China, almost as soon as an infant is weaned and can balance himself bowleggedly, he is made to stand on his own feet pedagogically. At an age when the Western child is confined in a nursery or classroom, the Chinese youngster is exploring the world on his own; and exploring it dangerously, so far as exposure to the hot sun, rain, sharp stones, thorns and thistles, inedible weeds, and mud puddles are concerned. He learns to put up with bruises and mosquito bites, with strange dogs and the lumbering water buffalo, with treacherous ditches and wobbly planks. He does all this barefooted and, in fact, with the minimum of covering of any kind in all sorts of weather.

The average Chinese village has literally a thousand hazards to life and limb strewn everywhere, any one of which would cause a Western grandmother heart-breaking anxieties. The infants play contentedly on the border of the village pond, deep enough to drown them at a single misstep. They toddle ahead of the cows and buffalo, pulling the unwieldy beasts by the nose with a rope too large for their tiny fists. They pass through an almost simultaneous succession of measles, eczema, whooping cough, and sniffles, and learn to take these maladies as the lot of man on earth. Their little siestas are taken wherever they happen to find themselves on the ground. In a word, they grow up as naturally as is possible in this world of original sin.

The Chinese boy learns enough natural science to qualify for several Boy Scout badges before he has ever entered a classroom. He knows the names of dozens of plants, what weeds are hurtful, where nettles lie, and the taste of various edible fruits and grasses and roots still without Latin names. He has explored the nests in tree and bush, caught snails and fish and butterflies, and snared birds as well as every sort of creeping life. He can distinguish at a glance the leaves of half a dozen kinds of trees, and he has helped in hilling the vegetables of his daily fare. A future farmer is already rooted to the soil, and takes an intelligent interest in the crops about him.

The most apparent result of this Chinese method of child training is that a Chinese tot, at five years of age, is a sturdy, self-sufficient little body who can handle himself creditably alone. He has learned to dress and wash, boy fashion, and to be content without adult approval or vigilance throughout his day. He has firmness of limb and surefootedness, hence, natural gracefulness and a supple body. A timid, awkward, helpless child is almost unheard of in China.

The Spartan toughening of a Chinese child, if not successful in smoothing the sharp edges of his world, has at least made him callous to its bruises. He has grown in infancy to depend on his own exertions and to be clear in his aims. At the first dawn of reason he has concluded that the only living the world owes him must come from his own effort. In short, the kindergarten of hard knocks that the Chinese urchin has graduated from has its decided advantages in character training. (1943)

A Family Affair

THE CHINESE MAKE MEALS THE CHIEF EVENTS OF THE DAY AND enjoy them as occasions for family reunions. Even in the boarding house that I am at present running for the students of the various schools of the city, the kitchen is the focal point in the house. I doubt whether anywhere outside of China two-score students ever rally in the kitchen twice a day to give active aid in cooking the food.

The cook's job appears to be starting the fire before the students return from school. Once they have returned, the boys take over in the kitchen—scrubbing pots, washing the rice, cutting up the vegetables, fanning the three firepots to intense heat, and scooping up water from the large urns that hold several hundred gallons. But their main delight seems to be watching the pots come to a boil.

An American cook might be driven out of her wits by a score or more of hungry young men in her kitchen, and tempers might boil faster than the pots. But in China all are good-natured and fond of joking, and they keep their ears and tongues active while doing the chores. Although only half a dozen can eat at a time or find elbow room at the stoves, the rest seem to enjoy the waiting. The secret lies in not considering it as waiting, but as part of the meal.

The students form a semi-circle around the fire and warm their hands while chatting over the news of the day. They step aside for the moment when a pot needs to be tended, and close in again automatically when the way is once more free. Chinese etiquette requires that meals be eaten in silence, so the time before and after eating is given over to conversation, and the actual eating is of very short duration.

Of course, these students are living as they would were they at home, and similar scenes take place at every fireside

128

throughout the length and breadth of China. At first glance, it seems a disorganized way of preparing meals, ill-suited to Western life, but a moment's thought shows it as not only primitive and natural, but rational and Christian as well.

Right through the Middle Ages down to fairly modern times the huge hearth was the center of family living, with little distinction between dining and kitchen room. Servants and masters ate at the same board and together. In the farming class the world over, there is even today that camaraderie at table that the snobbishness of town life lacks.

If introduced into American life in the cities, the Chinese way might not only solve the "servant problem," but focus the entire household in saner relations. Incidentally, it might be an eye-opener to many a good housewife, showing her how her husband and sons relish preparing the meals themselves. It might also change the gentlemen's attitude from chronic grumbling at the slowness of dinner, since it would give them an insight into the drudgery of the kitchen when this involves isolation from the rest of the family. It would elevate the status of the cook to queen in her special realm, with subjects under her. Although such a system would be hard on the dish towels and crockery, it would make the kitchen more comfortably messy and attractive to menfolk.

In short, making the hearth once more the rallying spot of the family would change the average house from a lodging place, with hasty meals, to a united home. The boys would learn economy and sociology more vividly than when these subjects are taught in school. It might even be claimed that the quality of the meals would change, even if not for the better at first. The best chefs the world over are said to be men.

But the chief attraction of this mode of living is the sharing of enjoyment among all the household. There is no earthly reason why the preparing of food should be considered more burdensome than the eating of it. Nor should marketing to procure the food be considered a dull chore. Most of the enjoyment of a flank of venison is in the hunting of the deer; the successful landing of a wily pickerel is more sport than the bone-picking contest afterwards; and any man would prefer splitting his own logs and feeding his own fire to lighting a gas range.

Man is by nature the provider for the family, and he should be allowed to exercise his right. It is human nature to enjoy the fruit of one's own toil, and the disadvantage of imperfect results is offset by the personal touch of even clumsy efforts.

The curse of city life is its artificiality. Let a housewife resign herself to amateurish meddling, call in the boys of the family to knead the dough and pare the vegetables, gather the entire family in the kitchen to mix the batter and grease the pans, and the household will vote the supper one of the happiest they have enjoyed together. The Chinese have tried this way for centuries, and no other race enjoys meals more humanly than do these citizens of the Orient. (*1944*)

A People without Pretense

THE DIFFERENCE BETWEEN WESTERN SINCERITY AND CHINESE IS strikingly exemplified in that phrase, "Keeping up with the Joneses," which so often is the American standard.

In China, dress and house are not merely scaled to income, but are unimportant and no index of the owner's self-esteem or local standing. A few instances to illustrate this may be more striking than a long argument.

A clerk in the mayor's office dropped in today on business. He wore no overcoat although the rain was chilly; his feet were shod in sandals without stockings; his clothes were neat enough, but faded by sun and rain; but the impressive fact was that he was unconscious of his appearance and entirely at ease.

Yesterday the principal of a high school called. He also was sockless; he wore the straw footgear, tied with cloth strings, that is common to farmers on these mountain roads. Both of these men would be classed among the notables of the city, but neither felt the need to dress better than his poorer neighbor.

A few doors distant lives a general. On duty he is resplendent in full-dress uniform and is squired by attendants, but at home he wears shorts as he putters, barefooted and mudstained, in his vegetable patch, in full view of passers-by.

Perhaps the supreme test the world over would be the womenfolk. In China, convention does not allow women even in the privacy of home to be in informal lounging attire, but the wealthiest of Chinese women, as well as the poorer class, dress for comfort more than Westerners do. They wear garments of sturdy, durable stuff, and marketing with a basket is not disdained by anyone.

It is in the home life particularly that this sincerity is portrayed. It is not parsimony, or even rugged Spartan living. The Chinese have feasts, as other people have, and they enjoy them thoroughly. But for feast or fast there is an absence of what, for lack of better term, might be called affectation or assumption of airs. There are frankness and simplicity, devoid of guile, in the genuine gusto of a feast, as well as forthright honesty in ordinary fare—such as the hearty meals of farms in Western countries.

Likewise, in the appointments of a Chinese house, honesty dominates the furnishings. In humbler homes, the unpainted wooden benches stand without apology, in company with cracked washbasin and earthen floor. In homes of better equipment, there is no reservation of "parlors" for formal occasion; the entire house is freely used by uninvited neighbors at any time of day, and the always-open door never discriminates against dress or social standing. It is presumed from experience that everyone knows and will practice the elementary rules of etiquette, in his own house or elsewhere; and even the beggar does not presume to intrude beyond the doorstep, no matter how open the door may be. The owner has neither anything to hide nor any pretense beyond the visible; he does not show off his house from vanity. Whatever beauty is present is for use by all.

Such hospitality would perhaps not be possible in Western homes, where many of the furnishings are fragile and easily broken by venturesome hands of children, or are of intricate and delicate material that soils in unwashed hands. Chinese children are much less restrained and even dirtier than Western children, but the treatment of a Chinese house, which builds its beauty into its walls or out of reach of urchins, prevents harmful use of the premises. The furniture is sturdy and solid; there is an absence of gimcrackery; and the result is soothing in its simplicity. In stores, too, there is a simplicity in salesmanship as regards the display, or lack of it, with no advertising. The cash-and-carry basis of sale, without charge accounts, also tends to make transactions commonplace.

Even in a Chinese theater, the audience is as enjoyable to an observer as is the play itself. Faces glisten and beam while friends are greeted; the mere settling into seats, the flurry of wraps, and the comments on the program are enjoyment enough, without orchestral prelude. The Chinese are honestly out to enjoy themselves.

This correspondence of heart and face is carried even into the public busses, with frank interest in fellow passengers and a good-natured tolerance of inconveniences that might easily cost the company a lawsuit in another land. China is probably the only country left in this world where pomp of state is refreshingly absent, where a man may lead his life unhampered by vitiated conventions. It is not that there are no standards, but that the supreme standard is sincerity. (*1944*)

Chinese Theater

IT MAY BE A BIT EARLY TO CRITICIZE THE THEATER IN CHINA. Like everything else in modern China, the drama is still in infancy, and only a doting parent can see features in a chubby infant. But, like all other modernization, the drama has taken hold quickly and spread rapidly.

The modern Chinese play has much in common with the centuries-old Chinese operatic drama. The old-style play, kept to narrow traditional themes based on classical romances and sung to tunes drowned by cymbals, drums, and shrill string instruments, at first thought has little resemblance to the modern spoken play, which seems to follow Western lines. But basically they both emphasize an historical, rather than a psychological, problem. In both, the Westerner waits in vain for a climax beyond mere chronological development of the plot.

In both, the plot is well known to the audience: in the old drama, from books read since childhood; and in the new modern play, from the story completely printed in the program. There is, therefore, little element of surprise from scene to scene. The hero or villain is such from the outset, and acts consistently throughout; the types do not develop, and suspense is absent.

It is true that many of the old-style dramas told a story with unity of cast and theme. But the vast majority are based on episodes from the heroic saga of the establishment of the

Three Kingdoms; they are more in the nature of an animated tableau such as was presented on the Western stage in *Victoria Regina*—the play that had such a long run in New York a decade ago. The old drama's semi-historical legends are well known to even the most rustic villager, and the Shakesperean absence of curtains or scenery allows dozens of episodes to follow one another without interrelation.

The modern play in China adheres closely to Western concepts of unity of plot and is restricted to one theme, but there is little evolution of character as the play progresses.

William Lyon Phelps characterizes Russian plays as centrifugal and European plays as centripetal, because the Western play concentrates attention on the actors' intimate, personal reactions, while the Russian play presents a problem of universal conditions. The Chinese drama also may be classified as centrifugal; this characteristic, common to both, may be found on study to be common to the whole of Asia. Strictly, Asiatic dramas are not "problem" plays that demand solution on the part of the individual, but statements of events without suspense.

One effect of such treatment is the quality of the attention demanded of the audience. With little need to concentrate on a problem, the audience becomes in reality visitors, and they contemplate the scene rather than listen to the plot. This may perhaps explain to the bewildered foreigner the freedom of speech and noise allowed and practiced by the audience in any Chinese theater, and the lack of clear articulation on the part of the actors.

Perhaps the most striking feature of the Chinese play, at least to a missioner, is its expression of the religious mind of the Chinese. The plays are strictly morality plays in a very broad sense. The old-style play is permeated with superstition, and whatever action is evident is the result of supernatural intervention. The modern play, of course, avoids superstition or introduces it only in derision, but unconsciously portrays the modern mind by its total unmorality. Emotion of any sort hardly enters into the theme; problems of love or sex or anger or murder are rarely, if ever, treated, nor is any attempt made to present the simple, happy, calm life of village folk. Family life is usually portrayed as a sterile relationship reminiscent of hotel existence. Women—a new element on the Chinese stage —are always vacuous though verbose, mere stage properties without influence on the theme, unemotional, and interesting only because of their numerous changes of costume.

The modern stage, it must be admitted, reflects accurately one phase of pagan life—that of the weak and numerically small element that lives in port cities. This is probably due to the fact that the playwrights of China are a narrow clique of city bohemians, whose themes are restricted to the unconventional and insecure life of commercial clerks. There is an honest attempt to portray such a life.

At first sight, it would appear that the Chinese theater is in its infancy and that this infancy is responsible for the immature, shallow themes. But such an explanation may be too simple. The answer might be that modern paganism cannot rise to the vision of great themes, and cannot treat simple ones profoundly, because all art is ultimately religious. (*1947*)

In Defense of "Face"

IT IS A CURIOUS QUIRK IN HUMAN NATURE THAT WE MUST BE partisan to view racial characteristics impartially. If that is putting it too strongly, at least we must love, before we can truly value, an alien culture. Ignorance of contributing causes is not the explanation of racial antipathies, but itself arises from indifference to the race concerned. Where indifference beclouds the intelligence, all alien cultures are judged outlandish and even inexplicable.

Travel easily tests this weakness. A hurried trip through foreign lands, with confusing glimpses of national customs, unless corrected by a willingness to understand, begets a spiritual pride that distorts the vision further. But granted a willingness to understand, which might be called national humility and really is the virtue of charity, even first impressions of an alien race may be very true ones.

Chesterton exemplified this in his first impressions of America. He came prepared in soul to understand baffling characteristics, and he found our good points of absorbing interest. Ireland, which he studied close at hand, he appreciated as few of his compatriots did. More impressive still is the fact that in everything he wrote about China, which he never visited, he valued her customs and culture with an understanding and sympathy often lacking in foreigners of long residence in the Orient.

With foreigners, mere length of residence is no antidote. When from the outset, judgments are jaundiced by antipathy or indifference, continued residence simply entrenches the prejudices. No more general condemnations of the devious guile of the Oriental may be heard than from the lips of liverish foreign traders in the East, whose generalities have gradually seeped into the Western concept of the Oriental, until it has become almost axiomatic that the Asiatic is odd, exotic, impenetrably different from the rest of men.

One example of this disdain relates to the matter of "saving face." Foreigners, with a bewildered chuckle, state as Gospel truth that the Chinese will do anything to "save face." And they instance compromises with truth on the part of servants caught *in delicto;* of pleas of ill health on the part of hastily retiring officials who cannot stand investigation; and many formulas of etiquette to spare the feelings of discomforted wrong-doers. Then the snickering conclusion is thoughtlessly drawn that the Oriental is mysterious, and that the white man can thank God he is not like the rest of men.

It is so easy to forget the thousand-and-one instances of similar "face saving" among Occidentals which we take for granted. But in the case of Westerners we ascribe the action not to nationality but to the individual, or we benignly see the underlying charity that wishes to cover a multitude of sins. When there is a reshuffling of a cabinet to palliate defeat, or an outcry against some poor scapegoat to distract attention from corruption, or when subtle pressure back-pages a threatened exposure, no one thinks to damn a whole civilization or ascribe the fault to racial characteristics. When an official is "kicked upstairs" to cover ineptness, or a corporation increases its vice-presidents, the action is apparently self-evident, and none marvel at the elaborate mechanism to "save face." When the bubble bursts at the beginning of a depression, and many men seek the "easy way" of suicide to avoid facing a grand jury, it is not looked upon as Occidental guile. When a corps of lawyers plead temporary insanity, and a thug has an airtight alibi, or divorces are granted for mental cruelty—when inconsistency and sentimental whims blur the policy of our education as well as our courts and politics—we rarely think of that conduct as evidencing a national trait; much less do we despair of understanding it as other than culpable individual weakness.

The situation is similar with the more homely practices of simpler folk. Chinese are noted for softening refusals in order to save face, yet gentle folk the world over charitably do the same, and no one is deceived or vexed by it. The stereotyped formulas of office procedure that excuse a man "in conference" or as busy; the social convention that permits us to be "not at home" or to have "a prior engagement"; the dunning bills that insinuate the debts were overlooked by mere mischance; or the distracting menu titles that disguise warmed-over hash—all testify to man's desire to live at peace with his neighbor.

In fine, the Chinese are as human as any other people, or even more so, but not to a startling degree. Special traits and national customs are often commented on by new arrivals to the Orient, and rightly so, for it is important for strangers in any country to learn immediately the conventions that govern smooth living. It would be a touch of Pharisaism, however, to conclude therefrom that the Oriental is mysterious or that "the heathen Chinese is peculiar." No race is composed of Nathaniels. (*1945*)

IN JOURNEYINGS OFTEN

"There is something superhuman in the Chinese ability to abstract time and urgency from motion. . . . The grace of our vocation accomplishes much in us, and not the least is its subduing of our Western restlessness and rash zeal to hurry the East."

The Sacramental Universe

"IT IS SAID THAT EVERYONE IS A MAN OF ONE IDEA, AND I SUPPOSE *I could say my idea is that everything in the universe is a sacramental,*" reflected Bishop Ford. *Three decades of crossing the hills and dales of South China left the American prelate as thrilled with the romance of mission journeys as when he had arrived in the Orient in his twenties. His vision of nature had a radiance possible only to a Christian poet.*

"When Christ came, He 'renewed the face of the earth.' In some mysterious way, all creatures shared in God's salvation of mankind," he wrote. *"Now, everything we see and touch and hear is given us as a message to remind us of His purpose—the salvation of the world."*

Bishop Ford frequently urged his missioners to visit as many pagan villages as possible. He said that a place is never the same after a baptized person has passed through it. The Desire of the Everlasting Hills has come close, and has transfigured every stick and stone of the countryside that thirsted for the splendor of God's presence.

Small Boat on the Ocean

A BOAT TRIP BY NIGHT, IN AMERICA, EVEN ON AN ORDINARY RIVER liner, means a cabin, deck chairs and promenade, dining saloon, and above all, a hundred miles and more between

141

ports. To some it may mean a rest from telephone or visitors, or a quiet spell to turn over the problems of the morrow; to all it means something unusual in the way of recreation, with a push button close by to satisfy our wants.

Over here, it has a meaning all its own that defies adequate description and leaves us helpless to express ourselves. A trip in the East is Oriental; so also are the boat and pilot; and the accommodations are for Orientals whose life is not obsessed with a mania for speed or luxuries. "A painted boat upon a painted ocean" might express the speed, but not the boat, for nary a dab of paint ever disfigures our junks at Chiklung. "Deliberate speed," if not "majestic instancy," is nearer the mark, for there is something superhuman in the Chinese ability to abstract time and urgency from motion.

I've made a dozen acts of faith in the superiority of the Chinese viewpoint in non-essentials. We are ready to grant that grace of motion lies in the absence of friction, but the Oriental reasons that the greatest beauty lies in the total absence of friction; viewed thus, our trip is the perfection of poetry and beauty.

Chiklung is only thirty miles from Yeungkong and I could have walked it in ten hours, but no Chinese reasons thuswise. By all means take a boat, if so our feet are spared; and, as I was not traveling alone, I readily agreed. We left after a Lenten breakfast, and we dined at seven in the evening on a bowl of rice and sea worms. The boat trip, by the way, included twelve miles on foot, due to the lack of water at both ports. This is the dry season and many rivers are not navigable at low tide.

However, you must not think I did not enjoy the trip, for Chinese travel has the advantage over modern craft in varying its experiences. This is the first time I traveled on a really small boat, on the ocean, for any length of time. We missed the usual vessels that ply the route, by miscalculating the tides, and we enjoyed the high-priced offer of an old man to take us in his private yacht. The boat was solely ours, except for the presence of a dozen logs that filled the available space and kept us from rolling with the waves. It had the essentials of a sailboat in a tattered sail—it is not unusual here to find the sail missing—and as the boat was seaworthy, despite a foot of water that leaked in, we gladly spread our blankets on the logs and were off.

It is hard to grumble when you realize you would make a splendid subject for a canvas; it is harder still, confronted with the happy wrinkles on the pilot's face who sees no lack of comforts in a starry night, a quiet trip, and a fare that will allow him two days' loafing afterwards. My smile of resignation was taken for delight and gave him courage, once we started, to assure us he had forgotten to lay in any rice for our supper. It meant a saving of twenty cents to him and did us no harm, as we had brought our own supply along. When he saw our store, he gravely stated he had not eaten yet himself and he more than graced our humble meal. Luckily, I had read my Office before we started, as there was no light aboard.

The starry night precluded any wind, and we skirted the shore so slowly that it was a treat for the mosquitoes to sally forth and overtake us. The lack of wind compelled the pilot to pole the boat. This he does by mounting the rim and walking its length with a bamboo pole against his shoulder. He earned his fare, and I've become so orientalized as to delight in watching him work. His walking gives a lilt to the boat that keeps him balancing in danger of a spill. It prevents his dozing on the job, yet gives a seesaw motion to the boat that wears my nerves into a stupor and lulls to sleep.

The long hours in a cramped position, where neither reading nor other relaxation may be indulged in, coupled with a somewhat fatalistic unconcern over other, if not better, use of time, and the utter impotence of worry to change conditions beget a numbness and stagnation which, frequently indulged in, might convert the most rabid Westerner into an apathetic, unruffled Oriental. The grace of our vocation accomplishes much in us, and not the least is its subduing of our Western restlessness and rash zeal to hurry the East. With the lips, we make profession of the truth that Rome was not built in a day; the Oriental has motived his lifework on the saying.

I took some consolation from Father Martindale's article in the latest *Dublin Review,* where he urges that Oriental stolidity and unemotional immutability are assets in our endeavor to Christianize the East; that Catholicism, unlike restless non-Catholic sects that shape their doctrine to the whim of the decade, has a starting point in its unchanging dogmas and mystic theology, where East and West may approach each other in sympathy and intelligence.

There was compensation for the tedious trip in finding, on arrival at Chiklung, that the boat I should have taken was waylaid, during the night, by bandits, and crew and passengers carried off for ransom. I would have been a white elephant on their hands, had I been there; and, as the pirates wanted the boat most of all, it is interesting to speculate what they would have done with me. It was mid-ocean and I fear me they might have made me walk the plank! (*1923*)

Why Hurry?

I'M ON A SICK CALL, AND HAVE BEEN SINCE YESTERDAY, AND won't arrive at the bedside till tonight, yet I have been traveling every moment of the time. Translate that into terms of modern travel, and my parish would extend over a good quarter of the United States, for even a taxi going steadily for thirty-six hours will register a fair mileage.

But China sets its own conservative pace, and I forget my good resolution of loving things Chinese to groan for speed. I don't know the Chinese equivalent of "time and tide wait for no man"; probably there is no such expression, for the Chinese have never experienced any agony at delay; they simply wait for the next time, or the next tide, and finally arrive.

This is one reason why sick calls are less frequent than the number of Christians would lead one to expect. The bearer of the news this time took three days to come to the mission, and, even then, we had to wait another day for a return boat. The entire distance, I'm ashamed to confess it, is only fifty miles, and I have covered it on horseback in two days—but that was in the dry season, in winter, during a spell of peace, and I had a hardy youngster who knew the mountain road, to run beside my horse. Now is the time of greatest heat, the roads are brooks, my guide is an old man, and I haven't any horse. So we must take two sides of a triangle, instead of the shorter base. The journey is an ordinary one, yet every inch of it is interesting each time we make it, and we manage to pick up stray bits of information unknown before.

First of all, any trip means a short cut through the city streets, and, as each of our companions has a favorite route, we often discover new alleys. This time I found that by boldly entering a certain house and passing through its courtyard, we saved a roundabout walk. Its only drawback is strange dogs. Each dog in China has a well-defined "beat" which he guards, and though he is moved to bark at any stranger anywhere, once you pass within his limits his bark becomes a snarl at your heels till his master silences him.

Walking in China is at best a feat: a hop to avoid a puddle; a side step where a child is sprawled stark-naked in the roadway; a jump over a self-satisfied pig whose two hundred pounds are stretched full length across the narrow alley; a kick at a noisy cur; hugging the wall as a long-horned buffalo swings by; dodging bamboo poles swaying carefree on a coolie's shoulder; a duck away from dripping spouts that are the limit of the city's drainage; a hasty glance behind to measure clearance for a sedan chair; a bobbing of the head in response to greetings from the merchants; tunneling through a group of open-mouths gaping at a cure-all vendor; an occasional slide and slip over wet flagging; a useless apology for bumping into gossiping old cronies—always accompanied with a wild search for your boy and baggage that have turned the corner.

I've battled on Park Row and on Forty-second Street for life, liberty, and the pursuit of a train, but in China the difficulty lies in racing along while everyone else ambles aimlessly. We are told by writers, if we wish to understand China, to set our pace by the man in front of us. At least it is a good rule for ease in traveling, because, despite our rush to reach the city limits and the wharf, we are obliged to cool off while we dicker a price for the boat. The old sailor can make but one trip a day, so he is in no hurry to close the bargain and sets a high value on his services.

But once squat down on the floor of the boat and watch the waves slap lazily alongside, after you have removed your shoes and hat and coat and lit your pipe, and you will sit and wonder why the West loves speed. Your progress no longer depends on self, and a carefree smile wipes out all wrinkles. (*1925*)

In Favor of the Horse

I'M BEGINNING TO FEEL LIKE ONE BORN OUT OF DUE TIME. WHEN China is going in for aviation and we have a landing field outside the city of Kaying, when motor roads are appearing in the valleys of our inland mountain ranges, and when autobuses are actually bumping their noisy way through the city streets, I am just discovering the beauty of the horse. Now it does no good to tell me that an auto on Broadway is worth a thousand cycles in Cathay, unless you have experienced Cathay and realize its vigorous living. The thrills of speed and travel are relative and personal; you may do seventy-five in a closed Packard on a straight course, without half the hair-raising, vibrating thrills that our mountain trails can offer on a muddy day. Even in travel, China scores a point in the variety of its means of locomotion—camel, sampan, wheelbarrow, rickshaw —any one of these will discover for you hitherto unused bones and muscles needing exercise, and you realize the joy of healthy pain.

But I plead especially for the horse, or, rather, the Chinese pony. A Chinese pony plays an exaggerated part in its owner's interests. The missioner is human, and so inevitably in his lonely life must have a dumb friend. I have tried everything, from an aristocratic heron, through parrot and pigeon, down to the lowly goldfish and mud turtle, but I have always found to my chagrin that they cared more for my food than for my company.

The dog in China is not a fireside pet, because he is as much a part of the household as are the pig and chickens; besides, his inherited place is at the doorway on the street, barking at all who pass; he attaches himself to the babies and womenfolk, and is not considered a man's pet. The cat is much less in evidence, and is fattened from purely utilitarian motives. Which leaves only the horse to be adopted by the missioner, and it meets his needs. The horse is rare enough and costly enough to come under the heading of a pet, while the spirit of apostolic poverty is placated by the need of locomotion.

147

I used to bolster my inferiority complex as a pedestrian by the assurance that walking was the only way to enjoy travel, but I must admit that in China the rule does not hold. With one eye strained to avoid mud holes and the other gauging the six-inch pathway, the pedestrian rarely lifts his head to see the view; ten hours of such walking is as much a strain on the nerves as on the feet. But just mount a sure-footed pony, and you rediscover the beauties of the Chinese landscape. Nothing can equal the joy of crossing a mountain pass and finding yourself raised high above the stunted pine, with a clear head and sparkling eye to appraise the distant view and with breath enough in your lungs to take in the cool, dustless, cedar-scented air; you belong to the scene and are not intruding. Or take the occasional long stretches of level valley road, especially a dirt road, when your horse without urging breaks into a canter and then into a gallop, and the steady pounding of his hoofs beats in rhythm with your quickened pulse. Ten hours on a pony, with an hour's rest at noon, is almost as tiring physically as walking, but for some reason or other your head does not ache, nor are your eyes bloodshot from overstrain.

There is vanity in riding that other exercise does not give. Who is there who does not throw out his chest and feel Napoleonic astride a horse? The Popes and Cardinals of medieval days must have presented a brave sight mounted on cavorting steeds. 'Tis a pity the horse has no longer a place in the liturgy! How our city youngsters would be attracted at the sight of their formidable pastor prancing by! Clerical conferences would partake of the nature of a rodeo, as they do in China! And, after all, the merits of horse flesh is just as debatable and wholesome a topic as many others; and even the Apostles did not disdain to use the horse as a simile in a sermon.

Apart from the harmless vanity of it all, the Chinese pony

has practical points for the missioner. On visitations of the district where it is customary for the Christians to hire a chair for their pastor, the missioner who rides in on horseback saves the village a welcome little sum that ensures a double welcome for himself; besides, it is easier on the villagers to put up a horse for the night or two than to feed and bed a couple of coolies.

Another point that should win favor and adoption by busy priests in America: greetings and good-byes are definite and quickly done on horseback. Your guest or yourself, once mounted, has no further time for dallying—the restive animal takes charge of the ceremony, and is soon out of sight! And the swinging of your leg across the saddle, no matter how awkwardly you do it, gives just that little touch of ritual that is lacking in modern manners.

I defy anyone to be grumpy, or out of sorts, or jumpy, after a brisk canter, no matter where he be; and, in China, where noisome smells and muddy underfooting are drawbacks to exercise, the little pony that raises you aloof from the sweltering crowd helps very much to make the out-of-doors attractive. (*1932*)

On a Chinese Bus

I'M WORRIED SOMETIMES WHEN I REALIZE HOW GOOD GOD IS TO us in China, especially in the little things of life; and it's the little things that make up life, for none of us is heroic for more than two minutes at a time. The latest instance of His goodness was on a bus trip I took this morning. I rarely mount a bus without a little prayer for help—not that I much mind the wild careening over rutted roads or the vaulting impetus of a sudden brake as two cars meet head-on at a curve where one has barely room enough. To be frank, I'm somewhat of a fatalist about accidents. Perhaps I lack imagination. What makes me anxious on a bus is the treatment I'll get from passengers.

A bus ride in these mountains is still enough of a novelty to make a trip somewhat exciting. First of all, the shortest bus ride is the price of a good meal, so we think twice before deciding on it; then, it always means an excursion away from home and even on business there's a holiday feeling about it, so that the mind is unusually alert for pleasant experiences and there is a natural wish that nothing may mar its pleasure.

Now, a bus ride could easily be chilling. Where all are strangers and you the strangest of them all; the Chinese reaction is reserve. Not the straight-lipped stiffness of the Nordic, or the demure side glances of a Filipino, but a sudden dimming of the eye and a waxy setting of the face and a rigidity of body that bespeaks a mind on guard lest it betray feeling.

The almost infinite difference, I am glad to say, between the aloofness of a Chinese and of other foreigners in the presence of a missioner is one of species and not degree. The Chinese distrusts, not the priest in the foreigner, but the foreigner in the priest. The priesthood is an asset that almost balances the liability; above all, there is no prejudice against the stranger's creed, but rather an eagerness to admit the moral goodness of our doctrine and a hasty conclusion that it is too sublime for adoption.

So the bus ride starts with stiffness, not merely in the unoiled mechanism of the motor, but also in the spinal columns of the passengers. But, fortunately, the bus in China is always packed. I've ridden in a five-passenger car with eighteen fellow sufferers; even in the larger bus they measure capacity by the number of shoes that can fill the floor. And I defy even the hardest shell not to crack in such a hot box; each lurch of the car releases a smile, and a sudden stop begets a chorus of grunts, and common suffering makes the whole bus kin.

I have found the secret of this kinship, and now no longer do I have to wait until the bus is under way. A shorter cut is simply to smile as you squeeze into your seat, with a grimace of apology as you wedge your elbow into your neighbor's rib. The smile works infallibly if you can catch the eye of any frozen face before you. The secret is not in the smile, but in the demonstration of your feeling that all are in the same boat and you are not claiming special privilege as a foreigner.

If you are traveling with a companion, the mere fact that you chat with him in Chinese is enough to set the bus agog at your fluency. The Chinese have poker faces when they praise, and it is only the absolute unanimity of the extravagant compliments that saves it from becoming a vice. You never have to fish for compliments in China, and our vocabulary is woefully lacking in enough self-abasing terms to counter compliments as etiquette demands. But, such preliminaries over, the conversation of the whole bus turns naturally to religion, and another onset of approbations is launched.

I remember that while I was walking as a youngster with a chum of mine, he explained his religion thus: "My folks are Episcopalians; we are almost Catholics." So, too, the Chinese on the bus, in somewhat similar strain, begin to boast of relatives who are Catholics, and those among them who are immigrants narrate the wonders of the splendid churches in foreign parts, so that the shortest bus ride is long enough for several points of religion to be discussed.

The curious side of this discussion is that it is almost always exposition of the doctrine, and only rarely an attack. The Chinese genius for compromise chooses safe topics for discussion, and the Chinese method of rhetorical questions allows plenty of assents from the listeners, as the bus raises its cloud of dust.

That any tangible effect comes from such talk is beside the point; at least a half hour is spent by a score of pagans in approving Catholic dogmas, and that is more valuable than the smoking room talk of American Pullmans. You alight at your destination with a slight pang of regret that you cannot continue the friendly conversation with such souls that are naturally Christian. (*1936*)

TOWARD AN INDIGENOUS CHURCH

"We are in mission countries, not to settle down indefinitely, as indispensable for the expansion of Christianity, but to build a nest for the fledgling native clergy who will one day replace us."

Memories of a Hakka Priest

In the October, 1952, issue of the American Ecclesiastical *Review*, *Reverend Mark Tsai, formerly one of the pioneer students in Bishop Ford's Kaying seminary, paid the following tribute to his late leader's zeal for the development of a numerous and holy Hakka priesthood:*

"After he arrived at Kaying in 1925, the first thing that he started was the seminary. To establish a good seminary for the training of priests, he considered no price too high. At first, he himself conducted some classes. Later on, these duties were passed on to someone else, but he still found time to give the writer daily private lessons in Caesar, Cicero, Virgil, geometry, and English. In establishing the curriculum of studies, he followed the most recent rules and regulations of the Holy See. . . . The spirit of those pioneering days was truly splendid. It was like heaven on earth.

"Bishop Francis Xavier Ford has passed on, but his spirit and heroic example remain with us all the time. He is South China's own glory. Kaying's first bishop became a martyr for the Faith; the entire Hakka people, therefore, will surely have a great future. He has indeed become 'the King's Highway in pathless China.' Te Deum laudamus!"

Chats with a Chinese Priest

Fr. Shi is tall and stocky, with a dignified walk. He would pass as a Senator from our Western states. While the average man in South China is undersized and wiry, he is big all around, with a smile that brings the youngsters toddling to him, and an alert sympathy that fills his room daily with students and older men glad of an hour's talk with him. Better still, he has an apostolic soul that is content with suffering. His lot has been that of a pioneer in building up new missions and never resting long in the enjoyment of his work. He has started many of the flourishing little groups of Catholics scattered over two or three hundred miles, and several thousands can turn to him as their first Father in Christ who poured the water of baptism on their heads.

It opened my eyes to his interest in his work when two hundred and more walked in on feast days from the surrounding district and he greeted many by name, after fifteen years of busy ministering elsewhere. I'm rather proud of the fact that I can distinguish one Chinese from another, and if I recall what particular village a man hails from my satisfaction is complete, but the intense love for his old-time flock that our visitor showed will henceforth silence any whisperings of vanity in my ability to "place" a strange face.

His thoughtfulness, too, was evidenced the first evening after supper. I like to light a pipe and catch the cool breeze that springs up after sunset, by pacing leisurely the common room which serves us as eating room and parlor. But the average Chinese doesn't see it that way; he takes no pleasure in unnecessary exertion, and among his friends he sits or stands, but rarely walks. His seventh heaven is a stuffy crowd of talking men, none of whom seems to listen to his neighbor.

Yet from the very start our Chinese brother in Christ was quick to fall in with my likes, and paced the narrow room as steadily as a Weston or O'Leary. And from eight to nine more regularly than the clock (a Japanese product) on the wall, we nightly met, and many were the sidelights thrown on

Eastern life and Western ways of doing. I found by asking, for he was not quick to talk about himself, that much of our territory is an open land to him; and village after village has had some curious fact to offer.

As a boy he left his home, several hundred miles southwest of us, to study at the diocesan seminary at Canton; after his classical course there, he was sent to the international seminary at Penang. There he sat side by side with Japanese and Korean lads, and Malays, and young men from India and Burma and Indochina, all eating the same kind of foods and speaking Latin as their common tongue. On big feasts as a special treat each was allowed to cook his own national dishes, though as a matter of prudence the Chinese were limited to eight courses—which in China is considered hardly a lunch, much less a banquet. He modestly claimed that the French missioners, who were the professors, always elected on those feast days to eat with the Chinese lads, as the other "nationals" put too much red pepper in their fancy dishes.

When he completed his theology course he went back to Canton. In his time men were not ordained immediately after graduation, but were sent out on the mission for several years' experience of its hardships to fit them better for their lifework. They could not do priestly work, but they journeyed from village to village instructing, preaching, forming boys' choirs and altar sodalities—in fact, doing the work of highly specialized catechists. They were especially useful as aids to new missioners, teaching them the language and customs.

After several years of this practical apprenticeship Fr. Shi was ordained, and then began an active life that called him to the four points of the compass within the Province of Kwangtung. It was before the advent of the little railway, and indeed before the steamboat's whistle woke these ports. Walking was the fashion then and Yeungkong was five days distant

157

from the capital. His first mission extended ten days west and six days north, but he seems to have lost no weight in the exercise and managed to be known by even the countless pagans hereabouts.

One night he landed at a seaport, drenched and hungry. He knew no one, and in those days, shortly after the Boxer trouble, strangers were eyed with suspicion. He stood in the street and said a little prayer, and then made for the nearest house to beg a night's lodging. But while he hesitated at the door, before knocking, the owner called out with a smile: "Aren't you a Catholic priest? I saw you last year in Yeung-kong; you gave some money to a beggar as I passed by. Come in, and welcome!" And the host soon had a hot supper ready for his wandering guest, who repaid him before the year was over by receiving him into the Church.

Another night, in a sailboat going to Tinpak, he woke up with his nose against the cold muzzle of a gun. He made haste to give the bandits all he had, but begged to be allowed to keep his breviary, as it was of no use to them. As the robbers were leaving they spied his suitcase that contained the Mass vestments and his chalice, and they took it along with them. Later, when they opened it, they were alarmed at what they had stolen and made a whole day's journey to the chapel to give back the sacred vestments.

Fr. Shi's mission now is three days' journey northeast of us. There he has several entirely Christian villages and, what is more striking, they are truly Catholic. It's refreshing to find in the midst of pagan China a village named "Sacred Heart Village"; here he has a hundred families and a chapel. A few miles away another hamlet is called "Three Cardinal Virtues Village"; and still another is named "Catholic Village." These villages are entirely Catholic. He started them by buying large tracts of ground and then inducing his Christians to settle there. This means a Catholic atmosphere for the growing boys and girls, who will see no pagan practices or vices as part of their daily life.

He is a student in his own way and for a score of years has been noting local idioms of the many districts hereabouts. His notes will be extremely valuable to future students of Cantonese. He told me the purest Cantonese is not spoken in Canton or in the other centers of learning, but on the waterfront among the sampan dwellers. This tribe of fishermen have never mingled with the polyglot landfolk, and have handed down the spoken word in its clear, musical purity.

As in the *Arabian Nights,* each evening's walk had its little stories, too numerous to note now. I am grateful for the opportunity of my evening chats with Fr. Shi. (*1919*)

Church Architecture

WE MARYKNOLLERS ARE BECOMING DEEPLY INTERESTED IN THE problem of Chinese church architecture. I suppose each missioner in China, during his lifetime, builds at least five churches. Most of these, of course, are simply village chapels; none of our larger churches will ever hope to compare in size with American churches. Yet the fact that we build at all gives ecclesiastical architecture quite a claim on our attention.

You remember a recent letter of the Apostolic Delegate to China, pleading for the expression of Chinese architecture in preference to imported types. We in America have had our experiences of poor taste in architecture, but most of the missioners in China are from Europe and have had glorious cathedrals in which to pray. Naturally, on coming to China and meeting the need of building, they have copied with more or less success the lines of the best European church architecture. What the Apostolic Delegate urged was a stimulating of effort to erect churches that would take Chinese artistic taste and ennoble it by consecrating it to God. Chinese art has served paganism for centuries; we must now baptize it.

This suggestion does not mean that there has been no attempt to build churches along Chinese lines. Most of our village chapels are Chinese in style, simply because they were built for small congregations by local masons; and the line of least resistance, if for no other reason, would naturally impel us to let the native mason plan his own way. But larger churches are a different problem.

Even copying pagan temples is impractical, for they were not built for liturgical services where several hundred worshipers must kneel as at Mass. They are simply receptacles for pagan idols and dwellings for their caretakers, visited by individuals who worship for a few moments, at no regular time. In shape they are foursquare, with an open court as a center; there are no windows, as the worship is physical and no books are read. They are hot in summer, cold in winter, and wet in rainy weather, but these inconveniences are not felt by the Chinese, who choose a clear day or hour.

To achieve, then, a practical building of Chinese style adequate for Catholic liturgy will demand much thought. The roof offers no great obstacle, for there is but one style throughout China. This style allows, however, no tower or dome; unless built high, it cannot be distinguished at a distance. The façade of Chinese temples is disappointing: it is the lowest of the walls, bare of ornament, and solid except for the doorway. The roof of the façade is supported by stone pillars braced by stone shafts, like goal posts; they are usually carved and offer some relief to the bareness of the exterior.

But the interior presents almost insurmountable obstacles. Windows are not native, at least exterior ones, although openings on the inner court are common. The interior of a temple is simply slender columns and flagged pavement. The sanctuary is raised above the rest, without a railing, and is similar to ours but for the fact that it extends the whole width of the building. The altar very often resembles a Catholic one, with table, flowers, candles, sanctuary lamps, and a canopied box within which the idol can be dimly seen through gauze curtains.

Summing up, then, there is no difficulty with roof or sanctuary. It is the nave which is lacking; in temples an enclosed, unroofed court is substituted. For a Catholic congregation, this must be roofed; but that would exclude light and air, and rob the building of a characteristic feature. Much of Chinese worship is done out of doors at roadside shrines and pagodas on the hills; so Chinese temples, with their open courtyards, have preserved much of the freedom of outdoor worship. The court is sometimes lined with trees, and contains a pond with goldfish and turtles.

The Apostolic Delegate did not urge a slavish imitation of Chinese temple style, but an adaptation of its best features. Curiously, he is the first, as far as I know, to view the possibility of a Catholic Chinese architecture. There is much weight to his pleading, in that he is an authority on the subject, and, hitherto, China has had few specialists to champion her art. As a prelude to a study of the subject, I scouted the chief bookstalls in Hong Kong and Shanghai for literature. Only one had any book on Chinese architecture and that sole book was priced at two hundred dollars; so the field evidently is virgin.

However, I daresay the next decade will show a decided change in church building here, for, though China's missioners are scattered far and wide, whenever they meet, the Delegate's letter is the inspiration for discussion and much wrinkling of brows that will result in a literal orientation of our churches of the future. (*1925*)

The Missioner's Ultimate Goal

PREACHING THE GOSPEL IS THE FIRST DUTY OF THE APOSTOLATE; but it is first merely in time, not in importance. The most important duty of missioners is to lay the foundation of a permanent indigenous Church. Over here on the mission field we are apt to lose sight of this double nature of the apostolate, because the generation of pagans living and dying all about us appeals so strongly for direct action in the work of conversions.

It is natural that the Holy See should be the first to be aware of the weakness of this stand, and recent Popes have again and again reminded missioners of their ultimate goal. We are in mission countries, not to settle down there indefinitely, as indispensable for the expansion of Christianity, but to build a nest for the fledgling native clergy who will one day replace us.

In practice, the twofold duties of the apostolate often appear to involve us in a dilemma. Work among pagans seems to limit work among Christians; the former is peregrinating for Christ, the latter is building. In so far as we give ourselves to the instruction of pagans, in just such degree we must curtail our labors for our Christians. Take, for example, a virgin field. During several years of friendly association with the pagans, the work of the pioneer is clear-cut and simple; he has but to instruct pagans. Once he has a few hundred converts, however, his anxiety is divided between forming in them a Christlike character, and continuing his former work with other pagans.

Both apparently are his duty, yet the daily building up of a strong parish, no matter how small the congregation, is work enough. He has his school and his catechizing, his need of revealing by individual and constant instruction the fuller Catholic life of the sacraments. Converts in the Orient are not, for the most part, an educated people capable of absorbing the spirit of the Church by reading. The Gospel must be preached to them; and the whole Gospel which we have imbibed from early childhood and insensibly is an elaborate system.

The problem of modern mission work in China has evolved various types of apostles; some have emphasized direct work among pagans, others have limited themselves mostly to the Christians in half a dozen stations, fostering an occasional vocation among the boys and girls. Outside the ordinary run of missioners, are those set apart by their bishop for higher education or literary work. Each of these various types has contributed to the spread and building of the Church in China. If they work together, they constitute a strong army battling for Christ.

It is easy to point out gaps here and there in the ranks, where missioners are scarce and overworked, but to the credit of the Church in China it can be said that a healthy advance is regular up and down the line. When it is noted that the present number of missioners is in proportion of one to eight hundred Christians, and that these Christians are scattered over large districts, we can justly admire the men who have accomplished this advance.

Now, the Holy Father again emphasizes the fact that missioners are not pastors; the pastoral work is to be done by the native priests, and the foreigner's work is in the front trenches. This directive does not involve a revolution in mission methods. Very often, our larger parishes are not in the big cities; our stations are but small islands in a huge sea of paganism, and without changing many missioners the effect desired by the Pope is accomplished. The larger parishes have not infrequently two priests, a foreigner and a Chinese, and the missions have anticipated the wish of the Sovereign Pontiff by giving the care of the parish work to the Chinese priest, thereby releasing the foreigner for work suited to his talents.

The real aim of the Holy Father in his latest directives, as I see it, is not so much a radical change in mission methods as a reorientation of our ideals. The problem is so complex that it is easy for us to become immersed in one detail, to the detriment of the whole. The Pope simply repeats that we must look for no final solution until an indigenous clergy is established. He reminds us again that our main task is to hasten that day, and that any venture which leads away from that aim is not success but failure. Indeed, he implies that our work will have been completed by the establishment of an indigenous Church, and that the conversion of China may then be safely left to the Chinese. It is of great value thus to recapitulate our aims, or, rather, to have them restated in clear terms by the one authoritative expert. (*1926*)

A Guardian Angel Smiles

WHEN WE BEGAN WORK IN HAKKALAND, IN 1925, WE FIRMLY resolved not to build anything anywhere till we were well settled, both in knowledge of the place and language, but more especially in funds. We made a solemn promise to ourselves not to take any forward step until our financial credit warranted it. We borrowed this axiom from Ben Franklin without blushing, for experience in the past had shown that early wrinkles and gray hairs are the result of living up to your income without reserve. It seemed a splendid chance to begin a new mission correctly from the very start.

The guardian angel of the mission surely must have smiled at our shortsightedness. We poor mortals were trying to imitate the "children of this world" in being prudent, but, that no flesh might glory in itself, Providence simply stepped in and ran things from God's viewpoint, and we were helpless. First, the wee, small voice spoke to the boys of our schools, and vocations to the Catholic priesthood superabounded. Then the Holy Father, as if he had seen the whole affair, wrote his letter to the missions, saying that we were not to refuse vocations.

There were ten boys waiting for us when we arrived in this hinterland of the port city of Swatow. Without budging an inch in our resolution, we gave the mission's guardian angel a knowing glance, and started the seminary in our own house. Of course, our conscience whispered that it would not do at all, but we were deaf. We took the boys in, and, as happened in the schools of Charlemagne, the youngsters became part of our household.

The rectory, with two bedrooms upstairs and three rooms on the ground floor, was not overlarge, but by putting the boys' beds on the enclosed porch and using one of our bedrooms for the teachers we managed to be cosy. The pastor made his bedroom in the hallway, by blocking off a corner with his bookcase. The next school term found us with thirteen boys. The hall room was released for the seminarians' use, by fixing up the attic for the pastor. We could still claim financial victory in the battle for economy.

Our defenses were rapidly crumbling, however. Before we could catch our breath, we had twenty-one seminarians. We crowded them into our two-bedroom dwelling, but at the expense of order and discipline. Only Chinese boys would have put up with the discomforts of those narrow quarters. We made

165

place for the latest recruits by sawing off the beds of the smaller boys, which gave us room for two more bunks. All spare clothing was stored in boxes in the yard. Outside of the hours for meals, the dining room served alternately as class-room and as study hall. Two Protestant missionaries from the Baptist university paid a call, and they had to be received on the porch. There was no room vacant except the pastor's bedroom, and three chairs could not fit in there.

At length, we conceded what we had known all along: a seminary is not a camp; and there were certain essentials which had to be provided. As we acknowledged defeat, we could hear the mission's guardian angel chuckling. "God has given you all those seminarians," he seemed to say. "Why should you be so stupid as to doubt that He would help you to build a seminary?"

The angelic chuckles did not irk us because we were remarkably happy ourselves. The joy of training Chinese youth for the Catholic priesthood far outweighed the sacrifice of worldly prudence. Under our fostering care, there would take place in China the miracle of the birth of "other Christs," all linked with Bethlehem's First-born. Each of those Chinese priests nurtured in our seminary would be God's "star in the East," calling men of good will from the shadow of death to the everlasting splendor of Redemption. (1927)

The Making of Chinese Priests

THERE ARE MANY INTERESTING SIDES TO MISSION LIFE, SO MANY that I wager we could find one to fit every mind; it is really an expression of the length and depth and width of the whole Catholic Church. The missions are the Church, not merely in embryo, but as a cross section of the full-grown body.

Grouped as nowhere else in the world, we find on the missions neophytes and baptized, confessors for the faith and apostles, virgins and even martyrs. We have, as it were, in one kaleidoscope the history of twenty centuries: the primitive Church; the age of persecution; the unfolding of dogmas; the questions of national rites; the incorporation of Catholic terms in a new language; the baptizing of pagan customs; and the development of a native Church. The Church is perennially young and a militant Church, because of its mission.

Yet the Church is so well knit together that its aim on the missions can be expressed in a single idea—the raising up of a native clergy. Given a clergy, China is as Catholic as Rome itself; and it is then only a question of time. Time is accidental; a clergy is the essential element.

And the question of a native clergy is one that can prove interesting to every mind. Some of us are interested in China historically, others linguistically, still others, psychologically; to some China means little else than a foreign land, to others a pagan foreign land, to the more thoughtful, it is a promising mission field. Whether we consider it from the religious, historical, or international point of view, the question of a native clergy meets us to be answered.

It is little to wonder at, then, that our first years in the Hakka mission have been wrapped up in the seminary. If I have written little of it to you, it was not from lack of thought, but perhaps because we were afraid to begin to speak. Catholic ideals are too sacred to be lightly spoken of, and there is a natural reticence in touching on the absorbing motive of our life over here.

Each must discover the Catholic Church for himself, and, having discovered it, the tendency is to be distrustful of one's powers of expressing its ineffable wonders to others. So it is with the establishment of a native seminary. We wish to exclaim: "Behold the tabernacle of God among men," and leave it at that. There is a strange equality in every Catholic work, an infinite equality that makes useless any measurement—it is work for God and therefore beyond all rating, so much so that superlatives are not strong enough in describing any effort to fulfill God's plan. But, even from the human point of view, the establishment of a seminary is recognized as peculiarly blessed.

Because of this, we feel our Kaying mission is well begun and solidly founded in our little seminary; without exception, our men have put their best efforts toward its success. Materially, as yet, it is a poor infant in makeshift quarters; financially, it has been a heavy expense to bear; and the running of it has demanded care. Yet the pain of its foundation is one akin to parenthood, an outlet for the love we need to express. We would not wish it otherwise. (*1928*)

A Chinese John Berchmans

THE KAYING SEMINARY, STILL IN ITS INFANCY AND BUT RECENTLY settled in its own buildings, has been called upon to make its sacrifice in the death of one of its students, John Yap Tet-hon. This young man was the first applicant for admission when the seminary was begun, in 1925. He was a boy only thirteen years of age, finishing his course at the parochial school in Kaying, but he had already entertained for several years the desire to offer himself for the priesthood.

He came from a family that has been Catholic for several generations, which is not unusual in this section of the mission. This particular family has, moreover, nourished a Catholic spirit that has sent the eldest son to the Catholic University at Peiping, while it generously encouraged the two younger boys in their vocation at the seminary.

John, although not a naturally bright student, often led his class because of his steady application. But, better still, as associated with the institution from its beginning, he was the leader of the other boys in a quiet, unconscious piety. He came from what would be considered one of the "better families" of our mission, and in China class consciousness is a strong element; yet in practice, he went beyond his classmates in little acts of humility and mortification.

The manual-labor period at the seminary—especially in its earlier days—was strenuous enough, and irksome to the average Chinese boy, who sharply distinguishes as a student between menial and other tasks. Yet John again set the example. He would work during the hour, digging in the garden or removing heaps of rubbish, in his bare feet. When asked why, he replied that the cloth shoes were too easily torn by such work, and he wished to save us that expense.

During his seven years with us, I never knew him to commit a deliberate violation of the rules; his interpretation of their spirit was generous and showed reflection. He could accuse himself occasionally of interior feelings of anger, though not of their outward expression, and in basketball or handball he had a mastery over his feelings even in moments of excitement. He entered into the spirit of any student activity, whether study or games, without losing himself in it, and he preserved a mature purpose in his actions rare in so innocent a life.

The scourge of the student class in China is lung trouble; and John developed symptoms. His lingering illness terminated in a characteristic act. He was conscious to the end, begging his father to be resigned to God's will. When his father finally assented, John, as though waiting for his permission, quietly closed his eyes and breathed his last.

He was the John Berchmans of the seminary, set in pagan surroundings where his virtues are emphasized by contrast.

God chose our worthiest. It is a reassuring thought that we are represented in the Eternal Sanctuary by one who was so grateful here below for what we gave him. (*1932*)

The Pope Leads the Way

WHEN ST. PAUL STARTED OUT ON HIS MANY JOURNEYS THROUGH Asia Minor, converting here and there small groups of Christians, he realized the fact that he could not take care of the new Christianities sufficiently well. So his first duty was that of selecting capable young men to carry on the priesthood. Thus, he ordained St. Timothy and St. Titus, and ordered them to continue the same plan of stimulating vocations locally.

The same policy has been followed by the Catholic Church ever since, and many of the letters that have come down to us from the Popes, written to the bishops of Asia, strike the same keynote: "Raise up a native clergy." At first glance it seems a hard problem, and almost a case of putting the cart before the horse, to try to develop a native clergy before the people are converted; it seems premature to take young men surrounded by the evil influences of paganism—with little of the grandeur and strength of a Catholic community to aid them— and to train them to the sublime life demanded of the Catholic priest.

Can the native priest measure up to the standards of the Church's requirements? I am able to speak for China better than for other countries, as my work has been there, but I feel sure that what I say of China is true also of Japan, Korea, India, and the adjacent countries.

At the Plenary Council of China held in Shanghai, in 1924, where all the bishops of China assembled, this same question was asked publicly, and each bishop was requested to state frankly his knowledge of the character of his native priests. One by one these heads of missions, many of them venerable old men who had passed forty and fifty years in China, who came from more than a dozen nations and represented every society in China, both secular and religious, and whose experience embraced the whole of China from Mongolia and Manchuria to Yunnan and Kwangtung (a territory larger than the United States), these bishops—starting from the eldest and passing slowly to the youngest—each in turn gave testimony concerning the native priest, and the tenor of their remarks was thus: Thank God, in my vicariate the native priests have been wonderful examples of zeal and piety.

As to their learning and mental ability, our Holy Father himself has said that he has found the Oriental students studying at Rome not in the least inferior to their European companions at the universities, and that the black seminarians proved themselves the equals in every respect of the white students. And it is clear that this should not surprise us. In the political world, in the field of diplomacy, in medical and scientific research, the so-called inferior Asiatic has shown himself the equal of the white man. Given an equal opportunity and similar environment, there is no reason why one race should surpass another.

The fallacy that the white man's burden is to rule the other races, because of natural superiority, is worthy of acceptance today only by backwoodsmen whose prejudice is the result of ignorance. The Oriental has exhibited as fine qualities as any other people; in the moral field, his restraint and steadiness qualify him to fulfill the demands of Western civilization.

Whether a Chinese or a Negro priest would succeed with a foreign congregation is another question, and one depending very much on the animosity and prejudice of the white man, but whether a Chinese or Negro priest would fit in with a congregation of his own people should not even be questioned. We are not entitled to attempt any Westernization of an Oriental people; and our charter to preach the Gospel limits our work to spiritual lines.

In practical ways, does the native priest show evidence of ability? Let me give you an example or two from my own experience. I have lived for several years near a Chinese priest, Father Wong. He taught Latin in the preparatory seminary, and later taught literature in a nearby college. He was pastor of several flourishing parishes, and then was assigned to initiate me as a newcomer into my district. While with me, he preached twice a day to non-Catholics, taught several classes in our seminary, rebuilt the rectory and school, translated a book, and wrote a series of lectures on apologetics. He speaks three Chinese languages besides his own, and takes care of a colony of French-speaking Catholics. He also reads English fluently, and speaks it fairly well. And he is not very exceptional among the native clergy.

I lived with another Chinese priest who converted 1,600 adults within five years. He built a church and school at the same time. He is now chancellor of his vicariate, yet he is not unusually outstanding.

All of which shows that our Holy Father is clear-sighted in urging the need of a native clergy. They are the real backbone of the local Church, and will guarantee its permanency; they are the pledge by which the native Christians are bound to the eternal Church.

A country without a native clergy, or having an insufficient native priesthood, is always in danger of being stranded for lack of a pilot. In time of persecution, the first to be wiped out or driven out is the foreigner. A tree that cannot keep its roots intact during a typhoon is doomed.

The problem, then, of a native clergy in mission lands is not one merely of logical need, but of expediency. The bishops have realized this, and during the past years of evergrowing self-consciousness on the part of Oriental nations they have multiplied their native seminaries and have more than doubled their students. While the education of native seminarians is a long and costly one, the standards have nevertheless been not only kept up, but raised still higher, and we are now witnessing the real beginning of the solution of the problem.

Pope Pius XI led the way by consecrating with his own hands the first Chinese bishops and the first native bishop of Japan; soon we shall see in every mission country a complete hierarchy of native clergy that will mean for the Church a new era, when the natives themselves undertake the conversion of their fellow countrymen. The consecration of the native bishops was but a simple step forward, yet, by turning the movement of mission endeavor in another direction, it re-orientated in a double sense the whole mission work, in such a manner that the successful evangelization of foreign pagan lands can be foreseen with a far greater degree of assurance than hitherto. The native clergy was the Pope's solution. (*1933*)

MISSION METHODS

"Novelty is useful to the Church after it has received her stamp of approval; if it is never assimilated, it is soon dated and its adherents become cranks. In trying out new methods, we should use them as makeshifts to lead our people into fuller, traditional Catholic life. Then we are on safe ground."

The Missions Are Not Static

SHORTLY AFTER HIS ARRIVAL IN CHINA, YOUNG FR. FORD WAS *conscious of the need of new life in mission work; but his adventurous zeal was tempered by a prudence rare in one of his years. "The vitality of a new missioner should find its exercise in zealously tackling the routine essentials of a regulated parish, with an alert eye to see fresh openings and a steady effort to equip himself to meet further demands on his talents," he later reminisced. "If his conviction of the need of reform perdures till riper years, he may then more safely risk his reputation as being eccentric."*

In his own riper years, Bishop Ford launched innovations in his Kaying diocese which won the approval of the highest mission authorities. He laid emphasis on the conversion of pagans rather than on the setting up of fine institutions. Schools, orphanages, and hospitals absorb the energies of foreign missioners, he said, whereas it is the Chinese Catholics themselves who must be taught to see the urgency of these Church institutions and the duty of subsidizing them.

"A mission should strive to be self-supporting wherever the local community can support its projects for the common good," he wrote. "But its direct apostolate among pagans naturally must be an obligation of the worldwide Church." He did not think that missions should place undue emphasis on economic security. "The curse of economic security is that it can too easily become a fetish that paralyzes initiative and

*confidence in God's bounty and tends towards a static con-
servatism," he explained.*

*Bishop Ford changed the constitutions of his parish sodali-
ties, so that the primary duty of every Hakka sodalist became
that of interesting his pagan relatives and neighbors in the
Church. Conversions in the diocese soon doubled. The spiritual
leader of the Hakkas desired that zeal be nurtured in his
Chinese seminarians and novices, not merely for the care of
Catholics, but also for the direct apostolate among pagans. "A
routine training along conservative lines suitable to an old
Catholic environment is not satisfactory for young Chinese
apostles surrounded by millions of their pagan countrymen,"
Bishop Ford often said.*

Do Missioners Get Results?

DO MISSIONERS GET RESULTS? IT ALL DEPENDS ON WHAT RESULTS
you are looking for. The missions, after all, are the Catholic
Church in pagan lands, and the work of the Catholic Church is
very hard to measure and weigh and put down in black and
white.

There are two sides to any work of the Church—the spiritual, and the material—and when dealing with a movement
extending over centuries, it is extremely difficult to pick out
any one period and ask if it is successful, even in a material
way. When it comes to measuring spiritual values we are still
more helpless, for it is a problem between God and the individual soul.

However, the question is a fair one in one sense. The
average business man, when he puts the query to us, usually
means: "Are you satisfied with mission work, or do you regret
it as a loss of effort? That is, do missioners achieve what they
are striving for?"

The Catholic Church, when she sends out her missioners to pagan lands, is not directly interested in the material welfare of the natives. She does not expect her apostles to become explorers or scientists, doctors or educators; she does not ask them to civilize the savage or Westernize the Oriental. The missioner to China does not go with a Bible in one hand and a mop in the other, to "brighten some little corner" of the world. Dirt and disease, and antiquated living habits, and inefficiency in business methods are not his special concern; nor does he bother himself whether the native wears trousers or not. He does not lament the fact that English is not spoken, even badly; that a radio is needed nowadays in every room; or that the natives never heard of halitosis.

Much less does he meddle in the local politics of his adopted country, or try by lobbying to influence its legislation. He is not there to reform the domestic or national habits of the native, nor is he a drummer for the imported products of his native land. It is not his mission to convince the Asiatic that the Western form of government and the Western taste in art or architecture or mechanics are preferable to the native style; he is not the advance agent for any government or manufacturing concern. He is not even authorized to express his own opinions and wishes in such matters.

The missioner is neither a private individual, nor an American citizen, nor a Westerner of any capacity—he is solely the representative of the Catholic Church in his locality, and has the care of souls entrusted to him. To some it may seem unnecessary to define thus closely the limits of his work, but the need to do so is clear when we realize how often and insistently the missioner has been awarded praise and prizes by governments or learned bodies, because of his contribution to scientific knowledge, and how often the accusation has been brought against the missioner by the Oriental that he is the

179

advance agent of imperialism. Too often the cross in the hand of the missioner has been quickly followed by the battleships or exploiting trading companies of the West, and the two have been so linked as inseparable that it is a relief to be able to repudiate the union.

It is bad enough to be misunderstood by the native who attributes mercenary or political motives to the missioner, but it is worse to be thanked by one's own fellow citizens as a valuable aid in stimulating Western business. It shows that the Western businessman can miss the purely spiritual aim of mission work.

Then there is another type of thoughtful Catholic business men who have been besieged by frequent appeals from mission lands. They put their question somewhat in this form: "Is mission work ever going to be self-supporting, is it always going to be a drain on the Church?"

That's a fair question in one sense, and one that's easily answered. Perhaps the major part of the work in mission fields is already self-supporting. But, in another sense, it is evident that mission work is inevitably a financial failure. Once the people are converted, there is a reasonable assurance that their parish needs will be met by themselves, but mission work also deals with pagans, and it is clear that when missioners devote themselves to converting pagans they must look for help elsewhere. A missioner opening up new territory in his vast district must first live in a rented house. He may pass years there before the number of converts warrants building a permanent rectory; in the meanwhile the rent must be paid, and not by the still unconverted pagans. While the Church is still vigorous and missioners can be found to open up new districts, the balance in our check books will always be written in red ink; to face the problem squarely, there are still a thousand million unconverted souls in pagan lands.

But, apart from this aspect of the work, the financial report of the missions has a gratifying sum of assets in mission properties that answer the question in another way. The missions will always need funds to start new projects, but there is a reassuring evidence of the financial health of the work, in the array of figures representing permanent gains already made in a material way. In the Catholic missions of the world there are about 100,000 institutions and places of worship. Most of these, with few exceptions, have been built during the present century.

If it is material progress we are measuring, we can truly say the Church in mission lands has indeed been well begun. Every one of these 100,000 buildings means much more than the mere brick and mortar. It means the conversion of souls sufficient to warrant the buildings; it means also the co-operation of the natives in their cost. We must not imagine that the missions are supported entirely by Catholics in America or Europe. The major portion of expenses is raised in pagan lands—not including the voluntary work of native teachers and catechists, which otherwise would be a heavy burden. Many of our missions are entirely self-supporting, while many others are nearly so. It is mainly the new missions of new societies, opened in a virgin field without converts, that depend on foreign contributions. The natives are generous in their poverty, and we can easily vision the day when the entirely dependent mission will be rare.

The question of the worth-whileness of mission work has still another form. It is this: "Why send missioners to places that are hard to convert? Why not concentrate them among the simple savages, where thousands instead of hundreds might be baptized each year?"

This, too, is a fair question; if the converting of souls were the main object of mission work, we should have to agree that missions in Alaska and Japan are less profitable than missions, for example, in parts of Africa.

But is the conversion of souls really the main immediate object of the Church? If so, why keep priests at home to minister to ourselves; why not send every priest to pagan peoples? Evidently there is a reason for the Church's present system, and it appears to be this: The object of mission work is not primarily to convert pagans, but it is to establish the Catholic Church in pagan lands. The purpose is to build up as complete an organization as possible, which will itself later continue with better success the work of converting its own natives.

While this method is for the time being much slower and can show fewer results, it really guarantees that whatever results are obtained will be permanent; a permanent Church will in the long run mean many more conversions and more stability and hope of perseverance than would be the case were missioners merely to convert souls and then drop them to go elsewhere. Intensive cultivation means years of slow labor with little to show in a spectacular way; it means that in a short while the Church in that region will have its own native priests and brothers and sisters; and, once a nation has its own clergy and hierarchy, it need not be afraid of persecution—it will weather any storm.

The history of our Catholics in the Western states shows us how disastrous is the result of leaving a congregation without pastors. Permanency and intense care will preserve a congregation faithful to the sacraments, and eventually produce vocations which will carry on the work without danger of lapsing.

For this reason the missions have concentrated, not on converting pagans, not on spectacular methods of modern advertising, not on many activities that are dazzling and transitory; they have built up a vast breastwork of seminaries and

182

convents in mission lands, with parochial schools and colleges to stimulate vocations. Already there is one vocation from every 400 families on the mission field. If we at home did as well in offering our children to God's work, many of the problems both at home and in the fields afar, which now hang fire for lack of vocations, would be solved.

Are missions worth while? I think you will agree with me that a work which really dates from the present century (which has realized almost a complete rebirth in mission work), and which has produced 12,000,000 converts, and is fast coming to the stage where there will be enough native priests to care for the Catholics and to release foreign missioners for work exclusively among pagans, that such a work—in spite of the poor resources and perpetual poverty that have characterized it—is eminently worth while.

Even were the whole mission field to prove a failure in converts, it still would be worth while, as following out our Saviour's command to preach the Gospel to all nations. But He has also promised those who leave dear ones and home for His sake a hundredfold even in this life, and He has redeemed His promise with abundant conversions and a growing army of native vocations.

Indeed, in all modesty, it can be claimed for mission work that it has been relatively about the most successful of all works—both as regards the financial returns for a small outlay, and the spiritual harvest of millions ransomed for Christ. (*1932*)

Some Tips from St. Augustine

THE FREQUENT PITFALL FOR THE MISSIONER, WHO IS INCESSANTLY reiterating in simple language the fundamentals of our faith, arises from the trite, hackneyed explanations of the Gospel story that must be repeated in scores of villages time and time again, especially in virgin territory where more varied deductions would be beyond the ken of the audience. This tedium begets listlessness, and the poor man begins to feel he is not doing justice to the Gospel. St. Augustine, Bishop of Hippo, seems to speak to the missioner when he says:

"I would not have you to be disturbed because you have often seemed to yourself to be delivering a worthless and wearisome discourse. For it may very well be that it was not so regarded by him whom you were endeavoring to instruct. For my part, I am nearly always dissatisfied with my discourses. . . . But often the eagerness of those who desire to hear me shows that my discourse is not so dull as it seems to me. . . .

"If it be distasteful to us to be repeating over and over things that are familiar and suitable for little children, let us suit ourselves to them with a brother's, a father's, and a mother's love, and when once we are linked to them thus in heart these things will seem new even to us. . . . Is it not a common occurrence that, when we are showing to those who have never seen them before certain lovely expanses, whether of town or countryside, which we, through often seeing already, have been in the habit of passing by without any pleasure, our own delight is renewed by their delight at the novelty of the scene? And the more so, the closer the friendship between them and us; for in proportion as we dwell in them through the bond of love, so do things which were old become new to us also. . . . How much more, then, ought we to rejoice when men now approach to study God Himself; and how much more ought we to be renewed in their newness, so that, if our preaching as being a matter of routine is somewhat dull, it may grow interesting because of our hearers for whom it is all new."

A very common objection, when missioners get together and

the more enthusiastic among them propose some detailed outline of instruction for adoption, is a refrain often heard in chorus: "That's all very well for your educated city people, but what about my poor farmers who cannot read or write?" It is truly disheartening, when breaking ground in a region, to discover that literally no one can read or write, and to realize that the missioner must somehow or other go over the whole complicated course of theology that is concentrated in our catechism and make it as plain as possible to them. "Born Catholics" in Western lands have had twelve or more years of school life in which to acquire the truths of religion gradually and according to their capacity; in China and other mission countries it is a problem to present the multitudinous necessary facts about God and the soul in a few months of instruction. And if, as in so many villages in China, there are a handful who are educated and the rest without schooling, the complication increases.

To show that the problem is no new one in the missions, and thus console the priest in his misery, let us see what St. Augustine adds:

"I can testify to you from my own experience that I am differently stirred according as he whom I see before me waiting for instruction is cultivated or a dullard, a fellow citizen or a stranger, a rich man or a poor man, a private citizen or a public man having some official authority, a person of this or that family, of this or that age or sex, coming to us from this or that school of philosophy, or from this or that popular error; and in keeping with my own varying feelings my discourse itself opens, proceeds, and closes. And since the same medicine is not to be applied to all, although to all the same love is due, so also love itself is in travail with some, becomes weak with others; is at pains to edify some, dreads to be a cause of offense to others; stoops to some, before others stands with head erect; is gentle to some, and stern to others; an enemy to none, a mother to all.

"There are also some who come from the ordinary schools of grammar and rhetoric, whom you would dare to class neither among the illiterate, nor yet among the very learned. . . . When, therefore, these men, who seem to surpass all other men in the art of speaking, come to be made Christians, we ought to convey to them more fully than to the illiterate an earnest warning to clothe themselves in Christian humility and learn not to despise those whom they know as shunning more carefully faults of character than faults of diction; and also that they should not even presume to compare with a pure heart the trained tongue which they had been wont even to prefer . . . thus they will not smile contemptuously if they happen to observe that some ministers of the Church either fall into barbarisms and solecisms when calling upon Almighty God, or do not understand and badly punctuate words which they are pronouncing."

The matter of mispronunciation is a tender point among us poor missioners, as dialects vary from town to town in China, and no one can be so snobbish about diction as a half-baked scholar. As St. Augustine points out, they are neither illiterate nor learned who are captious in such matters, but their presence in the audience sometimes makes exchange of thought much more annoying. Incidentally, it is consoling to know that St. Augustine himself in his discourses spoke with a Punic "brogue," and his critical students in Milan must have nettled him a bit about it.

As the whole treatise of St. Augustine concerns catechizing, it needs to be quoted entirely to do justice to the bishop's thoroughness of treatment. He even carefully gives examples of instruction to the various classes of catechumens; in reading them, we discover a practical side and deep insight into human nature of the common sort, of which his loftier mysticism in other works gives no inkling.

We are apt to think of the Fathers of the Church as battling for God on the grand scale, as they did; but St. Augustine shows he can stoop to the simpler problems of instructing catechumens with as sure a touch from the depth of his own experience. As a catechumen himself for half his life, he saw the Church from the outside as well as from within; as a school teacher for many years, he based his method of instruction on experience with minds of many nations; teaching in a language not his own, he paralleled the missioner's situation; and in manifesting throughout his treatise the need of warm interest in the catechumens and appreciation of their peculiar difficulties, he arouses the missioner to renewed efforts to better his work. While upholding the Chair of St. Peter, he has won a niche in the missioner's heart as the patron saint for catechists. (1940)

The Mechanics of Conversion

It may be news to Westerners that the average missioner is at a loss to explain his success in conversions. Asked how he manages to attain results that are, numerically at least, remarkable, he is apt to start off with the statement: "Apart from the grace of God—" Then comes a pause, and finally the confession that he does not know the answer. The science of missions has been studied for twenty centuries, but it is still in the experimental stage.

The missioner, like other scientists, plots and plans and endlessly experiments. He varies his method with each individual concerned, but, because he is dealing with human nature, the hundredth case is as unpredictable as the first, and

187

no method is certain of results. Yet, it is true that the average missioner will accomplish, over a certain period, certain predictable results. What may not be true in any one case at any particular time may still be found a valid conclusion in the long run of cases.

In spite of popular fiction, the average missioner rarely preaches directly to pagans. Here in South China, the people have no custom of listening to public speeches, and no assembly halls except in schools. So that, even were the method of public instruction attractive to the people, there would be no means of putting it into practice. How, then, are pagans brought into contact with Catholic doctrine? Mostly through individual introduction to the local pastor by Catholic friends.

Fortunately for the missioner, life in a Chinese village lacks all privacy. A convert to the Catholic religion cannot say night prayers with his family without arousing the curiosity of all his neighbors. A villager walking along the road in his best clothes is immediately asked by every passer-by where he is going. If the spruced-up man is going to Mass, the villagers will talk of little else that day. One or more of the convert's fellow villagers will usually seek to know more about the faith that attracted the new Catholic, and an introduction to the pastor then follows.

The fact that new converts in China are so closely observed puts them to a severe test. The public profession of Christianity implies, even in the opinion of pagans, a reformation of character in accordance with the new belief. Pagans are quick to criticize unbecoming conduct in a Catholic. Their attitude is somewhat akin to that of the world toward doctors and lawyers. So long as a man publicly sets himself up as an exponent of a high standard of morality, he is judged by his own scale.

For the missioner, then, the mechanics of conversion are largely a matter of interesting catechumens in further study, after they have been brought to him by their Catholic friends. At first, Catholic teachings must be couched in terms that mean something to a pagan. This is not an easy task, because paganism in China has lost much of its touch with the supernatural. It not only makes few demands in the way of worship, but it has no code of morality other than the somewhat vague dictates of a conscience frequently blunted in a materialistic environment. In China, there is no remnant of Catholic ethics such as survives in modern Western paganism.

In his instruction of catechumens, the missioner must start with fewer premises than would the priest in Western lands. Before touching on the complicated ramifications of Catholic worship and practice, the missioner in China must give a condensed course in natural theology and elementary ethics. His task is simplified, however, by the fact that the Church in China has limited religious observances to minimum obligations for new converts.

Mass is said regularly in the new convert's house, and this usually means that the missioner must arrive the evening before. The priest thus has an opportunity to talk privately and publicly with the convert, as well as with pagan relatives in the village. The perseverance of new converts in China is, perhaps, due mostly to this intimate friendship with the missioner. The interest shown in them by this intense cultivation begets loyalty and confidence far beyond what could result from more formal relations.

Conversions in China, then, are not a problem of interesting masses by public preaching, but of intimate attention to individuals. This intense supervision of the individual by the missioner enables the catechumen to persevere and to grow finally to the spiritual stature of a zealous Catholic. Gradually,

189

over a long period of years, a solid nucleus of Catholics is thus built up, even though these Christians may be scattered over an immense territory. (*1944*)

War and the Missioner

IN THE NEW TESTAMENT, AND IN THE WRITINGS OF THE EARLY Fathers, there is scant mention of war or peace. Our Lord did not castigate all warfare as an offense against God. He said, "My peace I give you," but He added, "not as the world giveth." So the mind of Christ on peace is not that of the world.

All through the Christian era there have been wars, many of them of the most devastating sort, but the successive Popes preached few, if any, sermons against war. In the Church's liturgy there is very little mention of purely material peace. There is, indeed, a prayer for peace, but for the peace which the world cannot give. The comments of St. Robert Bellarmine and of St. Thomas Aquinas on warfare justify war under certain conditions. The Church is, of course, in no way callous about the calamities of war. She is divinely guided to see things in true perspective, and to recommence her work as soon as pressure is relieved. The missioner must imitate her attitude.

Missioners have rarely preached the Gospel in surroundings of orderly peace. On the contrary, we find the expansion of Christianity proceeding in the midst of barbarous strife, annihilation of tribes, and enslavement of the conquered. All missionary work has been carried on with a sword hanging over it. The Church does not waste time lamenting the havoc of war; she begins immediately to reconstruct with whatever material has survived.

The missioner cannot afford to dwell unduly on war's mishaps, because his depression would soon beget the feeling that it is useless to plan anything for the future. Such a spirit is alien to the mind of the Church. It is for us to realize that our message is spiritual, and that the Church accommodates herself to every situation. She treats the conquered and the victors alike as her children.

Her missioners must take the same viewpoint, continuing on as Catholic apostles. War seems to be part of the growing pains of human civilization—at least it is the result of free will. God could have created a world without pain, but He gave us instead a testing ground where passions have full play. Perhaps God uses war to keep us reminded of eternity, and that nothing is an absolute evil except sin. We shall have fulfilled God's purpose if we continue doing His work.

"Seek ye first the Kingdom of Heaven." The missioner who puts first things first does not permit worry to interfere with hope. If tomorrow our work were wiped out, we would have only to begin again the day after. If we ourselves were slain, the deathless Church of Christ would have other apostles eager to repair the ruins. We should never consider material peace as necessary for our work. The peace our Lord promised His co-laborers is not that of the world, but interior peace of the soul—a peace that may include willingness to suffer. (1945)

The Dilemma of Mission Work

In the work of the Church, two extreme attitudes menace healthy progress. One of these undesirable attitudes is ultra-conservative, the other ultra-concessive. It might profit us in our work in China to study these two attitudes as the two dangers to missionary activities anywhere. There is, in fact, nothing startlingly new in these dangers. The Council of Jerusalem wrangled over the question of whether converts should observe the Old Law, and through the centuries there were controversies as to whether or not lapsed Catholics should be forgiven.

First, what is ultra-conservatism? It is the attitude of one who is easily scandalized, who instinctively recoils from innovation, who runs along in a groove, who not only prefers the safe, tried system, but considers it morally dangerous to experiment. Temperance and prudence are virtues; it is the extension of them beyond charity that makes ultra-conservatism.

In what ways can a missioner be ultra-conservative? perhaps he visions all the equipment of a well-appointed American parish as an indispensable requisite of working conditions, and is at a loss when such is absent. Again, he may become increasingly preoccupied with work around the sanctuary, to the exclusion of visiting the out-stations. He insensibly adopts a less friendly attitude toward pagan visitors who call at inconvenient times and upset his conservative routine. He entertains wealthier Catholics, to the inconvenience of the rest of the flock. These shortcomings are all symptoms of an ultra-conservatism that seeks "heaven on earth," in an impractical flight from the imperfect, rough realities of commonplace life.

Again, a missioner may adhere to such rigid rules of personal conduct in his effort to present an example to all that he becomes intolerant of human weakness and unenlightened pagan standards in others. An ultra-conservative missioner of this type attracts few souls.

The proponents of the other extreme attitude, the ultra-concessive priests, are found in every group of missioners, especially among the younger members. They wish to make the Church dynamic, and present her to the world as a modern challenge to present-days evils. The long yesterday of the Church does not interest them; they have an implicit belief that modern human nature is different from that of past centuries; they would prefer to simplify doctrine and accommodate it to the lower level of modern widespread, but shallow learning.

The danger of excessive modernization and simplification lies partly in the theological field and partly in practical education. Too simplified a Church, though more easily grasped by pagans and illiterate catechumens, is weak in supplying solid sustenance for Catholics after baptism. There can never be permissible watering-down of truth to suit weak stomachs. The real situation is that the Church does not alter her doctrine to fit circumstances, because her doctrine amply covers all problems. Her customs are ancient, but not antiquated. They are always malleable enough to respond to faults and inequalities in human nature, if we but study them properly.

The proneness to innovation may lie in a tendency to equalize religious teaching with other branches of knowledge, thus making it a purely mental process devoid of a supernatural content. We are apt to forget that, while imparting necessary doctrine, we are also giving our people a way of life and of worship that is the essence of religious teaching. And this reverence for the subject matter that we teach should carry with it a reverence, also, for the traditional methods and rubrics that have become associated with our creed.

Bishop Sheen remarked in private conversation that he has never yet found any non-Catholic with whom he needed to water-down religion, and that the deepest mystery of our faith is eagerly assimilated by even the illiterate. The weakness, then, may be in ourselves, not in the intellectual level of the people.

None of this criticism is meant to imply that no changes are necessary. Even the last stronghold of the faith, the holy Bible, is being put into a more accurate form by the Biblical Commission, and recently the number of Popes was diminished by dropping out several names. In similar manner, many of our methods may be improved in small ways and by local changes. It is the spirit which animates such changes that counts. Our purpose should be to deepen the knowledge of the faith in our Catholics, and to instil a greater reverence for tradition among our new converts.

The history of the Reformation is a sad commentary on private judgment run wild. Novelty is useful in the Church after it has received her stamp of approval; if it is never assimilated, it is soon dated and its adherents become cranks. We should, then, in trying out new methods, use them as makeshifts to lead our people into fuller, traditional Catholic life. Then we are on safe ground. (*1949*)

Modern Corporal Works of Mercy

THE CHURCH IS THE BODY OF CHRIST AND ALL HUMAN BEINGS are potential members of this Body. In order to reach these potential members, the Church must accommodate herself to living in the world and gradually bettering it. From the First Council of the newly born Church, the Apostles boldly faced the problem of making the world a better place in which to live according to God's precepts. The first laws of the Church were not only dogmatic, but social; money was collected for the poor of Jerusalem. The Church even experimented at the outset with a life in common, sharing equally whatever wealth was at hand.

In Europe, prior to the Reformation, all civic welfare was

194

in the hands of the Church; we are today profiting from her tremendous program of social betterment. Those economic and social systems that deviate from Christian laws have within them the vice of pagan materialism, which soon proves them unworkable. Such in modern times are the theories of Marx and Lenin, as well as the capitalistic economy of the industrial age.

It is true that first things come first. "Seek ye first the Kingdom of Heaven" is always our main directive. Hence, in this diocese of Meihsien, emphasis has been placed on direct evangelization as our primary duty, but this does not imply that the social and economic betterment of our people is not our concern. We might, then, ask ourselves what is our individual duty towards the community. Why is the Church in China seemingly of little importance in social projects?

We must realize that the Church in China is a comparative newcomer, introduced into a civilization little touched by Christian impacts. She is still of much insignificance to the great mass of the people, hence her influence must at best be weak. The Church has, nevertheless, firmly planted the germ of community ethics in China. Christian legislators made Sunday an official day of rest. During the past generation in China, the establishment of a system of education for the common people owed much to the example of the mission schools. Often, the only books in a village home have been the catechism and other Catholic texts. The institutions of mercy founded by the Church throughout China introduced by example the new idea that the sick and the poor deserve privileged attention, without respect to clan or family reputation.

It is necessary to recall that the Church is limited by her neutrality in promoting social reforms. She has to live under all forms of government, and she cannot afford to jeopardize her impartiality by favoring any one transitory economic revolution or reform, except where eternal principles are concerned. This is especially prudent where the Church is still numerically insignificant. She must tolerate much in China, for example, that is not ideal, and she must avoid inopportune attacks on existing conditions if she is to survive at all. In a pagan country, the Church must limit herself to prudent exposition of Christian principles, without burdening the consciences of her numerically weak Christians by unattainable demands.

Although officially the Church must limit her field of action to the enunciation of general principles, individual Catholics, and especially groups and communities, may more easily strive for their own welfare. In this field there is much that can be done by missioners toward civic betterment. The enormity of the need should not discourage us, because as mere individuals we are concerned only with small problems. Yet, were each missioner to improve conditions locally, the example might well be contagious.

What our people lack is not willingness to reform, but knowledge of how to go about it. History so often proves that one example of success is a stimulus to others. Were our Catholics in the thousands of villages in our parishes to become noted as civic reformers, the reputation of the Church would be enhanced, with consequent approval of her influence by outsiders. And this reform need not be more than local improvements of various kinds, almost too numerous to specify here.

Offhand, and starting with very minor reforms, our Christians could be encouraged to repair the local bridges and the paths in and around their villages. They could be urged, also, to plant trees on common land, to sew garments for the village poor, to visit sick pagans, or to buy a community

196

cow for ploughing. More ambitious programs might include irrigating projects, introduction of better crops, methods of village co-operatives, adult educational schemes, youth activities, and similar community improvements that would benefit the neighborhood.

None of these strivings for civic betterment need be on a grand scale, nor need they be closely identified with the Church. In fact, the more the undertakings remain a community effort, without clerical prop, the more they attain their purpose. True and lasting reforms begin with the small community in small ways; they will quickly advertise themselves to neighboring communities. Such projects should be modest, as befits a missionary Church that is still a stranger in the region, but we can be sure that, once the example proves successful, others will quickly copy, to the immediate benefit of the whole region. This is not primary mission work, of course, but it is a powerful natural aid to enhancing the position of the Church in the community. (*1949*)

The Young Missioner

AT FIRST, THE YOUNG MISSIONER IS ENGROSSED IN THE STUDY OF the language and the struggle to understand local customs, the character of the people, and the vagaries of household management. At this stage, a minimum of parochial work may test the limit of his ability. The new problems are a challenge at the outset, but familiarity soon reduces the work to a system that eventually runs smoothly. Then, unless the young priest deliberately seeks new problems, he may too easily become satisfied with this minimum of routine.

Experience shows that a leveling off of ambition may be reached when opportunities are no longer seen as a challenge.

If this settling down occurs when disillusion arises, or when no new problems are forced on the attention, a rigidity may ensue and a low standard be set that later will prove hard to change. It is well, then, to examine the nature of a missioner's duties over and beyond this minimum of parochial work.

In the first place, we have an obligation to know our Catholics—even the Chinese characters used to write each one's name. We need to know the background of each Catholic family, and this demands more than a brief visit to the various villages. In order to guide our people aright on the pathway of life, we must become interested in them as individuals. If we regard our Catholics merely as so many statistics in our parish registers, they will not become warmly attached to their mission center.

We have a further obligation of building Catholic character in our flock. We must fortify our laity by the establishment of sodalities, clubs, and Catholic societies of many sorts. As our people become strong in Catholic Action, they understand the importance of winning friends and relatives to the faith, and they endeavor to assume the financial support of their parish. We must seek and form religious vocations among our boys and girls, and raise up a corps of lay volunteer catechists. Youth is not attracted to the service of God by impersonal exhortation; everywhere, the cultivation of vocations demands intimate interest, patience, and enthusiasm.

Our schools require more than a cursory supervision. As a rule, our teachers lack training in the mechanics of their task, but under a zealous pastor they can be stimulated to improve their technique and to extend their influence over their pupils in extra-curricular projects. The truly apostolic pastor can inspire the Catholic teachers to make of their pupils messengers of Christ to many families.

The thousands of pagans in a Chinese parish belong to the

pastor's care. He must always be ready to invite the investigation of non-Christians, to satisfy their inquiries, and to instruct patiently prospective converts. This may sound unsatisfying to a fervent young missioner, eager to convert thousands all at once; but physical activity urged by impatience may overshoot its mark and deter fuller interest. Readiness to satisfy the inquiries of pagans often demands a thorough study of the doctrinal needs and modern problems of converts, a task certain to absorb the energy of the most ambitious missioner.

How, then, should a young missioner plan his work? Once the essentials of his duties are taken care of, he should cultivate, above all, a readiness of attitude to see openings and to prepare for them. As almost any skill can glorify God and we work best along our natural bent, the young missioner has a wide field to prospect. Enthusiasm (working along with God) can enter into every project and make it worth while.

The first requisite in a student priest in foreign countries is a prudent distrust of radical change—perhaps the hardest lesson to learn, while at the same time retaining enthusiasm. Young missioners are prone to criticize local social customs in the light of Western standards, unmindful of the strong hold ingrained tradition exerts in China. Nothing is dearer to a people than its traditions. Besides, radical change is rarely reform, as peoples are slow to concede value to novelty, and a stranger disregarding custom is merely dubbed uncouth. Courtesy will aid us to regulate impetuosity, and will deepen our understanding of the good sense of many customs.

The vitality, then, of a new missioner should find its exercise in zealously tackling the routine essentials of a regulated parish, with an alert eye to see new openings and a steady effort to equip himself to meet further demands on his talents. If his conviction of the need of reform perdures till riper years, he may then more safely risk his reputation as being eccentric; in the meantime, his program of work is extensive enough to exercise much of his refreshing energy. (*1950*)

THE KEYNOTE IS JOY

"It does not hurt us to dwell on the joys of our life on the missions, for they are inseparably joined with bitter failures and humiliations, and in themselves are not of a nature to nourish pride. It is God Who gives the increase. But, as we traffic with Him, He gains for us a wonderful inheritance— souls who otherwise would not know God. And when our inheritance fructifies in native priests and Sisters, we dare esteem our vocation as goodly indeed."

At Peace with God

BISHOP FORD WROTE TO A MARYKNOLL SEMINARIAN IN THE *homeland, in 1949: "I pity the missioner in China or elsewhere, who hasn't thought things out for himself, or who depends on exterior excitement for distraction. The veneer of locale quickly loses its glamor unless, as Chesterton suggests, we continue to see petty things around us as a child does, that is to say, as wonderfully exciting. In point of fact, our boredom is never caused by things or persons, but by our own thoughts (or rather, refusal to think).*

"In the United States, where distractions are always available, the vacant mind is not so easily noticed. But in China, where there is little light reading matter or other means of diverting the mind without any assimilation of ideas, the spiritual and intellectual vacuum is quickly apparent. My own conclusion, after three decades in China, is that locality means little in life. For a man who has learned how to think, even solitary confinement could pass profitably and pleasantly. What I really mean to say is that when our conscience is at peace with God, it matters little what kind of work we do or where—it's the why that counts."

A Goodly Inheritance

"THE LINES ARE FALLEN UNTO ME IN GOODLY PLACES: FOR MY inheritance is goodly to me" (Ps. 15:6). This psalm is on the lips of every tonsured cleric as he enters the course marked out for him, but it is an aspiration of a future. The missioner, with deeper feeling, recalls God's bounty as he surveys the field allotted him. It is a garden enclosed wherein he walks with God, and he finds that words are but a clumsy means of describing it, for on the missions God is our inheritance in a special way.

He is occasionally our sole companion, and then He must take the place of human friends. It is just in the hardest times that He proves Himself our Friend—especially so during two periods of our life here—at the very outset, when we find ourselves cut off for the first time from speech and books, and must become as little children and learn to lisp a strange tongue; and again later, when enthusiasm has cooled and experiments have come to nothing. In both cases, the missioner is favored above others in being made to realize that God is all.

It does not hurt us to dwell on the joys of our life on the missions, for they are inseparably joined with bitter failures and humiliations, and in themselves are of a nature not to nourish pride. It is God who gives the increase. But, as we traffic with Him, He gains for us another wonderful inheritance —souls who otherwise would not know God. And when our inheritance fructifies in native vocations, and we gather the young students about us and see them grow in the love of God, we dare esteem our vocation as goodly indeed. Any body of seminarians is a sacramental sight to the eyes of faith; but if they kneel before the Blessed Sacrament in a pagan land, they become heroic figures. They are facing the hosts of the Philistines as David did.

"And thou, child, shalt be called the prophet of the Highest: for thou shalt go before the face of the Lord to prepare His ways . . . to enlighten them that sit in darkness and in the shadow of death." (1926)

A Missioner's Day

WE HEAR A LOT ABOUT POLITICAL CONDITIONS IN CHINA, AND about the mission work in general—the schools and seminaries —and about catechists, so it may be interesting to hear something about the man behind the works, the ordinary missioner.

After many years in China, spent in several missions and with plenty of opportunity to see many missioners of half a dozen nationalities, I must begin by assuring you that the average missioner in China, from Manchuria in the north to Kwangtung in the south, is an ordinary common-sense individual, taking his work seriously, but not taking himself too seriously.

The strangeness of his surroundings is quickly forgotten in China, and he soon begins to think of China as home, and of the United States as "over there." This is as it should be, of course, and the more completely he considers China as home, the greater will be his success. Not that he forgets his parents or his old friends, but because he quickly identifies himself with his Chinese, and groups them with the Catholic Church the world over.

But what does the missioner do in China? How does he spend his time? How does he make converts among the Chinese? Well, roughly, there are two classes of missioners—those who have a thousand or more Christians to take care of, and those who have a lesser number.

Our aim in China is to set up a Catholic community somewhat like those you have in the United States. It would be better, perhaps, to speak of the Catholic Church in China, rather than of the Catholic missions in China, for, after all, that is the motive of the missioner—to build up the Catholic Church, to hasten the day when the Church in China may be like the Church anywhere else. In other words, our aim is to establish a strong body of Catholics, with parochial schools for boys and girls, to fill our Chinese Catholics with a love for the sacraments and God's law, to gradually develop vocations to the priesthood and the religious life; in brief, to duplicate the life of the Church in more favored sections of God's world.

You have but to reflect on the busy life of our priests and Sisters at home to realize very well the ordinary daily life of the missioner in China, who has a thousand or more Christians to serve. There are daily Mass, instructions in the catechism, sermons and services, similar to those in your own parish church. Unfortunately, the average parish in China is a huge affair, consisting of several thousand villages, twenty or more towns, and one or more large cities. The Christians are scattered in this large territory—ten in one town, fifty in another, a single family perhaps in a third. Usually, each town is made the rallying point for the surrounding villages, in the hope that soon it may develop into a large enough unit to be erected into a separate parish.

I mention here a personal experience for the sake of a concrete example. During several years I had a parish that was five days long by three days wide. I speak of "days" rather than miles, as miles mean little in this era of good roads. In our section of China we travel on horseback, and twenty-five miles is a good day's journey. In this rather large parish, then, of 10,000 square miles, I had Christians in seventy-six places, and it is the duty of the missioner at least once or twice a year to visit his Christians in their homes. That is the missionary work of a pastor with a thousand or more Catholics. He is like an American pastor, on a more extensive scale.

This visitation of the stations is the most interesting side of mission life. We send word by messengers to all the villages, announcing the date of our coming. The day before we start, we pay salaries to our home staff, and try to foresee necessary orders during our absence. Getting ready is easy: in summer our baggage is light, merely a Mass kit and a change of clothing; in winter we must also take along our bedding for the night.

In some sections the mule is better than a horse, as the mule is sure-footed on the narrow mountain roads, though apt to be stubborn in emergencies. There is no question of speed, as the roads are too narrow (often not more than six inches wide), and anyway the guide must walk ahead to show the way, and the mule resigns itself to the slow pace. We start just at daybreak, which means a still earlier Mass, and heavy breakfast (for there won't be any dinner on the road). Our trips are not fatiguing, as there are many stops along the way to drink tea and exchange a word of gossip with the passerby. Nothing is done very speedily in China; and the missioner soon learns to stop fretting at delays. The country through which we pass is rather monotonous, but so thickly populated with villages that you feel sad at so many pagan souls around you.

When the priest arrives at a village, he finds a crowd waiting for him. They have stationed the boys out on the hills to watch, and the lads give a signal of the missioner's approach by firing off crackers. As they often wait till the mule is in front of them, the firecrackers are a mixed blessing and the poor missioner's attention is taken up in quieting the balky mule. Then we go into the improvised chapel. Chinese houses in the South usually have a main sitting room, with the men's bedroom on one side and the women's room on the other. This sitting room, during our stay, is turned into a combination meeting room and rectory; sometimes (if the people are very poor), even the cattle are quartered there. As in another Bethlehem, I have slept with the cows on one side and the pigs in another corner, while the chickens and ducks roost under the bed. If we have brought Christians from other villages with us, sometimes they, too, sleep in the same room. It makes little difference, as there is absolutely no privacy in the village houses—the men will cheerfully sit on our bed and chat, while we are supposed to be sleeping.

However, before we turn in, there are confessions and a sermon, followed by night prayers; and the energy and zeal the barefooted farmers put into their prayers make up for any discomfort. It's a pleasant sight to see thirty or forty men kneeling on the floor in the semi-darkness—the men and boys up at the front near the makeshift altar, and the women down by the doorway. In China, the men have the place of honor near the altar, and we have no sharpshooters kneeling on one knee. The night prayers are said in common—the Our Father, the Hail Mary, Acts of Faith, Hope and Charity, the Creed, and the Ten Commandments. A pause to examine the conscience is followed by a good Act of Contrition, the Litany, and other prayers.

Although all are tired from a long day in the fields, they like to linger around and discuss the news from the city and exchange gossip, and their presence gives the priest a chance to question them one by one about their home affairs. Meeting them in their homes this way, the priest gets to know them intimately, and can stimulate any lazy ones or encourage those who merit it. Then we call the roll to find who is missing, and who has not made his Easter duty; we also arrange for the baptism of any babies born since our last visit, and we investigate the status of persons about to be married.

Gradually, by nine o'clock, the crowd has dwindled and the missioner betakes himself to his "downy couch." In the villages, the bed is simply two planks, placed on wooden horses, with a block of wood for a pillow. It sounds worse than it actually is; in fact, the heat of the tropics would make a softer bed uncomfortable. If our coming was unexpected, very often they take a door off its hinges, and it becomes our bed for the night. Of course a Chinese door has no doorknobs, so it makes a good substitute. Lying on such a bed, if sleep doesn't come, the missioner can count the stars through the holes in the roof, or listen to the cackling of the chickens. Long before daybreak, the Chinese are up again; and after an energetic wash at the village well they assemble for morning prayers, Mass, and Holy Communion, followed by another sermon before breakfast. Then the missioner mounts his horse and goes on to the next village.

That is the program for about three months each year in the case of priests who have large, scattered congregations. If the missioner is working mostly among pagans, or if he has finished his visitations of the villages, his daily work is different. At home, I rented a store down in the business section of Kaying; and we had three talks every day for non-Catholics. The store would seat about fifty, and usually every seat was taken. Between the sermons, the pagans would come in for a chat and a smoke, and listen to impromptu explanations of the previous sermon. Out of fifty who began the course, perhaps only three or four would persevere to baptism, but the others at least were not harmed by listening, and might possibly come into the Church some other time.

Besides this work of preaching, the missioner usually has a school or two, where he teaches on certain days. He also has a little dispensary, where from a dozen to a hundred or more patients may come daily for treatment. The priest, of course, can treat only minor troubles, and give the usual first-aid treatment, but even this is appreciated in a country where doctors are few and too far away. Well, that is our daily work on the missions. You can see there is nothing extraordinary or heroic in it—it is, in fact, simply a common-sense way of taking care of our Christians, and of trying to attract pagans. Conversions in China are not made as easily as some imagine; but neither are they harder than elsewhere, and the Chinese make very fervent Catholics after baptism.

I have not spoken about the happiness of our life in China, as that is something hard to prove at much length. But it is a fact that there is even a purely natural happiness in our life. The Chinese are lovable, intelligent, and have a sense of humor, so that our days pass all too quickly in attractive work. Instead, then, of pitying the missioner for his hardships, it would be more in order to envy him his vocation. (*1930*)

A Bishop's Life

I THINK THE AVERAGE BISHOP IN AMERICA WOULD ENVY US bishops in China, for even the most patient of them must hanker some time or other for a little of our informality and simplicity of life. To be treated, for a change, like any other man and to pass whole days of travel unrecognized, or, even when recognized, to be taken for granted without fuss; to have a seat in the bus depend on your elbows and not on rank; to sit on benches with seven strangers at a roadside table and dip into the common platters, each for himself and none who has heard of Emily Post; to be expected to help push the weary bus over rough hills too steep for the engine and then go without dinner because of the delay; to be physically tired from a twenty-mile walk and to really taste tea at the end of it—these, offhand, are a few of the downright pleasures rarely possible in America, which I am sure our bishops would enjoy.

I knew one cardinal of my boyhood days who used to bundle himself with sweater and cap and take stiff walks in the pelting rain along the seashore—the only chance the poor man had to escape admiring crowds; we in China on our mountain trails can smoke a pipe all day without causing the twitching of an eyebrow!

And the informality of our working hours! Doors in sub-tropical China are left open to encourage any breeze. And it seems to our Catholics so much more reasonable to go direct to the "boss" than to bother writing letters on the settlement of personal affairs that they step right in and tell their tale, unmindful of others who have preceded them. Fortunately, they like to stand, rather than sit, and their business is soon transacted. So a bishop in China does not lose the contact with his people that he had while pastor; the triviality of the business in question is a help also to keep in touch with realities.

Above all, a bishop in China enjoys companionship with his priests perhaps not realized outside mission countries. Where parishes are twenty miles apart and travel wearisome, both priest and prelate have a common bond of lonesomeness that levels the relation. The annual visitation is no formal ritual, but an eagerly sought chance to merely chatter for the first day of the visit, while succeeding days are spent in fairly minute details of budgets, plans, and theological cases to be solved. Perhaps a box of cigars has been bought months in advance just for the occasion, and the bishop is human enough to prolong his stay while they last. Confirmation is an added human interest, for most of those to be confirmed are adult converts whom the bishop meets informally and whom the pastor is secretly proud of and anxious to bring forward. Vocations are decided on the spot, and the bishop sometimes helps out in the confessional or on sick-calls. Then the nearby out-missions demand a passing visit, and the immediate future plans for them and other villages are discussed; the wages of the cook and catechists, the price of bricks and lumber, are brought out in the casual chats, and rough sketches of future chapels are noted down for action. It is all simple and minute and none of it momentous, but the bishop knows his clergy in a satisfying way.

The role of bishop in China has various other phases that give to the office a variety not found in many other countries. The peculiar danger for any one in charge of operations is to get out of touch with actual conditions and, working very much through bureaus and assistants, to remain aloof from realities.

Of course, the reason for much of his success is the relatively small group he works with and the simplicity of the enterprises that compare only faintly with the complex organization in the dioceses of the Western world. His problems are those of initiating new projects in a small way, and he need not vision too far into the future. Indeed, he is occupied perforce mostly with only the more immediate and pressing of needs, and his struggle is rather to get the infant Church to breathe at all than to worry over its higher education.

But, though the problems are simple, they are fundamental and vital; there is a faint aroma of the catacombs about them that connects us immediately with Peter and Linus and Clement and especially St. Paul. It is a refreshing thought that somewhere in the world always down the centuries there is a continuous beginning of new ventures that link us with the Apostles. The new-born faith in pagan surroundings gives much more meaning to the ritual in our simple ceremonies; the closeness of contact between bishop and flock makes emphatic the democracy of the Church's organization and her intention to have the laity united with the priest in the building of the Church. It is a relation that is enviable and scarcely possible in more sophisticated circles; but that makes a bishop's role in China, even from the human point of view, fascinating.
(1939)

Solitude

SOME OF THE EXPERIENCES WHICH WERE FAIRLY COMMON TO A
generation or two ago are fast vanishing from the world. One
of these is solitude. Our grandfathers knew it, ploughing the
fields, or in the lonely vigil of a snowbound winter's night. Now
it is found, perhaps, mostly among missioners.

To understand the deep heart of solitude, you have first to
silence the multiple machines about you. You have to dim all
light beyond a narrow radius. Above all, you have to be free
of obligations that may keep the mind taut or beget problems
that preoccupy. All this is well-nigh impossible in the twentieth century, except for missioners.

A missioner's solitude is not lonesome, though lonely. At
sunset, especially in the country parishes that make up nine-
tenths of China, his people withdraw to their homes. The chatter of children is stilled by early dusk; the cattle are bedded
for the night; and the doors are made fast against all prowlers.
The missioner sees the unlit houses in the distance melt into
the landscape, and an overwhelming silence, unknown to the
Western world, surrounds and penetrates. Gradually, the
steady flicker of the oil lamp liberates his mind to a relaxing
enjoyment of real solitude.

A missioner's day is peculiarly unselfish and long. From the
merest suggestion of dawn, he is at the disposal of his people.
In a democracy of living that has raised few barriers to close
association, among a people who have accepted him as sharing
their daily life, the missioner is immersed in activities throughout the day. Custom has put him at the call of all, and simple
folk who work for no one but themselves weigh time more
carelessly than do commercial-minded Westerners.

The solitude that is the missioner's lot from dusk to bedtime is, then, by contrast so striking and abrupt that it appals him at the outset. It's the rare man, especially in youth, who relishes an hour or two of absolute silence and inactive isolation in a dark too dense to focus the eye. In theory, the Westerner, harassed by tense activity all day, should yearn for absolute solitude; in actual experience, solitude requires an adjustment that drives hard against a lifetime of companionship and interchange of thought.

Like all habits, it is soon acquired, and its soothing influence on the spirit insensibly tests its worth. It is the brooding time of high resolves and clear logic, when the world and its ends are aligned aright, and the whisper of God is heard that steadies the morrow with fresh plans. It is the reason why old missioners are young and clear-eyed, and young ones can launch out into the deep. (*1943*)

The Beauty of Shadow

ONE OF THE DELIGHTS IN CHINA IS THAT THERE ARE SHADOWS everywhere. Our semitropical sun here in Kwangtung Province is merciless in flattening impressions; it reduces vision to a broad plane; it obliterates distinctions and individuality is lost in the dazzle of lineless brilliancy. Its steady glare dries up cool reflection and quiet meditation; and its very omnipresence defeats its power of illumination, as nerves grow tense in weariness.

As a corrective to this dazzling sunlight, China offers shadows to tired eyes everywhere they look. The twisting, shady lanes are bordered and topped with graceful bamboo. No red barns, gleaming white houses, or freakishly painted dwellings stand out on the landscape. Not even the lightning flash of racing vehicles wearies the eye. In China, man has so little modified nature's moods that traces of his work and his dwellings never clash with the scene. He has always sensitively adapted himself to nature, and has thus found poise.

Perhaps it is chiefly in the utilization of shadow that the Chinese has achieved affinity with nature. He leads an outdoor life in city or countryside to a greater extent than does the average Westerner, but he does so mostly in the shade of some protective covering. His city streets are arcaded; his umbrella is ubiquitous; and the farmer shields himself beneath a cool, palm-woven headgear.

The Chinese is master of shadow especially in his house construction. His guest rooms are not dustless, hygienic cubicles, devoid of character, but roofed angles, with an entire side open to a patio. The keynote of this patio is cool shade and a limited vista outlined in cold, green tile, with stone columns and intricate woodcarving rich in a blend of gold and colors that peep from the dusky background. The four guest rooms face on their open court, and at any angle there is a play of light and shadow as the sunlight filters through the tracery. In the evening, when flickering lights from lanterns throw the stone columns into relief, the scene is bewitching.

The hallways of a Chinese home breathe the same atmosphere of seclusion and rest. They derive their light from the open courtyards; but it is broken up by many archways that invite the eye to look beyond, yet cloister the space within. The Chinese house thus encloses permanent shadows that vary in depth with the angle of sunlight, and the filtered light from the courtyard enlivens a constantly changing succession of interior views that need little other ornament. Even the potted palms that thrive in such secluded light are strangely silvered by the angle of light from above. They cast a deeper shadow, unrelieved by any refraction.

This perpetually elusive, fluctuating permanency of ornament that is constructed into the house itself could never be realized in the flat-surfaced monotony of a Western boxlike structure. When this result is achieved, as in China, without any windows, the effect is one of rest and seclusion from an outside world. The eye is never enticed to the distractions of the street, but finds enjoyment entirely from the interior of the home. A Westerner chooses a house for the sake of the view from its windows; a Chinese builds his to enclose a view within, which is less subject to the vagaries of development.

The courtyard of our Chinese rectory is an ideal setting for night prayers with our Christians. Dim light from flickering tapers grades the shadows in a thousand shapes, restful to eyes strained by long hours of labor in sunlit rice fields. A single beam picks out the white statue of Christ, invested with singular beauty by its background of shadows. All the tired eyes focus undistracted on the Light of the World, and quiet peace soothes the souls of our Catholics. (*1944*)

China's Silence

I AM SURE IT DOES NOT HURT YOU IF WE IN CHINA CROW ONCE in a while over our advantages. There is pleasure in sharing joy; like mercy, joy blesses him who gives and him who takes, and it is good for the world outside China to know some of her attractions, especially when these are lacking in the West.

One of the penalties of modern civilization is the atrophy of the senses to some degree. Perception is dulled by tension. This may explain why city life is the death of poetry; God is not in the whirlwind. "While the deepest of silence calms all, and night has wandered through half its course, Thy Word, O Lord, in all His power comes." The rush and bustle of modern ways deaden acuteness in the senses, and much of the undertone is lost. "Be still, and see that I am God," sings the Psalmist.

216

Perhaps we need to live in China to appreciate silence, to become pagans in the primitive sense of village dwellers, although the civilization even in the cities here retains the silence of culture. For silence, after all, is evidence of art; man-made noises arise from friction, and are proof of imperfection in machinery. Nature at peace is silence or song or the steady hum of controlled energy that does not grate in stridency. And the Western world is never as still as China.

But China's silence is a thing apart; not mere absence of noise, or the lifeless vacancy of the desert or the ringing lull of suspended sound. It is not a manufactured silence or the deadness of a Puritanical Sabbath. It is silence as God intended it to be, the harmonious energy of man and nature living calmly.

China is a hive of industry, of physical labor continuing far into the night and starting with the dawn again. China is alive, as no Western land with all its noise is alive. It breathes and moves continuously like an anthill in systematic activity; it is an organism that pulsates and rests; but its sleep is tranquil breathing, and night comes as a nurse to lay a coverlet of mist softly and slowly over the sleeping city, so that its sleep is but a stage of life.

In the Western world, outside of convents and babies' cribs, night is a nightmare: long rows of deserted offices and shops, hard, glaring, empty streets, deathlike in exhaustion. Even dwellings, unlike those of the East, have not the restful look of huddling close to trees and ground, and in the moonlight stare through dark windows like gigantic skulls. The test of a city's beauty is at dusk or moonlight; if peace and life have fled its streets, the harsh electric light merely accentuates the corpse.

A Chinese city is at its best at night. The low-slung, sloping roofs of mossy tile silver the atmosphere, and the mingling cloud of fragrant smoke from the wood fires, eddying with the

217

mist arising from innumerable ponds, catches the first glimpse of the moon and gives ethereal beauty to the fantastic scene, like the court of heaven reserved for innocence.

It is a populated silence, instinct with life; the open courts within each house provide homes for countless birds nestling safely under the eaves; within doors the family and its pig and poultry—for the latter, too, have their place in genuine family life even in the cities—are bedded down in comfort; the dog in vigilant sleep is stationed at the doorway; while over every roof a myriad of bats, a fitting symbol in China of domestic happiness, flitter their silent vigil through the night.

But it is the unexpected silence of the day that surprises in China. Like the silent motion pictures of a generation ago, the figures move all day without much noise. The dirt roads and bare feet, of course, help deaden any sound, and the absence of vehicles gives an equal pace to the movement; long lines of mules walk daintily in single file, and poorer men, their own burden carriers, with heavier feet follow in the wake of the animals. Life is lived out of doors more in China than in most places, so that the roads and shops seem filled continuously with silent crowds. Small creeks as well as rivers bear laden craft that seem to drift along, their movement is so slow and calm. The bent figures and rhythmic plowing in adjacent fields do not distract the traveler's eye.

There is no frivolous gaiety in Chinese streets or fields, but everywhere placidity and smiles and unfeverish activity. Old cronies, warming themselves in the sunny angles of the houses and accepting the privilege of wrinkled age by sitting at their task, watch over the drying grain spread out before them; they are reposeful, but vigilant lest ducks and hens steal more of the grain than is indulgently allotted them. The only lazy being in China is the family pig, stretched out contentedly in a choice wallow, but even he preserves the silence.

218

Silence, then, in China is restored to its primitive meaning. It is not mere cessation of noise, as in the West, but an energetic co-ordination of smooth working without friction. It is akin to the silence of a Catholic church, or of a nursery where the cribs are filled with energy asleep. Like the energy of God working through the sap of trees, it is creative, not a void, a grace begot of centuries. (*1950*)

SISTERS AND THE DIRECT APOSTOLATE

"The 'contact apostolate' for Sisters is a peculiar battle of modern warfare. Like the sky fights of the twentieth century, it is a solitary struggle where the Sister must depend to a great extent on native initiative and the grace of the moment. Her confidence lies in the necessity of the work. China will never be permanently Catholic until her women take over their share in the Church's activities, and to do this, they must be given an example of women's sphere in the apostolate."

Testimony of a Sister-Apostle

As PASTOR OF YEUNGKONG IN KWANGTUNG PROVINCE, SOUTH *China, Fr. Ford built the convent for the Maryknoll Sisters' first mission band, and guided them in their initial apostolic endeavors in the autumn of 1922. He already had novel ideas for the work of missionary Sisters. When Mother Mary Joseph, the Foundress of the Maryknoll Sisters, visited Yeungkong in 1924, Fr. Ford obtained her wholehearted approval of his views.*

The following account of how Bishop Ford later launched the work of the direct apostolate for missionary Sisters in his own Kaying mission field is given by Sister Marie Marcelline, who entered the Maryknoll Sisterhood from Westbrook, Maine. Until she was imprisoned and then exiled by the Communists, Sister Marcelline was Mistress of Chinese Novices in the Kaying diocese. She writes:

"In 1935 the Kaying mission field had only a few thousand Catholics in a population of 2,625,000 Hakka Chinese. Bishop Ford saw the urgency of organizing all his forces for the direct aim of converting souls. He organized the Sisters under his direction as a band of consecrated women-apostles, sending them two by two among the people. In the course of the years, we grew to be a group of thirty Chinese and American Sisters, working in thirteen different missions, headed by either Maryknoll or Chinese priests. The aim for us all was not only that we reach into every village or town, but also that we enter into every house where the name of God was yet to be heard, and

in every house, contact every person who had yet to learn about Christianity. We were to establish a friendship between the people and ourselves, eventually to lead them to the sacerdotal hands of the priest-missioner, and ultimately into the Church, to the friendship of God and the Christianizing influence of the sacraments.

"Bishop Ford taught us the technique of the work which was the fruit of his apostolic genius and missionary experience. To this necessary training, our Mother General added the wisdom of her vision as a Foundress of missionary Sisters. With her approval, we were able to make such departures from the traditional religious pattern as were necessary to make us better fitted for as full an apostolate as possible.

"We had a section set apart in each of our convents as a rallying place for women and children. We were allowed to teach at night during a catechumenate if the people, because of the necessities of making a living, had to work during the day. We were permitted to live in the houses of the people and carry village catechumenates through, if the people could not come to the church for what we called a center catechumenate. Our habit was simplified for the conveniences of travel on flat sampans or bicycles, or of wading rivers.

"Meanwhile, the spiritual side of our lives was never lessened, though at times it had to grow strong on the sacrifice of deprivation of Mass and Communion during the prolonged stays in mission outposts. At such times, spiritual Mass and Communion, the divine Office, our Rosary and other spiritual exercises were unfailing standbys for us all. Periodical returns to a conventual center kept us fresh in the stream of religious and community ideals.

"The scheme of our instruction of the people was the catechism and the Christian prayer manual, explained by every catechetical device that we knew of. We followed up the regu-

lar catechumenate instruction of two months (at five hours a day) with post catechumenate courses, Sunday School courses, sodality, and Catholic Action group study, and other activities. In parochial matters, that is, in all the details of mission work, we were subject to the parish priest; in community or personal matters, we were directly under our religious superiors and Bishop Ford, who was our ecclesiastical superior.

"During the fifteen and a half years that it was my privilege to be in the Kaying diocese, it was our satisfaction to see the roster of Christians grow to the number of 22,819. As Communism began to infiltrate, many non-Christians saw through its insidiousness, and we witnessed to our great consolation in those latter months several movements for mass conversion in various sections of our Kaying diocese.

"The work that we did as Sisters met with the commendation of the Papal Internuncio, Archbishop Anthony Riberi. It was his plan that the other bishops in various provinces of China would train their Sisters to do just such work as Bishop Ford had guided us all to perform. The Chinese bishops of the northern provinces of Shantung and Shanshi had already designated candidates who were to be trained as future Sisterapostles. Archbishop Riberi felt that the Church in China would grow much faster if more Sisters were made to participate in the direct apostolate of converting souls.

"Then, Communism took over, and eventually we were expelled from the field of our apostolate. Bishop Ford died in the midst of this tremendous struggle of our time, the battle between Satan and the Church of Christ. Christianity has not failed in China. We hope that some day an army of priests and Sisters will be able to go back to that great land and to evangelize the Chinese millions according to the apostolic pattern set by our late inspired leader, Bishop Francis Xavier Ford."

Remedying a Serious Defect

IT MAY SEEM LIKE A RASH STATEMENT, BUT I THINK IT IS TRUE, that there is very little future for any mission in China that has not Sisters working in it. Critics have sometimes said that our missionary work in China is not efficient, and that we have very little to show for the three centuries of Catholic evangelization in this great country. Starting with the small beginnings of past centuries, we should by merely natural increase have trebled our Catholic population by now, they observe; instead of which, some old Christianities are barely subsisting without vigor.

Of course, we can always answer that there is leakage the world over, and that our Chinese Catholics compare favorably with Christians in any country. We can point out that China has produced its indigenous priests and martyrs, two good proofs of fecundity. We can remind our critics that the field in China is vaster than even the missioners themselves can vision, and the battalion of missioners has been fighting against legions, not to mention bitter persecutions. We can even produce less negative evidence in the hundreds of thousands of pupils in our Catholic schools, which is a big step towards stability.

But, to face the problem squarely, we must admit a serious defect in our system of evangelization. Until recent times, we had very few Sisters in China, and our work among both pagans and Christians was lopsided. Our neglect of the women aggravated the traditional apathy of the Chinese themselves for the welfare of their women.

Chinese women have never been debased to the level of Oriental women in some other countries of Asia, but their place and influence in the home have been subsidiary. Catholic missioners of former times have, perforce, concentrated on the conversion of the men, and thereby diminished still more the part that women might have played in a Christian family. It was not unusual to find a village of a hundred Catholic men, and but two or three Catholic women. The fault lay, not in the missioners, but between rigid Chinese etiquette and the absence of Catholic Sisters.

Formerly, only the men and our Catholic schoolboys went to church. The services were virile with the roughness, somewhat, of a lumber camp. Outside of mealtimes, the men and women did not meet on common ground. While the men and boys went to Mass, the women continued to worship idols. Indeed, the women constituted the backbone of idolatry; the men in general were more indifferent to pagan worship, contenting themselves with superstitions on a minor scale or on special occasions.

Had we won the women over to the true worship during the past three centuries, the Church in China would now have a far more glorious tale to tell. In winning the men, who are less stable and more easily converted, we built on a foundation much less solid than that of the Christian family. Missioners, of course, are not to be blamed for this. Chinese etiquette made it impossible for them to reach the women, and the idea of a missionary apostolate for Sisters had not developed to the stage where religious institutes of women could send many of their subjects to China.

Now that the Sisters are in China in considerable numbers, there has been an indefinable change in the Catholic life of our Christians. Women are instructed and converted, and a new recognition is accorded to the rights and duties of Christian mothers in safeguarding their children. We may look for numerous examples of truly Christian families, a better instructed growing generation, and a gradual refinement of thought and action. This will not be accomplished overnight, but it is inevitable wherever Sisters work. (1923)

A Memorable Visit

I DOUBT IF EVER ANOTHER MOTHER GENERAL HAD SUCH experiences and such a welcome, even though we say it ourselves. The more recent arrivals at Maryknoll know Mother Mary Joseph as superior of a thriving community. They see her in all the glory, as it were, of her leadership—if they see her at all, in these days of big mission activities. When we left Maryknoll for the missions, she had only a small group of Sisters to distract her, and she found time to mother every one of us boys. In fact, we still remember her Sunday desserts and feastday specials of a dozen years ago; we remember the lean days, too, when an unexpected influx of visitors taxed her ingenuity with hasty puddings; we recall the huge piece of pie that somehow crossed our path in reward for extra labor done—the thorough understanding of the growing boy. A Maryknoll Sister's vocation, though seemingly specialized, is extremely versatile, and the Mother General has filled every demand.

Our meeting, then, in China was a real Maryknoll reunion, with many a laugh over old problems. It is characteristic of our meetings over here that the gap of years is quietly bridged, and we take up threads of interest just where we left them off at home. Our thoughts of every one respectively were soon satisfied, and we began to realize how Maryknoll has grown.

Mother Mary Joseph's trip was unique in many ways, and, though she traveled the same route that is gradually becoming a Maryknoll pathway, I'm sure her observations were different from any preceding ones. We missioners see China close-up, with a quaintly interesting introduction and a more prosaic prolonged acquaintance; we are not mere visitors, but real friends of the Chinese. Mother Mary Joseph became one of the Chinese family, not a mere friend. She saw China from the inside of kitchens and the interior of the family quarters, cooed in unison with the babies, and smiled her way into the hearts of the women folk. She saw family life as we priests cannot see it, women smiling without restraint and unbashful girls. The women guiding boats or doing coolie's work would chat with her unreservedly, fully confident that she could divine their thoughts.

The crowning event of our visitor's month in Yeungkong was an unexpected wait of eight days in a village mission at Hoiling. We had safely left behind us four of the eight boats that we must take to reach Hong Kong, so there was no thought of turning back when we found Boat Number Five would not leave for a week. We settled down at the mission with the grace that holy indifference gives, to while away the interval. It could have been worse; it was winter, with a pleasant sun and tempered heat; there was an oceanful of seafood easily bought; we had more privacy than the average Chinese house affords; and the local catechist borrowed flowers to decorate our suites. We had the town crier, at night, to wake us at intervals, if perchance mosquitoes let us sleep; and during the day, the handful of Christians did homage with gifts of seaweed, lobsters, salted shrimps, and sun-dried eggs that taste no worse than do cheese or olives to a Chinese.

The little chapel was comfortably filled twice a day for Mass and morning and evening prayers, and we had a successful examination of thirteen catechumens for baptism. The travelers had a peep into the ordinary village life of a missioner. Hoiling was attractive in its poverty and in its cleanliness, and it had, in common with most stations, a pleasant courtesy, an unlettered delicacy, and genuine hospitality.

Natural Chinese etiquette is a marvelous rule of conduct. Here were so-called uncultured islanders in a situation never before experienced by them—the entertaining of foreign women. They had no parallel in their own life, for Chinese

229

women rarely travel, and then only to visit their relatives; the men do not associate with the women, and the women do not expect to be entertained even by the other women—yet these men naturally were masters in giving us just that degree of watchful attention that insured the satisfying of our wants, and protected us against annoyances.

The stay was a happy one for me, as the visit was unannounced and unexpected, and we caught the Christians off guard, as it were, yet faithful to their daily prayers. The pity of an ordinary visit is that we do not know how much is assumed for the special occasion. Like many a visitation, our official inspection is too superficial to be thorough, and I fear many a good soul graces the occasion who is not present at the more usual exercises. So, to "drop in" and find a good congregation is not often our experience.

The Sisters opened my eyes to another fact. A missioner, visiting a station, is often too easily resigned to the poverty-stricken look of things to attempt any remedy. The deft arrangement of a few pots of flowers about the altar, the smoothing ruffled linens, and the removal of incongruous litter that adorns the average Chinese room changed the appearance of our little chapel and helped devotion. What is better still, I'm sure the Christians will remember the points on cleanliness and keep the chapel in better condition.

But Mother Mary Joseph did more than this. She gathered the little girls about her and made them fearless in my presence. In the interior, the girls seem satisfied with peeping at the foreigner from unexpected angles. They shove their noses above the landing, if there is an upper story, and silent, persistent, heroically patient, they watch his every movement. He cannot turn a corner of the building without scattering a group of frightened but inquisitive little tots; he hears a whispering that he at first confuses with the buzzing of insects or the pattering of rats; he sees vigilant shadows or protruding eyes that betray the insatiable curiosity of children.

This is a blessing when a man wants peace, but when duty demands an examination in the catechism, it is as harrowing for the priest as for the children. Fear robs them of their voice, their eyes light everywhere but on the questioner; and all the coaxing that mothers use in dosing castor oil is overshadowed by our strategy in China. I always thought it was the foreign face and clothes that frightened them, but I look and dress more Chinese than the Reverend Mother did, and yet they ran to her and lost their bashfulness.

Her whole trip emphasized the hold our Sisters will have on Chinese women, and the utter need of such influence to gain these women's hearts. We men go through China and do some good in converting men, but the backbone of idolatry is the "devout female sex." The Chinese mother, despite her low esteem outside the home, is the real molder of the faith of her children, and an enduring Church is founded on her conversion.

The visit of the Mother General, then, in confirming the work begun by her Sisters in China, is really a milestone that will record the beginning of a permanent foothold of the Church in our missions. (*1924*)

The Message of Mary Magdalen

ST. PAUL SAYS: "THOSE WHO ARE ESPOUSED TO CHRIST THINK OF the things that please Christ." You Sisters engaged in the work of the direct apostolate here in the Kaying mission field are espoused to a missionary Christ. You have come to this particular section of China solely to preach Christ and Him crucified. In order to merit this grace of continually preaching the unsearchable riches of Christ, you have to be single-minded, always seeking your Lord and never letting Him go.

The Church gives us a model of this single-mindedness in St. Mary Magdalen; her whole life is a message to missioners, portraying the undeviating concentration of a loving soul on Christ. In the Office for her feast day, the Church applies the love song of the Canticle of Canticles to Mary Magdalen: "I have sought Him in whom my soul delights. . . . I discovered Him and have clung to Him and I will not let Him go."

Our first glimpse of Mary Magdalen in the Gospels is when she was going through the streets of Bethania, looking for the house of Simon the leper, who was giving a banquet for our Lord. There was a crowd gathered near the entrance, watching the guests arrive, and everyone recognized Mary Magdalen, because her life until then had been one of ill repute. She must have been tempted to turn away from those staring eyes and retrace her steps. But in spite of the mockery and sneers of the idlers, she made her way into Simon's house, mindful only of the urgency of her search for Christ.

After the body of our Lord had been laid in the tomb offered by Joseph, a rich man of Arimathea, Mary Magdalen was restless, seeking Him whom her heart desired. In the early dawn of the first Easter morning, before the world was astir, she went to the tomb, but angels told her that Christ had risen from the dead, that He was not there. Mary Magdalen did not give up the search. She saw a gardener and did not hesitate to ask him if he knew where the body of Christ had been taken. The single-mindedness of her quest touched the divine Heart. The One she had taken for a gardener spoke the single word, "Mary." She ran to him with the glad cry of "Master!"

It is thus that Mary Magdalen appears to us in the Scriptures and she really is a model for missioners, especially for you Sisters engaged in the work of the direct apostolate. The life is a hard one for women, so much so that the Holy See often doubted their suitability for the work. It is very difficult to be constantly seeking means of introducing strangers to the faith, to be seen daily in the public streets and the byways. Such an apostolate is against the natural reserve of women, and it demands above all a single-minded seeking of Christ in souls for whose sake He died on the Cross.

To be a pioneer in anything is hard, and it takes an uncommon single-mindedness not to worry about what people will say. The need of overcoming self-consciousness should make us turn to Mary Magdalen and take courage from her courage. If ever a woman forgot self, it was Mary Magdalen. She sought Christ "in season and out of season," whether it was womanly or not. She thought of nothing else, because she "loved much."

If our lives, like hers, are centered on the love of Christ, then He will manifest Himself to us in the humblest of his creatures. On the Day of Judgment we shall hear our Lord say to us: "I was a lonely little girl gathering firewood on the hillside, and you smiled at me. I was a dull old woman, and you taught me to hope. I was an ignorant, ordinary person whom no one thought anything of, and you gave me a rich inheritance. I was a homeless orphan, and you showed me the way to the dwelling of my Father in Heaven. And if you did it to the least of these, My little ones, you did it to Me." (*1940*)

The Type of Sister Needed

IT HAS ALWAYS BEEN MORE OR LESS A PUZZLE TO CONSIDER WHAT type of person is best suited to our work of direct evangelization. Although direct evangelization is basically a missioner's work, and should never be absent from whatever branch he or she is engaged in for the moment, it nevertheless has its peculiar phases that require special aptitudes, and these we can discuss.

Our work requires, first of all, making contacts. It is this initial step that is properly called "direct evangelization." To be fully effective, the initial step entails all the subsequent instruction of converts and the important "follow-up" after baptism. Making contacts, however, as a first step in the life-long acquaintance, is worth study.

Even in this matter of making contacts it is difficult to dogmatize, because much depends on the class of persons with whom contacts are to be established. The type of Sister required for very simple country women would be different from the one needed for well-educated schoolteachers; old women, or the practical mother of a large household, may be attracted by a type of Sister who would not appeal to young girls. The simplest statement we can make with assurance is that our Chinese women are as diverse as their Western sisters, and also basically the same as any women the world over. The superficial difference affects only customs; any Sister who does not realize this will be hampered in her approach to strangers.

The general characteristics of a "contact" Sister might be summed up in a person who is expansive, expressive, exhilarating, and exhibitive; in common language, a person who is large-hearted, ready-tongued, easily pleased, and not dismayed by crowds. This type is the opposite of one who is close-mouthed, distant, severe, and timid. Even Sisters who are inclined to be saving in words, cannot easily manifest warmth of feeling, are unbending in discipline, or find it difficult to be interested in worldly affairs may prove fit for contact making. But it is easy to exaggerate requisite qualities; zeal for souls will often be an ample corrective of imaginary lacks.

On the first thought, direct evangelization seems contrary to a religious Sister's field of labor, but when it is viewed simply as portraying Christlike character and restricted to the feminine world, it will be seen as eminently ideal work for Sisters of active congregations. The peculiar background of women in China especially demands such work on the part of missionary Sisters, at least until a nucleus of Chinese lay women will have been formed and stimulated to Catholic Action.

The weakest link in the missionary personnel is the woman catechist, chiefly because she is attempting work that has been without a model after which to pattern herself. With Sisters to guide her, not merely in the theory, but in actual convert making, she should prove fit for the task. But in order to guide her, the Sisters themselves should have experience in field work, and this means in direct evangelization.

The conditions of direct evangelization will emphasize more clearly than anything else what qualities are needed in the Sister engaged in this vital work. She is obliged to call informally on pagan neighbors (for practical purposes all women within a radius of five miles are neighbors), and often without previous introduction, though advantage is taken of any common friend. She uses every occasion of census-taking of Catholics to meet non-Christian members of families, and they are numerous in Chinese village houses. She angles at and accepts an invitation to repeat visits, and develops a personal interest in the pagan women. She is asked and prepared to give frequent informal conferences on religion to the small groups that gather on her arrival. In short, she becomes intimate with her neighbors.

As the main purpose of all this daily visiting is to make converts, the Sister does not camouflage her intention by carrying medicines. Her aim is to attract only those interested in religion, and experience proves that they are sufficiently numerous without other distracting side lines. Thus, no time is wasted in weeding out the merely curious or needy.

The great difficulty that the average Sister is apt to encounter in the work of direct evangelization is its apparent lack of immediate, tangible results. She has been trained to perform definite duties, limited to definite times, and usually in co-operation with other Sisters doing similar work. These duties have a direct bearing on spiritual values. Now, this same Sister is required to occupy herself in social visiting, to interest herself in the intimate details of family life, to use the graces of the world to attract pagan women. It would seem that she is asked to reverse all the rules and maxims she learned in the novitiate for her own sanctification. The work is disturbing and demands of the Sister hitherto untried powers.

The religious who has been carefully trained in recollection and the hidden life must now be *expansive*, but there is no real contradiction. Her frank open-heartedness arises from her conviction that all her neighbors are potential members of the Mystical Body of Christ and, therefore, in her keeping. While expressing outwardly herself the character of Christ, she continually seeks to make Him welcomed by others. She leads an active, outward life because she is a missioner entrusted with a message; she reflects the warmth of Christ toward all without distinction.

The "contact" Sister uses her natural talents for attracting others, by sublimating them in union with God's emptying of Himself. She is animated by the Holy Spirit, as was Mary when she "hastened" over the hill country to visit her cousin Elizabeth. A priest bearing Christ in Holy Viaticum through pagan villages knows a special joy nowhere else experienced, and it is this same joy that animates the "contact" Sister on her social visits. Her loving joy communicates itself to the souls of non-Christians, like a glowing spark leaping across a gap to bring life and light to pagan darkness.

The Sister engaged in the work of direct evangelization must be *expressive*; she is conveying a message that her listener has a right to hear. In the role of guest, she is not merely the passive recipient of kindly pagan hospitality. She is actually welcoming her neighbors into the Kingdom of God; hence, she must use all the arts of a hostess, although in another's house. The pagan neighbors, like the disciples who invited our Lord at Emmaus, should feel their hearts grow warm in pleasure at the presence of the Sister. She wins them by showing interest in their affairs and by linking herself with their concerns.

Unselfish interest always attracts, but to demonstrate this interest to best advantage the Sister needs facility in the Chinese language. She must learn to laugh in Chinese, as well as to teach or preach, and to laugh with the women at their own level. Her spirit must be infectious and arouse curiosity as to its source, and she has to rely on her ready tongue to satisfy the curiosity. First of all, however, the Sister must convince herself that apparently idle chatter is not a mere waste of time: this is one case where idle words are meritorious for Heaven.

The Sister should be *exhilarating*, by which is meant the opposite of the distant, impersonal, reserved, ethereal manner deemed characteristic of Sisters by those who do not know them intimately. Contact visits are to pagans who have never spoken to a religious before, and who have either no preconceived notion of how a religious should act, or some strange idea that we could never fathom. So, there is no question of giving scandal in acting towards these pagans in a perfectly natural, simple, sincere, friendly way. If they do not appreciate the significance of the habit or of the religious state, neither will they understand the otherwise legitimate reserve proper in dealing with persons in Catholic countries. The Sister, without sacrificing the least bit of self-respect by the spontaneous warmth of her natural friendliness, will thus meet the pagan women on the only level the latter can understand.

The "contact" Sister must also become *exhibitive*, in the

sense of becoming a spectacle to men and angels. Her work is out in the dust of the road, in the heat of the sun, in the midst of pigs and chickens and children, in the dark, smoky homes of the average Chinese village; her work is going among women wherever they are, and this means a sacrifice of clean quarters, quiet peace, recollection, and the sheltered atmosphere that has become part of her religious experience.

The work requires a discipline of the senses and an involuntary mortification of the more refined sensibilities that can easily become an adequate substitute for a hair shirt. Its publicity sometimes demands heroic courage. To be stared at, even by friendly but frankly curious women, to take for the moment the center of the stage, surrounded by strangers, to be confronted on all sides by unintentional outrages to Western forms of etiquette, is a severe trial of a Sister's zeal for souls.

In the Sister engaged in direct evangelization, all of the qualities mentioned above are the outward marks of an intense love of souls for Christ's sake. They are outward, not in the sense of being external only, but as actively proceeding from zeal and indicative of the apostolic nature of her work. She is the extern Sister of the Kingdom within us, the messenger to souls outside in the shadow of death; her cloister is not the oasis of the mission compound. As contact visitor to pagan women, she literally penetrates into the inner courts where superstition has its firmest foothold; she attacks the enemy at his strongest fortress and until this has fallen, it is vain to hope for a solid Catholic family.

The contact apostolate for Sisters is a peculiar battle of modern warfare. Like the sky fights of the twentieth century, it is a solitary struggle where the Sister must depend to a great extent on native initiative and the grace of the moment. Her confidence lies in the necessity of the work. China will never be permanently Catholic until her women take their share in the Church's activities, and to do this they must be given an example of women's sphere in the apostolate; they must have a pattern to follow and the inspiration and encouragement that only Sisters can give. So there is urgent need for "contact" Sisters; God's grace will enable them to measure up to their task, whatever their native abilities may be.

It is true, of course, that such contact work is but preliminary to the longer, more thorough, instruction of the new converts, and the lifelong initiation into deeper Catholic spirituality. Doctrine classes and Sunday School and parish routine will make further demands on the same "contact" Sister, and utilize all her skills along lines that are familiar and for which she was previously trained. But her hours of daily contact visiting should renew her joy in pioneering for Christ on new trails hitherto untrod, which had called forth her own initiative and creative skill in work that is peculiarly missionary and apostolic in character. (*1941*)

Kaying Lawn Party

OUR SISTERS HAVE EXPERIMENTED IN ALL MANNER OF PROJECTS —so vast is the field of their work among women, and so untried as yet are many ways of interesting women in the Church. The Maryknoll Sisters' hostel for girl students offered a good opportunity for getting in touch with the women teachers of the city, so a lawn party was undertaken.

In this homeland of Chinese lanterns, it seems odd that the Chinese do not use them for lawn parties. To the Westerner, the paper lantern is so fragile and dainty, and its light so enchanting, that it seems especially made for decoration. But the Chinese, practical as usual, think of it as a source of light, made beautiful only incidentally. The setting of the Sisters'

239

garden, sheltered by a dozen trees, needed little ornament to satisfy the eye; a few paper lanterns and streamers from last year's Christmas tree gave just the right touch of decoration to the chaste symmetry of the Chinese dwelling.

Like the answer to Sisters' prayers the world over was the weather. The heavy clouds cooled and shaded the lawn, and withheld their rain till all was ended. A lawn party in tropical China could be a warm event. And in this rainy reason, only faith would dare to plan such a gathering.

There were few onlookers as the hundred guests participated in the games. The dozen or so school teachers and other women notables soon lost their prim coolness in the atmosphere of friendliness. They were welcomed by the students and introduced to the Sisters, and they showed evident interest in all about them. Chinese school teachers traditionally are given a slightly formal deference that inhibits them from relaxing with their pupils, but under the Sisters' skillful casualness woman's delight in simple pleasure came to the surface, and they thoroughly enjoyed the novelty. The ingenuousness of a round of simple games participated in by everyone was beyond their ken or custom, but they entered into the spirit of the occasion gaily.

The Sisters themselves were rewarded by the hearty cooperation of the girls. The latter demanded the privilege of providing for the catering and the decorations, and they also acted as hostesses and prime movers of the games. The games were the kind that allowed all guests to participate: egg hunting, pinning the donkey's tail, musical chairs, and the like. They were reminders to the Sisters of parties at home, but were entirely new to the young generation of modern China.

Interspersed were folk dancing, and lively phonograph records, and a Maypole group, and much friendly chatting with the Sisters. The complete and unconscious frankness between the girls and the Sisters was a revelation to the visitors, and the unclannish mingling of sodality girls from all points of the compass was a sorely needed lesson against prevalent custom.

It may seem curious that in such relaxation the Sisters find their missionary work realized. Having the girls living with them in the hostel gives them better contact than can be experienced in purely formal school work. The girls' characters are formed as much outside of class as during school hours, and the hostel gives the refinement of home training that a day school cannot give. The association of the Sisters' influence with the girls' social pleasures, which subjectively are more intimate and important than mere study, gives the girls true values that will powerfully counteract the unsettled standards of modern emancipation.

The lawn party was an excellent occasion for practicing the virtues of a hostess. Young China is eager to acquire such, and the calm poise of the girls in placing doilies and serving tea, or conducting their teachers through immaculate bedrooms and study hall, gave no inkling of the careless habits that have needed wise correction.

To the girls the lawn party was an afternoon of happy excitement with their teachers. But to the Sisters it meant many an opening wedge for friendship with the non-Christian visitors, who have much influence over womenfolk in this region. To the visitors the lawn party was a revelation of the warmth of the Catholic faith and the joy of Catholic culture. (*1945*)

The Sister and the Direct Apostolate

IT SEEMS INCONGRUOUS THAT ALL THE WORKS OF THE CHURCH, except that of the direct apostolate, are, as we might say, well established, and are never entered into without previous years of training. The direct apostolate, which dedicates the Sister-missioner to work among women not for the benefit of their bodies or minds, but for their souls, is, however, given a different approach. In China and other missionary countries we can truly say, if we look at the statistics of religious engaged in such work, that this specialized field is not well known even to the clergy, let alone the laity; nor is it well established, as the few Sisters who are engaged in it here and there throughout China are, we might say, just emerging from the experimental stage; and the preparation for this work given to the Sisters on the part of religious communities is often faulty, lacking in practical methods when it is given at all.

Often, Sisters without any previous training are thrown into the work. The communities that send untrained nurses into the hospital or untrained teachers into the classroom are criticized severely and with justice. To repair human bodies, skill is needed which can only be attained by study coupled with practice. To fill the human mind with culture and education, another type of skill is needed, which also requires intelligent study, likewise coupled with practice. Does it not seem that to deal with souls in order to lead them to God, a more delicate work even than that of healing the body or educating the mind, there is then in proportion an even *greater* need of equipping the Sister-apostle with the proper knowledge and technique so necessary for the development of the work? Can we justly accept the erroneous attitude of many that anyone can be a catechist or that anyone can do the work of the direct apostolate? Or, as communities, are we aware of the need of the times, preparing our Sisters well for work among the people rather than sending them unequipped to face a task of such vital importance?

Perhaps we are not really at fault. If the field of the direct apostolate expanded on the missions and, as a result, became better known as a pressing need to be filled, then religious communities would in all probability stress the importance of such training as a necessary preparation for the work and take steps to attain it. But the field is apparently so narrow, and so few invited or sent into it that it naturally assumes an unimportant place and is relegated to the background.

It is also regrettable that missioners in China have concentrated almost exclusively on institutional works, and have absorbed the Sisters into works of this type. For the actual spread of the faith, of going about to preach the Gospel in towns and villages, they have engaged the help of lay catechists. To these paid workers, men and women, they have entrusted the catechetical work of the parish, contacting pagans and instructing them for baptism. Often, the priest's heavy parish work has permitted him to play only a supervisory part, so that the actual work of the conversion of pagans has been left more or less in lay hands. It has never occurred to the majority of these missioners to engage Sisters in works of this nature. Frequently the missioner prefers the lay catechist to the Sister and objects to "wasting" the Sister when there are lay catechists who, as they argue, can do just as well. Again, one meets the missioner who, through inexperience or ignorance, is opposed to having Sisters in his parish engaged in the work of the direct apostolate. They argue it is dangerous for the religious, too hazardous physically for the foreign Sister-missioner especially, too apt to fail, and so on. When one considers the vast, almost wholly untried field of Sisters in the direct apostolate, one is not surprised at such sentiments. They are a natural approach to work that is so new in actual experience in the field for most communities, even missionary communities.

The lay apostolate has been given great impetus by the

Pope's incessant plea for workers among the laity. The lay catechists on the mission field fill a need that is undeniable. But, what missioner has not experienced the feeling that they could do more if they were less worldly, less bound by home ties, a little more holy, a little more efficient—a little better trained? Has he not even had occasion to deplore scandals to his flock by lay catechists? A missioner, who was given Sisters for the direct apostolate by his bishop, threw up his hands in holy horror: "But what will I do with my catechists?" he cried, only to receive the answer: "Keep them, but let the Sisters work with the women lay helpers in training the new catechumens." He was the first to admit that his parish was a better one, his lay catechists doing more efficient and lasting work, his catechumens better instructed, and his new Catholics followed up carefully and intelligently. It was not an increase of numbers that he praised, although that was present, too, but an increase of quality. His parish was holier, more solidified, more apostolic.

To compare the work of the Sister-missioner with that of the lay catechist, or to feel that having Sisters one must "have naught beside," even lay catechists, is a fallacy that has no foundation whatever. The missioner who argued that his lay catechists can do just as effective work or even better than Sisters is making a mistake. The religious vocation, which is a gift from God, brings with it a certain unction which touches hearts. Certainly, if one is making comparisons, it cannot but be said that the Sister has access to the "secrets of the King" given only to the happy Bride. From these storerooms she will replenish the hearts of those with whom she comes in contact. The lay catechist, on the other hand, no matter how holy or zealous, considers his work in the light of a salaried position, and the sacrifices he is willing to make for souls are bounded at a certain point, aside from the rare exception.

If one takes into consideration the religious habit alone, it can readily be seen that it exerts a certain power to move hearts not given to the lay worker, who appears before the people as one of themselves. In pagan countries this power is very great, as the new and novel always create curiosity and lead to inquiry. Therefore, a mission would, to put it mildly, greatly benefit by Sisters engaged in the work of the direct apostolate. The women catechists would then have an example to follow in a country where there is practically no background on which the average catechist or Catholic Action worker can base his or her methods. The Sister-missioner does not supersede or oust the lay catechist, but rather becomes the answer to a well-trained body of Catholic Action workers, guiding them, working with them, inspiring them and at all times encouraging them in the often arduous and discouraging work for souls.

It has been said that the paid catechist is the weakest link in the work of the Church in pagan countries. The type of woman catechist one meets in almost all of China's missions can certainly bear witness, in most cases, to the truth of this statement. Often barely baptized themselves, they are engaged to teach others the truths of the faith. More often, with a background of a generation or so as Catholics, they bring to their apostolate an abundance of good will, but little knowledge of what to teach or how to teach it. Rattling off the catechism or learning a multitude of prayers often forms the only instruction the catechumens receive. As the majority of rural women are not educated, they memorize shouted formulas which have no meaning, so that often one comes across the newly baptized with beautiful faith but knowing little of what it is all about. They have no reason for the faith which is in them.

Efforts have been made to correct this situation by the formation of catechists' schools, wherein both men and women destined for the apostolate receive the necessary training to fit them for the work. But these schools reach only a small number of the catechists employed, and specialized training without an intelligent follow-up of their work again opens the way to criticism. The parish priest, with immense areas to cover, and parochial work absorbing and time-consuming, cannot in many cases give them necessary supervision over unbroken periods of time. The women form at least one-half of every parish. In the Sister-apostle, dedicated only to work among the women and freed from the absorbing cares of institutions the priest-missioner would find a valuable auxiliary.

"But," missioners ask, "what will the Sister do?" Accustomed as they are to the familiar picture they have of the Sister at the bedside of the sick, in the orphanage, or in the classroom, they are at a loss to find her a place in the missionary program. They fall back with a helpless shrug on the fact that all they have is a "parish"—or perhaps not even that—just a rented room for a Church and the beginnings of apostolic work. They could give her nothing that she wants more, if they only knew it! Does she not desire in her heart to go out among the people, loving them, desiring only to bring to them the knowledge of the Truth which they have a right to hear? What missionary Sister does not desire to be an apostle of the Word, the forerunner of Christ in pagan villages and homes? It seems only fair to her that she be given the opportunity to devote herself to the work of the direct apostolate.

That the well-trained Sister deeply imbued with the significance of her vocation can live so closely with the people and yet retain her dignity and a healthy combination of the contemplative and active life is nothing to be wondered at. Rather, it is a proof that she has a place in this specialized field.

The world needs the consecrated apostle as never before,

and the mission field especially has need of her in the work of converting a pagan world. Is it not time for all religious communities to study the question in relation to their own works, equipping the Sisters with the necessary training for work among the people, sending them "two by two" into every field and institution for the purpose of spreading the faith? (*1948*)

COMMUNISM

"Our hearts must be like the heart of Mary: anxious, yearning for the conversion of all our people—concerned particularly for the neediest, the purblind Communists."

In the Likeness of Christ

No one believed the trumped-up charges made against *Bishop Ford by the Chinese Communists. The leading citizens of Meihsien, Christian and pagan, petitioned the Communist authorities to release him. That must have been why the Reds transferred Bishop Ford and his former secretary, Sister Joan Marie, to a jail in Canton, where the Maryknoll prelate was not known to the people.*

On an occasion when Bishop Ford had an opportunity to speak briefly with Sister Joan Marie during their captivity, he used words similar to our Lord's expression of forgiveness for His persecutors: "We must not hate the Communists. They are acting according to their lights."

However Bishop Ford's lonely death came to him, it received the welcome of a familiar friend. In a conference to his missioners, he had said: "Death is the one thing that we should glow over and exult in. . . . It brings the day of our nuptials, of union with God for all eternity, the day of release from imperfect intercourse with God to a life of understanding and immediate assimilation."

Mary and the Communists

In our mission work, we have to show a human interest in people as well as a supernatural one. We have to learn to put our feet on the ground, and not to live entirely in the clouds. Our Blessed Mother is our model in that combination of the supernatural and the natural. When she told Bernadette that she is the Immaculate Conception, she had reference to the supernatural grace which elevates the Mother of God above all other human beings. But in her revelations to the children at Fatima, Mary said that she is the Immaculate Heart. Her heart is full of concern for the world—concern for the need of reparation.

The word "Immaculate" might terrify us, as being too much beyond our comprehension, but we can hold on to the word "Heart" and realize that it is a bond of union. Now, the heart of our Blessed Mother was concerned not merely for the sufferings that would come upon millions of her Catholic children if reparation were not made for the sins of the world. She also had loving compassion for the blindness of the very Communists who were persecuting her divine Son. Mary said that the Holy Father must consecrate the world to her Immaculate Heart, and this has been done. She revealed that the special purpose of this consecration was the conversion of Russia.

The people in the Middle Ages would have understood the revelation at Fatima much better than we do. They realized more vividly the meaning of the Communion of Saints, and the relation between Heaven and earth. How little of our lives is spent in reparation for the sins of others; how few of us concern ourselves with the insults to God committed by unfortunate fellow men. The whole world has become selfish in its devotions, as well as in everything else.

A good test of whether we personally deserve this accusation of selfishness is our own attitude toward the Communists in this territory and elsewhere throughout the world. Do we not tend to become impatient when confronted with the apparent stupidity of their logic, and are we not angered by their seemingly senseless attacks? How often do we think of having pity for them, of making atonement for their blindness, of looking upon them as sinning against God rather than against us? Yet the Immaculate Heart of Mary yearns over those same deluded Communists; she has expressly told us so.

Our Blessed Mother wants us to share her anxiety for the conversion of the world, to feel the agony of the crown of thorns pressing into her Son's Head, and of the sword piercing her own heart. She wants us to carry about with us in our daily work this deep anxiety for the conversion of souls, and a corresponding generosity in offering reparation for the sins of the world. Nearly a quarter of a century ago, Pope Pius XI decreed that the prayers recited by Catholic priests and faithful after daily Masses should be offered for the conversion of Russia. I wonder how many of us have said those prayers with a really fervent awareness of Russia's tragic needs?

The little addition that we make in our Chinese prayers in calling upon the Immaculate Heart of Mary to convert China is right in line with the revelation of Fatima. We are dedicating ourselves to the winning of this section of China to Christ. We are not merely physically present in China. Our hearts must be like the heart of Mary: anxious, yearning for the conversion of all our people—concerned particularly for the neediest, the purblind Communists. (*1947*)

The Challenge of Communism

IT WOULD BE WELL FOR US TO CONSIDER COMMUNISM IN relation to our own lives, because over here it is gradually becoming a great force, a terrible danger. Communism has infiltrated all through China. How are we to meet it? The Holy

Father says that Catholics must become aggressive in the spiritual warfare, and must not be afraid to try new methods in the immense struggle against the inroads of atheistic Communism. In this world crisis, each and every Catholic is obligated to battle for the faith even, if, in so doing, he become a fool for Christ's sake.

During the past three decades, Communists have gained many millions of adherents, even if we allow for the fact that terror has motivated countless "conversions" behind the iron and bamboo curtains. What is the secret of this success? It may be ascribed in part to the colossal optimism of convinced Communists. They are radiantly confident that their system is going to produce heaven on earth, to change the whole world. They refuse to consider obstacles or failures; their gaze is always fixed on the Red millennium just around the corner.

A second reason for the success of Communists is that they are not afraid to try new methods of propaganda. They refuse to abide by international laws; the only laws they abide by are those expedient for furthering their cause. They seek to infiltrate every foreign government; they send their agents into every country to agitate in secret. We would call their methods underhand, but they do not see it that way. The Holy Father has pointed out the efficiency of their so-called cell method, making converts one by one, and acting in small groups.

A third factor in the success of the Communists is that they have convinced themselves that their system is a real democracy, is what the people want, and that it answers humanity's needs. How they arrive at these conclusions is a mystery to us, but, if questioned, they answer that their system works, it produces results. Of course, despotic regimentation and slave labor do produce tangible results in a material way. Right here in Meihsien, for example, if the Government were to compel 50,000 people to labor for a month at dredging the river and building bridges, the city would be appreciably improved. But how about the individual laborers? The system would not take into account their neglected farms and hungry families, because in a Soviet "democracy" the individual rates only as a cog in a soulless State machine.

Finally, Communism appeals strongly to downtrodden people who have no happiness. It appeals to them as a last desperate remedy. Things cannot get worse than they are, they wrongly think, and perhaps conditions might improve.

The Holy Father says that we must use new ways of countering the methods employed by the Communists. In the first place, we must manifest our zeal for Catholicism as openly and fearlessly as the Communists labor for the advancement of their system. In the Western world, it is not considered good form these days to show enthusiasm; I think we are apt to be timid in preaching our religion. In my hostel for students it created quite a furor when one of the boys knelt down on the ground to say his prayers before getting into bed, in spite of the cold floor and the pagan students in the room with him. I realized then I had forgotten to tell the boys that praying in this way is a Christian custom. The example of this one Catholic student had a very good effect.

If we only had five minutes to say something to the world, we would certainly urge all men to acquire knowledge of Catholicism and seek salvation in the true Church. Well, we only have the time on hand, let us make the most of it. It would do us all good not to be afraid to manifest our joy in our religion. We cannot afford timidity in preaching the faith to pagans. Of all the people in the world, Catholics should be radiantly confident that the Church founded by Christ can triumph over all evils.

As for new methods, we can put them to good use, as do the Communists. We can counter the cell method by urging

255

each of our Chinese Catholics to win new converts for the Church. The average new catechumen is especially anxious to tell others about the wonderful religion that is now his. We should try all sorts of schemes, even if some of them fall flat at first. One of the weaknesses of Communism is that it is not based on reason, its arguments cannot stand up against a real test. But we Catholics have reason behind us. If we equip ourselves with all sorts of arguments, and study ways of propagating them, that method should have a telling effect.

Of course, we cannot adopt the underhand and unethical methods used by Communists to attract people to their form of government. But we can be more vigorous in searching out men of good will who have a basic desire to lead decent lives. We must feel ardently that we have been divinely commissioned to revolutionize the world. This is what St. Paul meant by saying that we must preach Christ "in season and out of season."

Let us, then, not be afraid to try every way of bringing people to think about God. At the same time we must avoid throwing cold water on ourselves or others, by foreseeing disaster or complaining of lack of success in previous efforts. In other words, keep a radiant hope. If our Holy Father, after 2,000 years of Catholicity, can tell us to start over again in the endeavor to spread and defend the Kingdom of God, we cannot say that he, our leader and model, is afraid to try new methods in meeting the challenge of Communism. (1948)

Hope

WHAT IS, PERHAPS, THE MOST STRIKING CHARACTERISTIC OF POPE Pius XII is his fighting ability. With half of Europe already in the bear hug of Communism, with thousands of priests and religious killed, and tens of thousands imprisoned or deported, with millions of Catholics homeless and hungry, the Holy Father does not take time off to lament. He challenges Catholics not to waste energy in merely denouncing Communism, but to demonstrate in their own lives the Christian spirit of hope.

We are apt to think of hope as resignation, as a grim virtue of hanging on in spite of difficulties, as perseverance in its negative aspect. Our Holy Father shows it as an active, positive virtue, as a fighting quality, as faith in action that leads to charity. Hope is a joyous confidence, a warm unhesitancy, an almost instinctive facing the future with assurance.

Hope, then, should be the spirit animating us in this beginning of a new year. Like the Crusaders of old when Catholic Europe was threatened by Moslem invasion, we take up arms with the cry: "God wills it." God put us here, in these conditions. So be it. He has overcome worse in the past, and He is with us.

There is a human tendency to imagine that we could do better work if we only had peace; that is, if we only had things the way we should like them. A little reflection will show us that not only is ideal peace never realized, but that perhaps it would even be dangerous for us, allowing us to settle softly into ruts and grooves of our own making. God's Church is a challenge to the world, not a compromise, and judging by the facts of history, God seems to have chosen pain and suffering as His way of winning souls. We must share in the Sacrifice of the Mass in order to apply its infinite merits to our ministry.

The virtue of hope is expressly reliance on God's power, rather than on our own efforts. Leaning on our own strength always begets discouragement, shame, frustration, and inevitable failure. Leaning on God's goodness towards us and on His power turns these same handicaps and drawbacks into purifying demonstrations of His assistance.

Hope at all times, not merely in a crisis, is an essential missionary virtue. In our work, we are thrown very much on our own resources. Consequently, we are prone to experience elation and pride when our judgment proves for the moment right, or dejection and discouragement when our project is hampered. The virtue of hope is the remedy for these weaknesses. It lifts us above the natural, and makes us lean on the omnipotence of God. It makes us wary of temporary and temporal aids and gives us, as it were, a sudden insight into God's vast plan of creation that settles everything into a correct perspective.

Hope is the most delicate compliment we can pay to God; it is akin to the entire confidence babies show in the sure protection of their mothers' arms, and God is bound to react to it. As the Old Testament puts it: "No one hath hoped in the Lord and hath been confounded." And our Lord says: "If you ask the Father anything in My Name, He will give it to you." The certainty of victory is a tremendous source of energy. "If God is for us, who is against us?"

When we hope, we are Christians; despair is simply another name for paganism. We are God's coadjutors, and He will make up what is lacking in our strength. To yield to downhearted fear of the Communist menace would be to succumb to the temptation of taking a pagan view of life. Such an attitude would frustrate our missionary vocation and defeat the very purpose for which we are battling.

We begin our year's work, then, confident in God's power. In fact, I am sure God wants us to have big ambitions for Him. We should even have what the world would consider overconfidence that God wants the millions in this mission field to be converted. We know it is God's plan; we know that it is within God's power; we know God can accomplish the seemingly impossible, even through us. So there is no need of calculating on defeat. There is nothing to fear. There need be no hesitancy in giving ourselves entirely and with assurance to the conversion of our people. (*1949*)

Perseverance

NOW THAT WE HAVE A LULL IN THE THREATENED PERSECUTION of the Church, it might not hurt us to take stock. Probably all of us felt a twinge of conscience when the Communists took over this region, and, in consequence, we experienced new fervor in our prayers and motives. Even the best of us, no doubt, gave a sigh of relief when our region was again retaken by the Nationalist troops. The natural reaction to this relief would be to settle back into routine, postponing the execution of whatever good resolutions we made.

It may be, however, that God has allowed us this lull in order to ease us gently into the path of persecution. Certainly it is only a lull. To face probabilities calmly, we may consider it likely that our section will be retaken by the Communists within a few months. This should not mean dismay, nor should it discourage us in any way from persevering in our appointed duties. God needs us; He needs us here in our mission, and He is with us and knows our condition.

At this time, it might help us to recall that God has been called the "Hound of Heaven." We have shirked pain and humiliation, and have tried to fashion our lives according to our own wishes; but the Hound of Heaven persists in pursuing us and gives us no rest in our daydreams. This does not mean that we have to forego joy, but rather that we must learn to joy in being allowed to suffer with Christ. It means interior peace in restraint. Instead of shirking inconveniences, we have to train ourselves to welcome them, as coming from God to purify us.

If persecution is swift and clear-cut, there is no chance for preparation; indeed, there is less need of preparation under such circumstances, for God tells us what to say and do. But we need to steel our hearts to gain merit from a tedious, petty persecution that never builds up to an acute crisis. It is then the natural virtues fail us, unless they are based on supernatural motives.

The pierced Hand of Christ extended to us may well be hidden under annoying and ugly derision. We may not recognize our Lord's Passion in the vexations of impediments to our work, and each incident may seem so obviously motivated by human hatreds that it may be hard to receive it as God's will. It needs more training to seek God among the rough stones of a dusty road than in the beauty of a sunset, and in the case of man-made harshness, we are further blinded by our own human pride. But perseverance in seeking Christ in His more baffling disguises will make us keen in knowing Him, when He calls us to share in the drinking of His chalice.

Perseverance is a Latin word that means "going through to the truth"; the underlying truth beneath all petty and severe persecutions is God's will. The motto of our diocesan shield is *condolere,* which means to "feel with," to share in suffering, to see all human passions from the viewpoint of Christ's Passion. If we go through to the underlying truth in all that befalls us, we shall preserve true peace of mind in the days ahead, no matter how our Saviour manifests Himself.

This does not necessarily mean a change in our conduct. Indeed, where we are facing in the right direction, perseverance almost implies continuing in the same path. But it may mean perceiving, instead of merely gazing—seeing through to the truth, instead of shying off at appearances. We Americans are unaccustomed to putting up with inconveniences, and we are not exercised in the natural virtues of patience and humility, so for us the going may be harder.

In any event, our vocation implies immolation, and our lives are no longer ours to dispose of. We have offered ourselves to be used as God sees fit, and those words are not empty formulas. We have no natural or supernatural right to lives free from persecution. Persecution was given us as a legacy and a promise by our Saviour, and a mark of identification with Him. When the Church challenges force incarnate in Communism, she invites persecution.

If persecution comes, we will persevere in our present work so far as we may be allowed, sure that it is God's will and that He can turn evil into good. The world-wide persecution of the Church, and her sufferings in which we have so small a share, may bring about in God's own time a rebirth of the faith in all nations. If we share in Christ's Passion, we shall also share in His Resurrection. (*1949*)

The Church in Communist China

COMMUNISM IN CHINA TOOK ADVANTAGE OF THE DISORGANIZATION of a very loosely knit country that was toddling in its first steps towards democratic, responsible government. The people did not welcome Communism; they tried to remain merely passive. If in civic-minded Europe the Soviets discovered that a handful could control a region, so much the easier was it for the Communists in China, where concerted resistance is unknown and united action untried. Then, too, the Chinese is tied to the land almost as closely as agricultural laborers were in feudal Europe; he is not free to move elsewhere, and, hence, he submits to any officialdom without much thought of resisting graft or redressing wrong.

The real strength of Communism in China is absolute suppression of freedom of expression, coupled with a mastery of propaganda. In the past, national and provincial affairs were unknown to the people to an incredible degree, except through rumor by word of mouth. Communism capitalized on this vacuum, by infiltrating fifth columnists into all ranks of society.

Thus, it was left to the Church to voice the sole articulate opposition to the underlying evils of Communism. And the Church in China, though rooted in a sound farming class, is numerically insignificant and lacks the means for quick, efficient propaganda. Nevertheless, almost overnight the Catholic body was recognized, even by puzzled pagans, as the one anti-Communist force in evidence throughout China, clearly taking a stand on moral and doctrinal grounds. Foreign bishops, priests, and religious stood steadfast at their posts. The devotion to their faith of both Chinese priests and Chinese Catholics parallels the most glorious annals of Christian martyrdom.

Communist persecution of religion in China follows the same tactics as elsewhere in the Soviet world. Freedom of religion is promulgated, but this illusory proclamation is immediately followed by a program of anti-religious propaganda, coupled with absolute suppression of adverse criticism and a rigid control of information. As the controls press deeper, we foresee a more severe persecution.

Can the Church continue to function in Communist China? The answer is yes, provided continuity be not lost and the minimum of tolerance allow the administration of the sacraments. The Catholics of China are not, for the most part, city dwellers. They live in small towns and villages fairly evenly distributed over the vast land, and history has shown that the

Chinese farmer depends on his own resources to survive all hardships. Even if persecution reaches the stage where the Church can no longer function openly, the stamina of the sturdy Catholic farmers will aid them to persevere in the faith. The traditional Catholic life of Chinese villagers has been centered on family prayers rather than on Church services. It is more independent of the liturgy than in Western lands, and thus more capable of survival under persecution. (*1949*)

LITURGICAL YEAR IN CHINA

"In these days we need to think of the Passion of Christ. We do not know how God is going to test us. . . . To daydream about martyrdom is not enough, we have to gain the grace of so inestimable a privilege, we have to be worthy of it. We must be wholly laved in the Blood of Christ, our garments must be red."

"Live the Truth in Charity"

The conferences in this section of the book were preached by Bishop Ford to various groups of his priests and Sisters, and circulated among the others in their mission outposts. Bishop Ford was a realist who faced squarely the fact that missioners engaged in the direct apostolate are often, during long stretches of time, deprived of the usual external aids to the spiritual life. He was consequently untiring in the sharing of his own deep spirituality with his co-workers.

He taught them to consider spiritual deprivations as part of the mission vocation, because apostles must be constantly at the disposal of the people. It is for the missioners to grow strong in a sacrificial inner life of close union with God. Bishop Ford seemed to sense the least sign of timidity in apostolic action, and he vigorously instilled the courage and confidence befitting those who labor for Christ and so can do all things in Him who strengthens them. Among his favorite expressions in conferences were: "Live the truth in charity," and the words of our divine Saviour, "Learn of Me, because I am meek and humble of heart."

Advent

The word Advent indicates the approach of someone, and has the underlying significance that this approach is an adventure, something daring and bold with an unforeseen result.

The descent of God the Son from Heaven to earth was a coming, rather than a going, for His delight was to be with the children of men and He saw this world as His. It was a coming to take possession of His kingdom, not an attack against us; it was a homecoming. Advent implies not a state but a movement, not an arrival but an adventurous journey. That is an aspect of the Saviour's coming which should inspire in us anxiety and loving longing, as if we were watching the first unsure steps of an infant.

God has set forth to become incarnate on earth, and all Heaven holds its breath in watching the experiment. All other adventure that can befall mankind is as nothing in comparison with this surpassing manifestation of God's tender longing for the fallen human race. God humbles Himself and empties Himself of His majesty to win a way among strangers. He comes to men as an Infant with wavering step, that they may rush forward to pick Him up. The issue of His coming in our case lies with each one of us, not with Him, for He has taken the first step and is toddling toward us.

How human is our religion, how homely is truth! False religion cannot unbend, because it is a dead skeleton; it cannot cry or laugh, because it has no heart. The pagan gods are represented as being coarse and brutal, violent or deadly calm, even as being dignified in a cold, heartless majesty, aloof from man. Only we Christians have a God so near to us that He can be cuddled and cradled in His daring adventure into our hearts.

It is the risk of this adventure of God into men's hearts that gives us missioners warrant for our vocation. We are heralds of a King who asks, not demands, allegiance. Our human willingness must clear and straighten His path, so that His coming may not be impeded. He gambles on our co-operation, as well as on the hearts of pagans. The King has left His heavenly home with confidence in our generosity; He ventures forth, counting on our care—God has placed Himself in our keeping. Was there ever another adventure so risky as this one?

"The weak things of the world hath God chosen that He may confound the strong." Both in His own coming, and in us, His instruments, the daring adventure of God becomes a series of heroic little acts. He asks of us missioners fidelity to duty in the small acts that make up our day. God is saving the world as an Infant, and only in childlike humility can we succeed in making straight His way. Our daydreams of grandiose accomplishment fit in ill at the crib, where the Christ Child's delight in just being with men is a rebuke to our impatience of results. He learned how to walk the small ways of human life, and we must keep step with Him.

Advent, then, is a time to renew our youth spiritually; to learn to stretch out our hand tentatively, as He did, to the strangers around us; to break the crust of our grumpiness and try a smile. It would not hurt us to remember that our religion is the only source of this world's joy, and it is both natural and supernatural to smile with the Infant Adventurer.

Advent is an adventure for us as well as for our Saviour, a time to serve Christ with an alert spirit and a changed heart, risking ourselves and forgetting ourselves as we make way for His coming into Chinese souls. If we make this an adventurous Advent, the Christmas crib will find us breathless with joy. Indeed, not only this beautiful season, but life itself, is meaningless if it is not an adventure, because our time on earth is a test and trial, not an end in itself.

At the Christmas Crib

THE CLOSING DAYS OF DECEMBER ARE CHILL, BARREN, AND DARK. The year is drawing to its end, and it is natural for endings to bring solemn thoughts of the finality of blasted hopes. But God chose to be born at this time, and thus to transform the dark days into a season of radiant joy. By His coming He "renewed the face of the earth." In some mysterious way, all creatures shared in God's salvation of mankind. There is a unity in God's working. He is consistent in the use of simple things. He makes use of simple elements for His sacraments, and of simple people as his instruments.

In the cave-stable at Bethlehem, so many centuries ago, Mary knew that the Child to be born of her womb was the Second Person of the Blessed Trinity, the Expected of the Nations, He who would shine forth as the Light and Life of the World. But the coming of the King of kings was devoid of all pomp and majesty; in the midst of the silence of the night Divine Wisdom came down to earth. His throne was a couple of pieces of wood nailed together, like the wood later to be fashioned into His cross. His bedding was straw, the food of lowly animals. He was wrapped in simple swaddling clothes, like the bands which would enshroud His wounded Body in the Holy Sepulcher. Poor as it was, the stable was a better shelter than Mary's Son would have while He went about calling men to the heavenly Kingdom. Then, Jesus would have no place to lay His head.

Mary was full of grace, which means full of faith. Her selfless humility was in no wise scandalized by the simple surroundings God had chosen for His Son's first earthly court. Nor was she dismayed when the first who came to worship the infant King were poor shepherds from the neighboring hills, rather than the potentates of this world. St. Ambrose tells us that Mary united in faith with the shepherds, and that thus her own faith acquired new vigor. If we share some measure of Mary's humility, we have had similar experiences. How often our faith is strengthened by some simple observation made about God by our Chinese catechumens. The profound truth of their insight is so simple that we did not hitherto perceive it.

Mary and St. Joseph, the devoted guardian of the Holy Family, were completely attuned to the message brought to mankind by the Divine Infant. His message is one of peace. Not merely cessation of human warfare, but the peace of union with God in His plan for the renewal of the face of the earth. At Bethlehem the wood and the straw of the crib, and the swaddling clothes, shared in God's plan by their service of the Infant Saviour. God's peace was upon the cattle and the sheep, as they drew near to warm the Child with their sweet breath.

A far greater share in the peace of union with God is offered by the Christ Child to the souls of men, ransomed and renewed at so infinite a price. Let us, then, confirm at the crib our understanding of God's plan for us. The loved and simple surroundings of the Saviour's birth will help us to realize that everything we see and touch and hear is given to us as a message to remind us of His purpose—the salvation of the world.

New Year's Eve

ON THIS LAST DAY OF THE YEAR IT MIGHT BE WELL FOR US TO ask ourselves in what spirit we go about our work. Have we the same spirit in us that is in Christ Jesus? When we first took up this active apostolate we experienced a natural exhilaration and pleasure. In the early days we rejoiced over even the promise of a conversion. If someone smiled at us, we came home full of enthusiasm over the prospects in such and such a village. After a while, however, a good deal of the first buoyancy of spirit disappeared, we began almost to take our mission work for granted. In any phase of life there is a danger of losing the appreciation of the sacredness of our task, when doing it becomes mere routine.

It may help us to readjust our viewpoint if we consider our work as Christ sees it. After all, we have the most thrilling vocation in the world, the privilege of making straight the way of the Lord in towns and little villages. Do we appreciate the fact that the manner of our apostolate is patterned on the active ministry of our divine Lord Himself? He did not settle down and wait for the multitudes to approach Him.

In the scenes immortalized by the New Testament, we see Christ on a road, walking through fields of grain, on a boat, or, if He is in a house, it is always someone else's home. He even partook of His last supper and instituted the sacrament of Holy Eucharist in an inn, which proves that He had no place to lay His Head. All the while He was teaching His Apostles and founding His Church, but it was the Church of the wayside and of homes where He was made welcome.

Our Lord went wherever He was invited, and He always granted some grace to His hosts, as He did at the marriage feast of Cana. He did not refuse the advances of Gentiles. At the well of Samaria He used the pretext of asking a woman for a drink of water, in order to be invited into a pagan city. Christ yearned to bring grace into every town and hamlet, but He waited for an invitation. He did not force Himself on deliberately unwilling souls.

Now that He has ascended into Heaven, our Lord depends on the co-operation of His missioners for the growth of His Church of the wayside in pagan lands. Have we ourselves ardently invited Christ to help us in our apostolate? Our hearts, too, can burn with the joy of His presence, if we entreat Him to abide with us on our mission journeys. We are apt to associate the presence of God with our chapel, but perhaps He wants us to find Him by the wayside, in the homes of pagans. It may be that He is saving the grace He desires to give us for those moments when we are really founding the Church with Him—out on the road.

This coming year, then, let us renew and deepen the joy of our apostolate by selfless invitation of Christ into our own hearts, in order that His power over the souls of pagans may operate through our labors. Above all, let us be grateful that our Lord has given us the sublime vocation of co-operating in the growth of His Church of the wayside among China's pagan multitudes.

The New Year

WE COULD NOT TALK ABOUT GOD IF WE DID NOT TALK ABOUT Him in a human way; so God used our vocabulary in His dealings with us. In the terms of that human vocabulary, we are justified in saying that God likes to be thanked. Surely, He must like to be thanked above all on New Year's Day, at the turning of a new page in our lives.

In his Epistle to the Ephesians, St. Paul told his converts to be thankful always to God for all things. If we wanted one single phrase on which to model our lives, perhaps we could find it in those words, "be thankful always to God for all things." When we give thanks to God we forget our selfish interests and think of others; then our whole being becomes lightsome and joyous.

These are difficult times in China, but our thanksgiving must not be dimmed by discouragement. Imagine our Lord on the night before He died. He took bread, broke it, and gave it to His Apostles. Then, raising His eyes, He gave thanks. He instituted the Eucharistic Sacrifice, the Sacrifice of Calvary, perpetuated always on the altar; and the word Eucharist means "thanksgiving." At the supreme moment of His earthly life, when He was about to face the world's greatest tragedy, Christ gave thanks to His Father in Heaven. He gave thanks for the benefits of the Cross, benefits which at that time looked like pure calamity and were later to be revealed as the salvation of the world.

Thanksgiving is the most unselfish, the most Godlike, act of which we are capable. We have to learn how to give thanks. Of course, the ideal way of rendering thanks is by sharing in the Holy Sacrifice of the Altar. Only in the Sacrifice of the Mass is God fittingly thanked. Therein, as Man, Christ thanks His Father for every trial that has been given to humankind. We become truly a part of the Eucharistic Sacrifice by uniting with Christ in thanking God for everything that has happened to us. Then all things are seen in their correct perspective. We acknowledge that everything that befalls has been willed by God out of His love for us, and so we thank Him for the bitter as well as for the sweet.

That is what prayer consists of, the recognition of our dependence upon God. Our voluntary recognition of that dependence gives us a share in creation, and we make the new year a truly new season. The fire of the Holy Spirit burns up in us everything against His will and we become wholly attuned to God. We are renewing the face of the earth. Nothing can befall us in the new year that is not according to God's plan, and if whatever befalls is according to His plan, it is the most perfect thing that could happen to us.

The Epiphany

THE EPIPHANY IS AN ANCIENT ORIENTAL FESTIVAL ON WHICH baptisms took place in the East, and in earlier times it was not even celebrated in the West. The word Epiphany means "shining forth" or "shining through," a light which transforms. Originally, the reference was chiefly to the star—"We have seen His star in the East."

One day, when I was in Rome with our Father Founder, we went into a sculptor's workroom. He showed us an alabaster Madonna, and when he turned on an electric light behind the statue, the dead substance was transformed. You could almost see life in the statue, because the light shone through. It is said that everyone is a man of one idea, and I suppose I could say my idea is that everything in the universe is a sacramental. Our Lord insists so often on light and life. He called Himself the Light and Life of the World.

On this Feast of the Epiphany, the Godhead shone forth and was revealed to the Gentiles in the Infant Saviour. Christ became incarnate, suffered the death of the Cross, and rose again from the dead, in order that the beauty of the Godhead might shine also through us. Everyone in the world, every Christian and every pagan, is called upon to show forth God. That is the sole purpose of all human life, and without it our missionary vocation would be meaningless.

We have dedicated ourselves to revealing the Epiphany to those who have not seen its splendor. But unless we ourselves receive actively the Light of Christ, it will not shine forth through us so that pagans may walk in its radiance. "To those who receive Him, He gives power to be sons of God"—and to draw others into union with the Trinity. By a deepening of our active union with Christ on this Feast of His Revelation to the Gentiles, we are reborn as missioners of the lifegiving Light of the World.

The Church Unity Octave

DO WE STOP TO REALIZE THE EDUCATIONAL VALUE OF BELONGING to the Catholic Church? No other organization has so perfect an instrument for teaching as the Calendar of Feasts. In the hands of a devoted teaching brother or Sister, the Calendar becomes a fruitful adjunct of history, geography, social science, and general culture; its saints and events should be the chief inspirational matter presented to our parochial-school children. Especially is this remarkable about the missionary side of the Church, for the lives of her Apostles and pioneers and martyrs will open the minds of our children to the important thought of the universality and continuity of the Church's mission.

The Calendar is fittingly divided and the feasts are psychologically well seasoned. After Christmas, when our thoughts are focused on the Infant Saviour, when our hearts have been quickened with love and the interchange of gifts with friends has drawn us outside ourselves and petty preoccupations, the Church gives us the Epiphany to direct our thoughts to the East, and continuing during the month of January she offers us the Church Unity Octave.

During these eight days of the Church Unity Octave, January 18-25, starting on the Feast of St. Peter's Chair at Rome and ending on the Feast of the Conversion of St. Paul, our Holy Father and the bishops of America exhort us to unite in prayer for the conversion of the world. On the opening day the intention is a general one, for the return of all the "other sheep" to the one true fold of Peter. The feast itself is a call on all of us to offer homage to the center of Christendom, and when we join with this our prayers for those outside the fold we testify to the universal jurisdiction entrusted to Peter by the Lord of all.

The nineteenth is the Feast of Sts. Marius, Martha and their sons, Oriental noblemen who came to Rome and then were martyred. The octave intention of this second day is the return of all Oriental Christians to communion with the Holy See. The twentieth is the Feast of St. Fabian, the martyred Pope who sent St. Dionysius and other missioners to France, whence England was converted. The intention, then, on the third day of the octave is the submission of all Anglicans to the authority of the Vicar of Christ.

The Feast of St. Agnes on the twenty-first glorifies virginal purity, a stumbling block of the Protestant Reformation, and our prayers on this day are for the conversion of the Protestants of Europe. The twenty-second is the Feast of St. Anastasius and of St. Vincent. The former was a Persian soldier who, through curiosity as to the meaning of the cross, was converted and became a missioner in Syria, where he suffered martyrdom; St. Vincent, a Spaniard who showed courage while being roasted on a gridiron. During the fifth day of the octave we are asked to consider the millions of Christians in America who are not Catholics.

On the twenty-third the Church celebrates the Feast of St. Raymond, the zealous preacher who went throughout Europe and inspired the hearts of an almost incredible number of lukewarm Catholics, and on this day we are called upon to pray for the return to the sacraments of lapsed Catholics. St. Timothy, the companion of St. Paul, and a Jew, is commemorated on the twenty-fourth, on which day we are asked to pray for the conversion of the Jews. The last day of the

277

octave falls on the Feast of the Conversion of St. Paul and fittingly strikes the keynote of our prayers for the conquest of the whole world for Christ, the King of kings.

If the Catholics throughout the world, as is the wish of our Holy Father who is offering Mass during these days for the intentions of the octave, were to redouble their prayers for the conversion of those outside the fold, the united prayers that would storm Heaven would without doubt mark the year as a Pentecostal renewal. Our participation in this octave will at least enlarge our viewpoint, broaden our charity, and make us see in every man a brother whom Christ is yearning to welcome to His sacraments.

St. Patrick

In the fourth century of the Christian era, the pagan Irish made slave-hunting raids on England. During one of these raids, it is said, Patrick, then a boy fifteen years of age, was captured and taken to Ireland. He himself tells us in his autobiography that he had been baptized, but knew little about God. In Ireland the boy was put to work as a pigherd, his life was hard and his food of the meanest. For ten long years, Patrick led the lonesome, hard life of a pigherd—which was not a bad preparation for a missionary career. Missioners need to depend as little as possible on social life.

Then Patrick escaped, by walking 200 miles through an unknown country until he found a boatman willing to take him across the sea. The boatman intended to resell the young man as a slave, but Patrick escaped again and gradually worked his way back to his home in England. It was while he tended pigs on the hillside in Ireland that he had first thought of becoming a priest and a missioner. But now he was twenty-five years old and had never studied; he was brave to begin his education from the lowest grade.

Overcoming the reasonable objections of his relatives, Patrick struggled through the elements of education and then crossed over to France to continue his studies. When he disclosed to the authorities in the French monastery his ambition to return to Ireland as a missioner, he was laughed at as an ignorant man and an escaped slave who would be in constant peril of recapture. Patrick persevered in his intention, however, and finally won his superior's consent to his ordination to the priesthood. The tenacious man was later raised to the episcopate, and set out with a small group of fellow missioners to the pagan shores of Ireland. On landing, he was twice recaptured as an escaped slave, but was fortunately each time released.

There had already been apostles in Ireland along the east coast, but they had made little impression. Patrick, knowing the customs of the country, adapted Christianity to the people. Ireland was a land of clans, and by setting up churches, monasteries, convents, schools and catechumenates for each clan, Patrick soon organized the Church in each valley. We must not think of him as a great patriarch with brilliant abilities. He plodded along persistently, and finally so successfully that he built several hundred churches, ordained about 5,000 priests, and consecrated over 300 bishops.

St. Patrick introduced many human touches into his apostolate. He had wooden swords made for the children, on which were written the catechism and prayers; as the little ones played they memorized the doctrine. He took his seminarians around with him during his ceaseless missionary journeys. In fact, he traveled with quite a large group of teachers, cooks, and even girls to sew vestments. His miniature migratory congregation served as a visible example to the new converts.

Patrick's life as a missioner packed tremendous work into

his travels; he covered the length and breadth of the island. The people were not easy to convert; they tried to assassinate him on the road, and he was often robbed. But there was something harder still to endure. One of his bishops accused him to Rome of a fault committed in his early youth. He was demoted as leader of the Church in Ireland, and even his best friends turned against him in his ignominy. Fortunately, he lived to be reinstated and vindicated.

It seems to me that our lives here in China parallel that of St. Patrick in many ways. We, too, experience somewhat the lonely life he led and adapt ourselves to a strange environment. We have many misunderstandings, petty though they may be, and the magnitude of the work ahead is a temptation to discouragement. We might ask ourselves whether or not we are prone to exaggerate our own difficulties all of which are picayune in the light of St. Patrick's life. His missionary career tells us how to face daily discouragement, tedium, and apparent failure. Like St. Patrick, we must live with Christ before us and behind us, all around and within us, to the right side and to the left—we must make Christ our sole friend and helper.

The Annunciation

THE FEAST OF THE ANNUNCIATION FOCUSES THE ATTENTION ON obedience. "Behold the handmaid of the Lord," says the Blessed Virgin, "be it done unto me according to Thy Word." Obedience is something fundamental. Every work of the Creator is called to perfection, and perfection consists in obedience. Imperfection is "I will not serve"—the sin of Lucifer, of Adam and Eve, and of each one of us. It all gets down very simply to nothing more than that. The heavens and the earth inevitably announce the glory of God, but He has granted us free will. By a free, creative act we manifest God when we serve Him in glad obedience.

The great Rule of St. Benedict, founded on that of St. Augustine, deals wholly with the vow of obedience. It does not mention the vow of chastity or the vow of poverty. That is because St. Benedict sees obedience as the foundation of all virtues. There are, of course, various degrees of obedience. Perfect obedience is conformity not merely of the will but also of the emotions. When a mother is out walking and holds out her hand to her child, the little one can put his hand in hers reluctantly and be dragged along, or he can take her hand unquestioningly, confidently, and gladly. The latter sort of obedience should be our aim.

Obedience of any kind requires sacrifice. The very belief in God, in His Church, and in His sacraments requires more than a mere rational, natural act. It demands our creative will to obey, the sacrifice of our own proud judgment. But we as Catholics have believed all our lives in God and His Church. When we are dealing directly with God, we normally find satisfaction in obedience. He has promised, "You do this, and I will reward it." The sacrifice really pinches, though, when we are called upon to obey other human beings as the representatives of God's authority.

It goes truly against the grain to give unquestioning and glad obedience to another human being with whom we rub elbows, perceiving all too clearly his faults and apparent lack of judgment. We know a better method of doing a thing, or a more practical solution of a difficulty. So we think, and it may be true from a human viewpoint. But from God's viewpoint, we do not know better than our superiors. He chooses the weak things of the world to confound the strong.

St. Catherine of Siena knew that Pope Gregory XI was not a strong character. She did not hesitate to tell him plainly that it was his duty as Pope to leave Avignon and take the Papal Court back to Rome. Nevertheless, Catherine was always mindful of the fact that Gregory was the Vicar of Christ. She ended one of her letters of exhortation with the words: "Take care, or else I will have to complain to Jesus Christ about you, because you have no other superior on this earth." It took perfectly obedient faith on the part of the saint for her to recognize in the vacillating Gregory XI her highest superior in this world.

Obedience is a double-edged sword, and I can assure you from personal experience that I was happier when I could just obey superiors than I am now, when I have to give commands. In the seminary obedience was easy for me, though it was a real stumbling block to some of the others. That was because I grew up as a very junior member of a large family. Now, on the other hand, I find it hard to issue commands. Obedience is easier from the giving than from the receiving end.

Obedience is seeing God in everything—"I live now not I, but Christ liveth in me." On the Feast of the Annunciation, the obedience of Mary brought Christ down on earth to save fallen humanity. We, too, are called upon to co-operate with God in His creation. The glory of God awaits our human word of obedient consent. With the help of the Mother of Christ may our response be, like hers, not slavish, but humbly exultant in the wonder of the divine will.

Easter

THE VERY NAME OF EASTER, WHICH IS THE MOST IMPORTANT festival of the Church, is borrowed from other religions, whether we call the feast the Pasch or Easter. Pasch is the name for the principal festival of the Jews, the Passover, while Easter was an Anglo-Saxon goddess of light or spring-time. The Catholic Church is so sure of herself that she can afford to tolerate the Christmas tree, holly, mistletoe, the Easter egg, and dozens of other pagan additions to her feasts. She has adapted pagan incense and candles and her basilicas were made-over pagan buildings. Only a Church sure of herself can be indulgent in minor importations; it is the weak State that must guard its frontiers and employ hordes of secret police.

This toleration of harmless, or potentially harmless, pagan customs might even be a deliberate use of material at hand to show us that matter in itself is God-given and to be used for God, even though it have pagan associations. It seems to be common-sense that the Church must build on the natural material at her disposal. When you are trying to explain prayer to a pagan, you must start with terms that are familiar to him and 'baptize' them. Even our term for 'God' in Chinese is an example of this; pioneer missioners chose the nearest approximation to Catholic orthodoxy from among the many pagan terms of the spirit world. So it was natural for the early Christians to talk of the festival of our Lord's Resurrection in terms of somewhat similar feasts with which they were familiar.

This assimilation of pagan natural to supernatural ends is even in line with the Feast of Easter itself. We commemorate the resurrection of our Lord's human body and, in consequence, mankind's resurrection from the dead. Perhaps, falling back on my usual habit of renaming things, if we were to call Easter the "Feast of New Life" we would be more conscious of its meaning. It is the victory over death. Perhaps, after all, the "Victory" might be the most appropriate name for Easter. "Victory" is related to the word "victim," and at Easter we exult in the Paschal Victim, while we cry with the Church: "O Death, where is thy sting?"

We Catholics, then, are familiar with the belief in the life beyond the grave and, perhaps, are not conscious that the fact of survival after death can be startling news to those outside the Church. Recently, Soviet students were electrified on coming across a Christian statement of belief in a future life after death. But do we ourselves have the correct viewpoint. about death? The inevitable fact of death, the only sure event in our existence, is so completely avoided in our thoughts that we must consciously use effort to direct our attention to it. Perhaps this is because we are affected by ambient materialistic abhorrence of death, and we have dropped the early Christian custom of saying that it is "sleeping in the Lord."

Should there be anything sad about death? There is a physical dread of death that has little or nothing to do with moral values, except to enhance the courage in one who physically dreads yet endures for higher motives. We are men, not angels, and can rarely escape the penalty of having nerves and an imagination. So, if the thought of death is depressing and disquieting, this may be a salutary sadness not incompatible with warm acceptance of God's Will. If sacrifice were pure joy, it would lose its meaning.

Yet I cannot help thinking that St. Paul would have little sympathy with such feelings, that he would counsel us to face death as God's method of making us victims, that is to say, consecrated to Him. Death is God's way of purifying earthly life, of rendering mankind adjusted to life in Heaven. And Easter, the victory over death in our Lord's Resurrection, is a pledge of our own future existence, a guarantee by God that death is not the end, but the entry into a new life.

In our active missionary work here in China we can all too easily become absorbed in preoccupations with petty trivialities, and thus subordinate God's view to urgent local problems. We should welcome the long-range view that the thought of death supplies, as a needed corrective of distorted myopia in daily concerns. Death is the one thing that we should glow over and exult in. It is the one guarantee that justifies our dedication to our religious vocation. It brings the day of our nuptials, of union with God for all eternity, the day of release from imperfect intercourse with God to a life of understanding and immediate assimilation.

The Ascension

THE FEAST OF THE ASCENSION IS OF GREAT MISSIONARY significance. On this day, before our Lord ascended into Heaven, He constituted His Church as a missionary organization, saying: "All power is given to Me in Heaven and on earth. Going therefore, teach ye all nations, baptizing them in the name of the Father and of the Son and of the Holy Ghost."

This command must have been a startling revelation to the Apostles and disciples gathered on Mount Tabor. At that time religion was considered a national affair. Even the religion of the Jews, of those who believed in the true God, was clannish and restricted with few exceptions to the Jews themselves. But the distinguishing mark of the true Church of Christ was to be catholicity, universality. The mission of this Catholic Church was to penetrate and to transform the whole world.

Unhappily, the Church has had its periods of lassitude in one part of the globe or another, but each century has shown it conscious of its duty to some extent. Deeper clarification of the history of the so-called dark ages and of the Renaissance is gradually proving that the Church has always been active in propagating the faith. The Vatican Archives have yet to yield their story of continual and continuous apostolic efforts.

Even here on the missions we should constantly keep before our minds the apostolic vocation of the Church. Why is this necessary? Because history shows that human beings always have a tendency to relax, to attain equilibrium, to settle down, to become static—and this is fatal to our calling. Once the brick-and-mortar stage is attained, there is a tendency to halt in admiration of what has been accomplished, to assume an historical viewpoint, and thus soon to become a museum piece ourselves.

The first stages of this decay are insidious, because they appear more or less justified. Having attained our first objectives, we want to dig in, on the pretext of holding them. Soon, our dug-out is enlarged, and then our energies are consumed in embellishing it. But the routine of city parishes in the more luxuriant days of a Church that has settled down is not for mission countries. We are the itinerant salesmen of a Church on the march, using wind, water, alleys, and byways to spread the Gospel—nature's method, so to speak.

This must always be our way of life. We cannot afford to look back, to ease up, and to settle down. Even in well-intentioned concentration of our efforts on a home base, there is danger of forgetting our Lord's command. Let us beg God, then, to grant us a constant appreciation of the splendor of our missionary vocation, a vocation that demands delivery of a message to the thousands in their villages who sit in the shadow of death.

Pentecost

ADORATION OF THE THIRD PERSON OF THE BLESSED TRINITY IS less emphasized in popular devotions than adoration of the sacred humanity of Christ, because it does not lend itself so readily to simple explanation. It should be a special devotion, however, of priests and Sisters engaged in apostolic work. Ordinarily, when people are buying a new automobile, they are much attracted by the outward appearance of the car—its neat lines and roomy seats and its upholstery—but a scientist gives attention rather to its engine and chassis. The Holy Spirit is the motive power in the Church, and as specialists in religion we should study His actions.

Let us try to picture the first Pentecost. Our Blessed Mother and the Apostles were gathered together in the cenacle in prayer. The Apostles, still simple fishermen unskilled in dealing with a hostile hierarchy and government, were agonizingly aware of their own weakness. They had recently passed through the harrowing experience of persecution, betrayal, denial, and of seeing their Divine Founder crucified. It is true that our Lord had later spent forty days with them, thus clarifying their doubts and focusing their minds on their future apostolate, but they were still timid, very few in number, and entirely surrounded by enemies beyond the locked doors.

Our Lord had left the Apostles principles, but theirs was the appalling task of applying the principles to immediate problems. They had been assured that the Church would overcome all enemies, but they did not have the advantage we possess of twenty centuries of proof. They confronted a greater problem of conversion than any other missioners; it was their task to lay the foundations and to speak of ideas hitherto unknown. No wonder their hearts failed them. God chooses the weak things of this world to confound the strong, and the Church was at its very weakest before Pentecost.

This is the first lesson we can learn from the feast, that

God the Comforter gives us our strength, and it is only when we realize our own weakness that we can lean on His might. When conditions are beyond our power to overcome, when we have done our poor utmost to co-operate with the grace of God, then we can confidently expect the Paraclete. It is useless to worry about the future, about things that may never happen. If, realizing our own weakness, we throw ourselves wholeheartedly into God's work, then God and we are invincible, because nothing is really important when measured against His strength.

Another lesson we may with profit derive from this Feast of Pentecost is that suffering may be God's plan for the purifying of our motives. It is human to avoid suffering, but pain accepted in advance may be God's way of uniting us more closely to Himself. Our Lord said: "If the world hate you, know ye, that it hath hated Me before you." As Christians we should share in the Cross, expiating our own sins and those of other men. This need not worry or terrify us, we have but to recall the tremendous words of St. Paul: "I can do all things in Him who strengtheneth me."

Our Lady, Queen of China

ON THE LAST DAY OF MAY, WE CELEBRATE THE FEAST OF OUR Lady Mediatrix of All Graces and Queen of China. Today's Gospel shows us that our Blessed Mother was made the dispenser of God's favors, not when she was gloriously crowned in Heaven, but when she stood on Calvary at the foot of the cross. She was officially appointed as Queen of China by the Pope, Christ's Vicar on earth. Neither of these titles is an empty one; Christ and His Church do not bestow meaningless titles.

In these troublous days, when China is cut off from the free world and difficulties abound in our apostolic work, we should thank God wholeheartedly for the favors we continue to receive daily through our Lady, Mediatrix of All Graces. I am reminded of an occasion when St. Francis of Assisi and Brother Giles went out begging. Brother Giles talked much of where and how they might successfully beg for food, but St. Francis interrupted his companion every moment with praises of God for the weeds and flowers along the wayside. When we become too absorbed in the practical worries of the good Brother Giles, then it is time to listen for the joyous interruptions of St. Francis.

The sufferings of the present time are not essentially evil, because it is during pain that individuals and nations turn to God. God's favors, bestowed on us through Mary, come to us in ways we could not have foreseen. World War I stressed the need of an indigenous clergy in mission lands, and the Pope began to appoint Asiatic and African bishops. The Church became young and apostolic again, with the stirring of new missionary energies throughout the world. During the recent war, Maryknollers exiled from China by the enemy invaders were invited to Latin America, and the opening of missions there now may mean the salvation of millions of souls. God's ways are inscrutable, known only to Himself.

Now, Mary, Mediatrix of All Graces, is also the Queen of China. I won't dwell on what the Communist regime may do to this ancient country, but we know that in the years ahead Mary will have the Chinese people in her special care. Perhaps the first crown our divine Lord has given His Mother in China is the present suffering of the whole nation. We missioners are privileged to share in this pain, and thus to have our small part in the splendor of our Lady's Chinese diadem.

The Precious Blood

THE FEAST OF THE MOST PRECIOUS BLOOD WAS INSTITUTED ONLY a century ago, but the devotion is as old as Christianity. We may even go further and say that it dates back to the origins of Judaism, because everything in the religion of the Jews foreshadowed Calvary. The sacrifice in the temple, the sprinkling of doorsills, of clothing, and even of food, with sacrificial blood—all the Jewish liturgy was concerned with the shedding of blood.

The New Testament dwells constantly on the salvation of the world by the cleansing Blood of Christ. This is the glorious theme of so many of St. Paul's Epistles, the very burden of his missionary message to mankind. There could not have been a New Testament without the shedding of the lifeblood of the Testator. Devotion to the precious Blood might be called the one link uniting Jews, Catholics, and Protestants. Protestants, indeed, sometimes seem to have appreciated this aspect of the Redemption better than many Catholics.

To make pagans understand the foulness of sin, and the cleansing, redeeming power of the precious Blood might well be the successful approach where other means have failed. The evident burden of guilt is so fundamental to conversion, and the doctrine of the precious Blood so directly applicable, that even to the least thoughtful of pagans it should appeal strongly. This teaching should bring forcibly home to them the price of their Redemption.

The early Fathers say that the Church was born from the pierced side of Christ, and that the sacraments were brought forth through His Blood. The beautiful Office of the Feast of the Most Precious Blood tells us: "You who sometime were afar off are made nigh by the Blood of Christ; for He is our peace who hath made both one . . . making peace through the

Blood of His Cross, both as to the things that are on earth, and the things that are in Heaven."

We cannot rightly esteem Divine Providence, the Fatherhood of God, our adoption as sons, or the love of God expressed in His revelations, unless we know the ugliness of sin and the price of Redemption, that is to say, unless we meditate on the precious Blood of Jesus. The only value any of our missionary work has is that it has been baptized in the Blood of Christ. The special beauty of this Feast of the Most Precious Blood, as I see it, lies in its concentration on our Lord. The whole tenor of the feast seems to center our attention directly on the Blood of Christ, a short cut to the heart of revelation, to the quintessence of the New Testament.

In these days we need to think of the Passion of Christ. We do not know how God is going to test us. The devotion to the precious Blood is a fundamental, sane approach to God. It is hard and painful; it will help us to steel our own hearts against weakness. To daydream about martyrdom is not enough, we have to gain the grace of so inestimable a privilege, we have to be worthy of it. We must be wholly laved in the Blood of Christ; our garments must be red.

The Assumption

OUR LADY WAS ACCLAIMED AS MOTHER OF GOD AT THE COUNCIL of Ephesus, in 431; shortly before Bernadette's vision at Lourdes, the Immaculate Conception was defined; and now her glorious Assumption into Heaven has been revealed to us as a dogma. In her Immaculate Conception, Mary was "our tainted nature's solitary boast," the sole human being who perfectly fulfilled God's will; hers was a unique personal relation with God never repeated. As Mother of God, Mary became the co-redeemer of the human race. At the Assumption she was the first to enter, body and soul united, into the final glory awaiting redeemed mankind after the general resurrection. Thus, all through her temporal life, Mary was the expressed ideal of God's plan of creation.

Our Lady's Assumption is one of the oldest Christian feasts, celebrated especially in the Eastern Church. Its centuries-long observance is a wonderful instance of the value of tradition as the deposit of faith. Dogmas usually tend to widen the breach between the Church and schismatics, but this new dogma of the Assumption draws us closer to the Eastern Orthodox in a common, ancient, deeply inbred devotion to our Lady as the embodiment of Catholic culture.

The dogma of the Assumption is, moreover, the Church's answer to a materialistic world. The nations are engaged in the pursuit of progress without formula or definition, except their implicit theory of inevitable advance. Our Holy Father replies to the muddled thinking of the secular world by pointing to the final destiny of mankind as exemplified in our Lady's Assumption. The dogma implicitly states that the perfection of our faculties and bodily skills will be fully exercised only in Heaven. It might be called a corollary of the dogma that we are made to know and love God, that our intellect, will, and senses, which grope experimentally through life seeking their various aims, attain fulfillment only in contemplating God in Heaven.

Our Lady was the first of creatures to reverse the curse of original sin and its penalty of death. How beautiful she must have appeared on the threshold of Heaven with a body fitted to enjoy the presence of her God—a mind and heart that from conception throughout life were always directed to union with God, a will that had never deviated from His purposes, and senses that had been continually attuned to her sublime vocation. The very word "Assumption" throws light on our Lady's status. Its Latin derivation betokens choice, the deliberate purchase and drawing to one's self of what has been won. God drew our Lady to Himself, His purchased prize; the choice was His, and His title was Mary's redemption by her Divine Son.

The Flesh and Blood Mary had given Jesus had already entered Heaven, and the God-given instinct of maternal kinship thrilled our Lady's body and soul as she came into the Divine Presence to receive the embrace of her God and her Son. As a perfect creature she was best fitted to contain the overwhelming love poured from the Heart of God, and the union with God renewed afresh her capacity to enjoy God and give joy to Him.

The Assumption, then, was the moment of creation's fulfillment, the vindication of God's Incarnation and Redemption of the human race, the first fruit of God's plan for mankind— a plan which includes our own appearance, body and soul, before the throne of God. May the Immaculate Mother of God and our co-redeemer, in the renewed glory of this revelation, draw the Russian and other Eastern Orthodox into union with Christ's Vicar, and focus the mind of the world on the true aim of progress toward the goal of union with the Creator of the universe.

The Most Holy Rosary

IF WE WERE TO SUM UP, FROM A CATHOLIC VIEWPOINT, THE knowledge a missioner should possess, we could find it all epitomized in the prayers of the Rosary. The Breviary is a compendium of the teachings and writings of the true Church, and the Rosary is a compendium of the Breviary. You could meditate on the Rosary for the rest of your life. Our co-founder, Fr. Thomas Frederick Price, often used to call the Rosary the missioner's Breviary, and, in fact, the Church has raised the Rosary to a high status by allowing us to substitute it for the Breviary in certain cases.

In the long history of the Church, many devotions have captured popular attention. Purely emotional devotions take the world by storm, and then often fade away, but the Rosary perdures. The Rosary is a Catholic, universal devotion, and the Church wants us to rise above the personal viewpoint in our prayers. In reciting the Rosary we say, "pray for us sinners," not "pray for me." The prayers of the Rosary take us out of ourselves by adoring and thanking God, and they please our divine Lord by praising His Mother.

The very fact that we have such a prayer as the Rosary seems to me one of the proofs of the divinity of the Church. In its simplicity and stupendous universality the Rosary could not have been solely the product of human genius. Because the Rosary is inspired by God, taken from sacred Scripture, and confirmed by the decision of the Church, the Spouse of Christ, it has a most pleasing sound to our divine Lord. It has been fittingly named a Rosary, a beautiful garden of roses. The Rosary is the biography of Christ, as told by His Mother.

It would be well for us missioners to make simple, child-like use of the Rosary. It is the universal prayer that farmers, peasants, housewives, and children are saying all over the world, and praying in unison with them becomes the happiest prayer. The Rosary is a sturdy, sensible prayer, a prayer that can exercise all our faculties, all the knowledge we have of God from the Scriptures and from personal experience of His infinite love. The Rosary is a prayer that is suited alike for the wisest and the simplest.

All Saints' Day

THE BEATIFIC VISION THAT THE SAINTS IN HEAVEN ENJOY HAS A twofold relation: they not only see and possess God, but He also sees and possesses them, in some mysterious manner not as yet revealed to man. Perhaps it is important to dwell upon this aspect of celestial life, because we may have rather strange ideas about it. Fr. Martindale remarked somewhere that, as a child, he had been terrified at the thought of God's seeing him. He pictured God as a big, glaring, disembodied eye, which hypnotized him during the day and formed his nightmare as he closed his own eyes in sleep.

The thought that God is everywhere and always sees us should not be terrifying to children; it can just as easily be exciting, alluring, and a source of strength. The little one can be told that God looks at him because He is always watching over us to protect us. He calls to us, warns us against danger, and gives us just the strength we need to escape it. A child who has been taught to think of God in this manner is not afraid of going to bed in a dark room, because he never feels alone.

Spiritual books urge us to cultivate the "presence of God," which is another way of saying that we should realize constantly that God sees us. I find great happiness in recalling the interview between our divine Lord and the young man who came to question Jesus about his vocation. The youth represents every one of us, and the Scriptures record that Jesus looked at him and loved him. In that manner does God always see us, a look that is constant, continual, and motivated by love. The Heart of Jesus speaks to us and invites us through the tender patience in His eyes.

When I first arrived in China, I was somewhat puzzled by the absence of the outward signs of affection that are common among us in the West. I asked one of the schoolboys how he and his friends showed affection. He replied in a rather surprised way that people show affection by looking steadily at each other. The boy did not realize that he was describing accurately our Lord's manner with the young man in the Gospel. The eyes are in truth the windows of the soul, and grow limpid with love as in no other way.

In Heaven, the love in God's eyes is answered by the enraptured gaze of His saints. And we on earth can also direct our vision upon the Desired of the Nations, the Light that illuminates every man born into this world. We are esteemed by God as precious, and also reflected in the pupil of His eye. It is an image that passes from the eye to the Heart of God. In this sense at least, we can begin our Heaven on earth by gazing back at Him.

Our vocation as missioners is to show God to others. He is our divine Model in everything. If we are to enjoy Heaven on earth, it must be in our work with Him and especially in how we look on others. When our Lord dwelt on this earth, preparing souls to people heaven, He manifested an ever-understanding Heart and the patient forgiveness that anticipates the faltering words of contrition. Imitating Him in this, we can begin to reflect the light that attracted souls to Him.

Our eyes must not look on pagans and catechumens with cold, impersonal severity. In His dealings with His fishermen and country folk, our Lord showed us how to accommodate our manner and speech to the ignorant. "He who sees Me, sees the Father" was the mild reply of Jesus to the importunate questioning of His Apostles. Would that we might say the same. Our catechumens can readily believe that God sees them and watches over them with love, if they perceive that our motives are directed by the same love.

Above all, our manner of looking at our pagans and our

catechumens must give them confidence in forgiveness. All our work is useless if they do not realize that God glories in forgiving them, that there is joy in Heaven, over each sinner's repentance, and that we, like God, can forgive them seventy-times-seven. An oration during Mass tells us that God's omnipotence is manifested rather by forgiving than by creation. This supremely divine attribute must be reflected in the loving expression of our own eyes.

The goal of our earthly life is to attain the beatific vision of God in Heaven, so that throughout eternity and with increasing clarity we may feast on the sight of God. By directing our eyes steadily now to the Face of God, we but begin here what will absorb us in Heaven. How slight, then, is the partition between the saints and us. They form with us one chorus of admiration and love, lost in the vision of God. On us on earth rests always the patient, forgiving look of God, an invitation of utter love: "Blessed are the pure of heart, for they shall see God."